Produce Your Own Damn Movie!

Produce Your Own Damn Movie!

Lloyd Kaufman
with Ashley Wren Collins

NEW YORK AND LONDON

First published 2009

This edition published 2013
by Focal Press
70 Blanchard Road, Suite 402, Burlington, MA 01803

Simultaneously published in the UK
by Focal Press
2 Park Square, Milton Park, Abingdon, Oxon OX14 4RN

Focal Press is an imprint of the Taylor & Francis Group, an informa business

Notices

Practitioners and researchers must always rely on their own experience and knowledge in evaluating and using any information, methods, compounds, or experiments described herein. In using such information or methods they should be mindful of their own safety and the safety of others, including parties for whom they have a professional responsibility.

To the fullest extent of the law, neither the Publisher nor the authors, contributors, or editors, assume any liability for any injury and/or damage to persons or property as a matter of products liability, negligence or otherwise, or from any use or operation of any methods, products, instructions, or ideas contained in the material herein.

Library of Congress Cataloging-in-Publication Data
Kaufman, Lloyd, 1945-
Produce your own damn movie! / Lloyd Kaufman with Ashley Wren Collins.
p. cm.
Includes index.
ISBN 978-0-240-81045-4 (pbk. : alk. paper) 1. Motion pictures—Production and direction. 2. Low budget films. I. Collins, Ashley Wren. II. Title.
PN1995.9.P7K386 2009
791.4302'32—dc22

2009024692

British Library Cataloguing-in-Publication Data
A catalogue record for this book is available from the British Library.

ISBN: 978-0-240-81045-4 (pbk)

DEDICATION

This Book is lovingly dedicated to my beautiful wife, Pat Swinney Kaufman. She has produced my own damn life for the past 35 years.

Pat Swinney Kaufman circa 2005

Table of Incontinence

Introduction:	**Charlie Kaufman Is My Doppelgänger *or* Why I Want to Blow My Fucking Brains Out**	**xiii**
Chapter 1 Preamble:	**Penniless in Pittsburgh Asks Lloyd**	**1**
Chapter 1:	**Producing Models and Car Models *or* Producing America's Next Top Tromodel**	**3**
	Producer Vocabulary Lesson #1: Executive Producer	5
	Out with the Old. . .	6
	. . .And in with the Who?	6
	The End	7
	Five Producing Models	7
	1. The No-Budget Model	7
	2. The Credit Card Model	8
	3. The Troma Model	8
	4. The Presale/Cross-National Model	10
	5. The Big Hollywood Movie Model	10
	• Attempt #2 to Define "Executive Producer" *by Avi Lerner*	11
Chapter 2 Preamble:	**Nervous in Naples Asks Lloyd**	**13**
Chapter 2:	**How I Got a Rabbi to Hate Jews *or* How I Let Oliver Stone Beat the Crap Out of Me to Hone His Producer Skills**	**15**
	Producer Vocabulary: Co-Executive Producer	15
	Speaking of Yale. . .	16
	But Enough About Halitosis	17
	• Mark Harris Finds Art in the Passion, Not Necessarily the Deal	21
	A Possible Reversal of Fortune?	21
	Don't Believe in the Top 100, Top 10 or Top Anything Lists	22
	Just Like *JFK* and *Nixon*	22
	• How Steven Paul Got Started at the Ripe Old Age of 12	23
	• Joe Dante Explains the Ideal Relationship	27
	Back to the Big Fuss	27
	• Mick Garris Distinguishes the Masters of Horrors	31
Chapter 3 Preamble:	**So Close in So. Cal Asks Lloyd**	**33**
Chapter 3:	**Film School or Porno? Taint No Difference *or* My Dinner with Louis Su**	**35**
	Producer Vocabulary: Producer	35
	Sage Advice from Roger Corman—Also Some Oregano Advice	37
	• Who Is Louis Su?	38
	• Ernest Dickerson Does Not Dickerson Around	47
	• The Core of More from Corman	49
	• In the Trent-ches with Trent Haaga	52

Chapter 4 Preamble: **Losing It in Las Vegas Asks Lloyd** **61**

Chapter 4: **Producing Movies Inevitably Gets You Stoned (And Is Really, Really Hard) *or* A Union Dose of Some Shirley Jackson Optimism Goes a Long Way** **63**

Producer Vocabulary: Co-Producer 63

A Note from My Editrix 64

- Who Is John Carpenter? 65

The Ultimate Self-Stoning Job, or There's a Hole in My Begel ~~Bagel~~, Man: A Short History of David Begelman 68

A Lottery Ticket with a Big "?" on the Prize 69

- How Shanley Gave Lloyd the Shaft . . . ley *by Matt Lawrence, Resident Troma Bitch* 70
- Getting Stood Up by Oscar 72

You Don't Have to Be a Shithead to Be a Producer 74

Which Way Went Blair Witch? 74

Climbing High Up at IHOP: Lessons from Stan Lee 75

- Terry Jones Tells Us Why His Producer Was Not the Messiah, Just A Very Naughty Boy! 77
- Quoth the Draven, Evermore 80
- Why Tamar Simon Hoffs Always Makes Up Three Different Budgets for the Same Film 81

The MPAA Lottery 82

- Paul Hertzberg Advises Against Falling in Love with an Un-Commercial Project 85
- Avi Lerner and Buddy Giovinazzo Say Unions Cause America's Lottery 88

My Perfect Night In 90

- Making a Movie Sucks: "Why Are We Doing This—We Hate Making Movies!" *by Stoning Victims Trey Parker and Matt Stone* 90

This is Fucking Depressing . . . Anybody Else Want to Stop Reading and Go Out for a Beer? 91

Chapter 5 Preamble: **Eager in Erie Asks Lloyd** **93**

Chapter 5: **Is There a Business Plan? Is IMDB Ass? *or* Secrets of Financing and Producing from the Pickled Brain of an Elaborate Non-pyramid Schemer** **95**

Producer Vocabulary: Line Producer 95

A Note from My Editrix 96

Line Producer 96

A Few Words via E-mail from my Co-Author Ashley 97

- Compare, Contrast, Coagulate: Lloyd's Producing and Acting Resumes on www.lloydkaufman.com and www.imdb.com 102

The Accidental Business Plan 117

- Roger Corman Puts His Finger on the Money Question 119

Real Talk About Real Estate and "Reel" Mistakes 120

- Avi Lerner Reminds Us That Producing Is Not Just an Art: It's a Business 121

Simple Math is My Favorite Kind... Call It Tro – Math 123
- Brian Yuzna Tells You How Money Has Changed Over the Years 123

A Little More Exploitation for the Road 124
Jist So This Chipter Don't Seam *Two* Poifect... 124

Intermission: **Andy Deemer's Production Diaries** **125**

Chapter 6 Preamble: **Starstruck in Starbucks Asks Lloyd** **131**
Chapter 6: **Pre-Sell Your Flick in a Game of Five-Card Stud *or* Go For a Straight *Flush*** **133**
Producer Vocabulary: Associate Producer 133
What Is the IFTA and Why You, Mr./Ms. Producer, Ought to Give a Shit! 135
- Just How Does the IFTA Define an "Independent Film"? 136

Why the Heck I Ran for IFTA Chairperson 137
- What's so Friggin' Important About the *United States v. Paramount Pictures, Inc.* (1948)? 138
- What Are the Financial Interest and Syndication Rules? 140
- Comedy Central Proves My Point 146
- Brian Yuzna Gives You a Lesson on Evolution from the Video Boom to the Modern Age 147
- What *Is* Pre-Selling?: Lloyd Asks Paul Hertzberg 148
- More on That Pre-Selling Thing from a Sales Agent (Who, In My Opinion, Is Also a Producer): An Interview with Kathy Morgan About Her Game of Five-Card Stud (Actor, Director, Producer, Script, Domestic Distribution) 152
- But Why Would I Need a Sales Agent? I Know How to Hustle! *by Jean Prewitt* 158

Chapter 7 Preamble: **Anxious in Anchorage Asks Lloyd** **163**
Chapter 7: **Fuck Me Jesus on a Pogo Stick! Where Am I Going to Produce My Own Damn Movie? *or* The Secrets of the Location Vocation** **165**
Producer Vocabulary: Location Manager 165
Producer Vocabulary: Unit Production Manager 166
Location Locution: Choosing a Location and Getting It in Writing and Lots More 167
Hanger: A Case Study and Melvina Gets Her Groove On 169
What *State* Are You In? 172
- The Unstoppable, Legendary Pat Swinney Kaufman 173
- Paul Hertzberg Gives Us a Reason to Stop Making Fun of Canadians 180

Bunny-Hopping My Way to a Movie of the Future 182
My Catering Standards 184
How Do You Even Pay People to Begin With? Setting Up an LLC 184
Whatever You Do, Get Insurance! 186

- How Debbie Rochon Did Not Get a Hand *or* Can You Digit? *by Debbie Rochon* 186
- Brian Yuzna Also Defects North 192
- Trent Haaga Gets Thrown in the Trent-ches on Location 193
- Brian Yuzna Ran From the Indies to the Andes in his Undies—or at Least From Indonesia to Spain 194
- Long Before There Was Charlie Kaufman, There Was Charles Kaufman *by Charlie Kaufman* 197

Chapter 8 Preamble: Pumped Up in Peoria Asks Lloyd 203

Chapter 8: How to Do It Hollywood-Style *or* I am the Herpes of the Film Industry: I Won't Go Away 205

Producer Vocabulary: Assistant Producer 205

- Producing, Directing, and Lloyd, Oh My *by James Gunn* 210
- Working at Troma Isn't Always Toxierrific! 215

The Two Heads of Lloyd Kaufman 216

- Avi Lerner: A *Rambo*-Style Rebel in Hollywood 217
- Mark Neveldine and Brian Taylor *Crank* It Up 221
- The Duplass Brothers' Motto: "Make Movies, Not Meetings" 222
- *Kingpin* Brad Krevoy Unmasks the Hollywood Mystery 223
- The Way In: High-Voltage Wisdom from Mark Neveldine and Brian Taylor While Larry Cohen Says "God Told Me to Write a Great Script" 232

Chapter 9 Preamble: Frustrated in Frankfurt Asks Lloyd 237

Chapter 9: Face the Music: Post-production and Distribution *or* Pump Up Your Production to a Higher Level 239

Producer Vocabulary: Internet 239

- Joe Lynch Likes Makin' Music (Videos) *by Joe Lynch* 246
- The Duplass Brothers Say Go for the Volume (and Neveldine and Taylor Interject) 250
- Thank You for the Music *by Dennis Dreith* 252
- Editing and Post-production: A Troma Fan Teaches You Everything You Need to Know About Free Software to Produce and Edit Your Own Damn Movie *by Daniel Archambeault-May* 256
- Herschell Gordon Lewis Says "Distribution, Distribution, Distribution" 259
- Doing the Distribution Dance *by Mark Damon* 262

A Late-Night E-mail from My Former Assistant and Former Co-Writer, Sara Antill 265

Afterword Preamble: Frugal in Fargo Asks Lloyd 269

TromAfterword: Dammit! Why Are You Reading This?! 271

A Trio of E-mail Exchanges Among Ashley, Elinor, and Lloyd, *and* A Final Final Ending to This Book About Producing 279

Index Gyno's Bitchin' Index 285

Acknowledgments

Ashley Wren Collins, I apologize for driving you insane.

Sara Antill will not want to admit this, but she made a valuable writing contribution to this book. Thank you, Sara.

Michael Herz and Maris Herz, thanks for producing the warm and gentle environment that is Troma.

Jerome Rudes, who directed me toward writing my own damn book.

Elinor Actipis
Michele Cronin
Amanda Guest
Pat Swinney Kaufman
Charles Kaufman
Susan Kaufman
Lily Hayes Kaufman
Lisbeth Kaufman
Sigrun Kaufman
Charlotte Kaufman
Roger Kirby
Matt Lawrence
Scott Langer
Eckhart Tolle
Annie Cron
Erin Sparks
Evan Husney
Matt Manjourides
Maria Friedmanovich
Travis Campbell
Robert Frost

Matt Hoffman
Nathan Shafer
Allan Carroll
Jean Prewitt
Ben Cord
Marianne Williamson
David Chien
Marcus Lesser
Megan Silver
Cathy and Ron Mackay
Richard Saperstein
Tyra Banks
Amy Adams
Emily Blunt
Faith Preston
The Manhole Club
John Rieber
Jean Cheever
Tom Polum
Oprah Winfrey
David Bryan

Joe DiPietro
John Rando
Gabe Friedman
Giuseppe Andrews
Avi Lerner
Mark Harris
Dr. Phil
Steven Paul
Joe Dante
Mick Garris
Reed Morano
Ernest Dickerson
Roger Corman
Trent Haaga
Stan Lee
Terry Jones
Danny Draven
Tamar Simon Hoffs
Paul Hertzberg
Buddy Giovinazzo
Trey Parker
Matt Stone
Brian Yuzna
Barack Obama
Kathy Morgan
Debbie Rochon
Nina Paley
Billy Baxter
James Gunn
Mark Neveldine
Brian Taylor
Jay Duplass
Mark Duplass
Brad Krevoy
Robby Benson
Larry Cohen
Joe Lynch
Dennis Dreith
Daniel Archambeault-May
Herschell Gordon Lewis
Mark Damon
Jack Gerbus

And I'd like to direct a special thanks to the "Exit 47" sign on Route 95, which has produced some valuable and practical direction throughout the years.

Introduction

Charlie Kaufman Is My Doppelgänger *or* Why I Want to Blow My Fucking Brains Out

Everything I touch is fucked. No, seriously. I could take a piece of gold and, with enough effort and influence, turn it into a shiny pile of bona fide chicken shit. I have been aware of this sad fact for over 40 years, yet for some reason I continue to touch stuff and fuck it up. This is the curse of Lloyd Kaufman. Let me give you an example of why I want to blow my fucking brains out.

A few short weeks ago, I rearranged my schedule to attend Spain's prestigious Sitges International Film Festival. I love Sitges, and was especially inclined to go because they were presenting me with a lifetime achievement award. My trip to Rio was abandoned and my appearance on Conan O'Brien[1] postponed indefinitely, but dammit,

[1] From what I hear, Conan O'Brien was so upset about the cancellation that he stormed off the *Late Night* set and had to be replaced by Jimmy Fallon.

I was determined to get that award. Seventeen hours after leaving New York City, I sat in a darkened room with 2,000 other Sitges attendees and listened closely as an old man, speaking in broken, somewhat unintelligible English, went on and on about the genius of *Tromeo & Juliet* and Troma's latest masterpiece, *Poultrygeist: Night of the Chicken Dead*. My heart swelled with pride as 2,000 people applauded me and the little company that Michael Herz and I started in a Hell's Kitchen broom closet in 1974. It was truly a beautiful moment. Before the award was presented, the auditorium lights dimmed and a hush fell over the crowd as they prepared to watch a short video of my career highlights.

And then, as 2,000 pairs of eyes gleamed, transfixed by the images flashing before them, the career highlights of another Kaufman—Charlie Kaufman, to be exact—started rolling in sequence on the big screen. As *Eternal Sunshine of the Spotless Mind* played before my eyes, my pride-swollen heart dropped into my groin. Welcome to the Kaufman Curse. The good news is, for the remainder of the weekend, most of those 2,000 people thought that I was, in fact, Charlie Kaufman, so at least I got a few job offers out of the whole ordeal. But that's not the point.

The point is, as much as I consider myself a director, I am also a producer. And in this case, I hadn't produced. Being the pessimist and control-freak that I am, I had considered sending my own reel of career highlights to the festival coordinators, but, in the end, had decided to be hands-off. The end result was five minutes of *Adaptation* and a trailer for *Synecdoche, New York*. But hey, I'm not complaining. Considering that 2,000 people had gathered to honor me with an award, I'm just lucky an asteroid didn't aim itself for Spain and choose that moment to strike.

But don't get me wrong. Being a lazy producer isn't always a bad thing. Just look at the George Street Playhouse's recent production of the world premiere of *The Toxic Avenger Musical*. I am listed as "Based on Lloyd Kaufman's *The Toxic Avenger*," because I created the characters and basic story, but I have had very little to do with the actual production. Let's face it—as good as the songs in *Poultrygeist* were, I'm not going to tell David Bryan of Bon Jovi, who wrote all of the show's music, how to write a hit song. Furthermore, the George Street Playhouse is all the way in New Brunswick, New Jersey. And I think I've already told you that I'm lazy.

In fact, that's one of the best things about producing! You can choose to be as involved or uninvolved as you would like. You can be the hands-on, detail-oriented, script-shaping, director-controlling type of producer, or you can write a check and go on vacation. The producing style that Michael Herz and I tend to lean toward is the latter. In other words, we respect the Kaufman Curse and tend to stay out of the way, such as with *The Toxic Avenger Musical*. However, there have been several instances where we have done the exact opposite, with varying degrees of success. When we produced the two sequels to *Class of Nuke 'Em High*, I was incredibly hands-on.

What I'm trying to say is that your role as producer is really up to you. It obviously wouldn't take an entire book to teach you how to be lazy, so I intend to focus more on the role of active producer. But then again, I've already told you that everything I try to do ends up fucked, so by the end of this book, we'll probably end up with 312 pages on the art of check signing.

But stick with me, kid. I've got the greatest signature in showbiz.

XOXO,

Lloyd Kaufman, AKA Uncle Lloydie

Penniless in Pittsburgh Asks Lloyd

Dear Lloyd,

How do you get people motivated when you aren't paying them?

Penniless in Pittsburgh

Dear Penniless,

1. Fear.
2. Guilt.
3. Threats of suicide.
4. A demonstration of how much you believe in the project.
5. Alcohol.
6. Yelling.
7. Fire the naysayers.
8. Lips.
9. Campfire sing-a-longs.
10. Repeated viewings of *Poultry in Motion: Truth is Stranger than Fiction*, the documentary chronicling the making of *Poultrygeist: Night of the Chicken Dead*.

xoxo,
Lloyd

Chapter | one

Producing Models and Car Models *or* Producing America's Next Top Tromodel

When I married my amazing and adorable wife Pat, she came with a 1969 Ford Mustang convertible. Of course, that's not why I married her, mind you, but I won't deny that it sure did sweeten the deal. When your two great loves in life are musical theatre performed by young hairless boys and a Southern belle with a kickin' car, a decision must be made, and I made it. Ten years after we tied the knot, however, I was inspired by a Sally Struthers commercial late one night, and donated the kickin' car to an orphanage ~~for a giant tax deduction~~ to help the poor orphans. Pat did not agree with my benevolent decision to donate her car to ~~get a giant tax deduction~~ help those poor, less fortunate souls. I stood my ground, and for the last 20 years, I have lived with her endless scorn. So, a few months ago, I decided to do something about it. I made a few calls[1] and arranged to buy a 1969 Mustang to replace the one that I had so graciously given away 20 years earlier.

The dealership was in Indiana, so the entire deal was conducted over the phone[2] and essentially in good faith. When I finally arrived in Indiana to pick the car up, I was in awe of the beauty before me. The car was perfect. The red paint glistened under the neon lights. The rims of the tires sparkled. A tear formed in my eye as the jovial midwestern used car salesman handed me the keys and title. My marriage would be back on track in time for me to retire and die peacefully. With nothing between me and the open road ahead, I slid into the sweet-smelling leather seat and began the long drive back to New York.

The next several hours were spent in a haze of self-congratulation. The engine purred like an alley cat in heat. The sun smiled at me, just like Pat would be smiling at me in about 14 hours. Everything was going well, but because I'm Lloyd Kaufman, something of course had to go and get fucked up.

The moment came just as I reached my first traffic light. Suddenly, the engine's purr shifted from that of an amorous kitten to something resembling an 800-pound man with bronchitis, as if he were choking on a wiffle ball. Smoke appeared from beneath the shiny red hood, and the arrow on the engine thermostat, which had been resting comfortably between "Cool" and "Hot," swung definitively toward "Hot." My instincts—as well as my eyes and ears—told me that something was wrong. I pulled over, jumped out of the driver's seat and opened the hood. All around me, cars began honking at the billowing smoke coming from the engine. Once it cleared, I could see exactly what the problem was.

The problem was that I didn't know anything about cars.

I tapped on something with my finger and pounded something else with my fist, a fine strategy that usually worked well when my TV screen turned to snow. I closed the hood and kicked a tire, just for good measure. I got back in the car and, lo and behold, it was working just fine again. In fact, it worked all the way to the next traffic light, where Mister 1969 Mustang and I repeated our Smoke

---

[1]What I really mean by this, of course, is that my assistant made a few calls.

[2]Again, entirely by my trustworthy assistant.

Gets in Your Eyes tango. In fact, we continued to tango like this for the next 14 hours. Along the way, I also discovered that the passenger side door refused to open and the glove compartment flat out refused to stay shut.

But still, nothing could bring me down! Who cared if I had just purchased a car that broke down in traffic? Everyone knows that there is hardly any traffic in New York City! And so what if the passenger door didn't open? Once I handed the keys over to Pattie-Pie, I probably wouldn't be allowed back in the passenger seat anyway! I had set out to buy a car, and dammit, nothing was going to ruin my high!

You may be thinking to yourself right about now, "Gosh, I've read only a few pages of this book, and already I've learned so much about film producing!"

Of course you have, but fasten your seatbelts, because you are about to learn *even more*! You see, film producing models are a lot like a 1969 Mustang. What worked in 1969 might not work as well now, 40 years later. Producing models are in constant flux. And always remember, as Marie Curie was fond of saying, "You can't fuck with the flux!" To be a great producer, one must keep up with the times.

PRODUCER VOCABULARY LESSON #1

When it comes to defining the term "producer," things can get complicated. There are many titles, responsibilities, and people involved in a film production. Throughout the coming chapters, in the spirit of learning, I will provide detailed, scientific descriptions of different titles commonly used in production. That way, you can pretend you're a big shot by showing off your new vocabulary. You're welcome. Let's begin:

EXECUTIVE PRODUCER: This can be anyone from the CEO of a major studio to the Estonian owner of a chain of dry cleaning stores to the schmoozer in the apartment next door who can sucker some poor saps into funding *your* movie. These guys are the Harvey Weinsteins, the James L. Brooks, or, if your karma is down the shithole, the Kaufmans and Herzs.

Synonyms: The Money Guy, The Big Cheese, The Guy You Want for Your Best Friend.

Example: "Today the Executive Producer called and told me that we were $80 million over budget, and he sounded a little upset."

OUT WITH THE OLD. . .

For more than 40 years, I've been able to produce, direct, write, and make my own damn movies in 35 mm with almost total freedom. I've also been able to produce each one, with a few exceptions, for roughly the equivalent of $500K, including all production, marketing, and distribution costs. Several of these movies have gone on to receive worldwide acclaim and a loyal fan following, and all of them have gone on to break even—sometimes even making a few bucks.

Under the Hollywood producing model, this is nearly unheard of. Studios spend millions of dollars—sometimes hundreds of millions of dollars—on a single film. And although a handful of these films are remembered 10 years later, most will be forgotten like last week's leftover egg salad, slipping into film limbo along with unbaptized children and Times Square pickpockets.

Troma films compete with the giant studio films by containing commercial elements like a cool gun, a monster, or a naked person while still retaining their edge, whether it be satire, horror, or even both, as with my latest fowl movement, *Poultrygeist: Night of the Chicken Dead*. Although some people may not "get" the movie, there is at least one thing in it that will appeal to a wider audience, such as large amounts of naked people. This appeal allows the film to be at least somewhat entertaining to everyone, and with a little luck, it will make some money over time. This is the model that has always worked for me, but with *Poultrygeist*,[3] that model may be like a 1969 Mustang.

. . .AND IN WITH THE WHO?

The films that we see in theatres today are all owned and controlled by five or six megaconglomerates.[4] These companies own and control not only the movies, but also in many cases the theatres that play them and the television stations, newspapers, and magazines that review and advertise them. With that type of industry consolidation,

---

[3]The original title for *Poultrygeist* was *Good Night and Good Cluck*, but George Clooney got there first!

[4]I am referring, in no particular order, to evil corporations such as Sony, Viacom, Time Warner, News Corporation, and Disney. Their mere existence is why we are force-fed so much shit in the entertainment world today! Actually, they have so many marketing dollars that they make us think we need their crap.

even independent theatres are scared to take on a film not supported by a kabillion dollar ad campaign. Even though *Poultrygeist: Night of the Chicken Dead* is usually the highest-grossing film in each city in which it is allowed to play, we are still turned away by theatres unwilling to take a risk. We have reached a point where unless a film is released through a major distributor or studio, it is economically blacklisted and therefore unable to sell tickets, much less make a profit. Even direct-to-DVD is no longer much of an option, as the mom-and-pop video stores that flourished in the 1980s have been hijacked by corporate chains, which are, oddly enough, owned or controlled by those same five or six megaconglomerates.

So the reality is that *Poultrygeist*—although it was the highest-grossing "screen" in the United States on its opening weekend and received the best reviews in Troma's 35-year history—will most likely not make one cent.

And that is the end of this book.

THE END

Well, not quite. . .

This change in the industry could be the end, but it doesn't have to be. After all, not all of that 1969 Mustang is bad. The car is beautiful to look at. The tires don't leak air and the windshield isn't cracked. It's great for picking up young boys at the 7-Eleven, and on a short drive around the block, it drives like an absolute dream. The trick is to take the parts of producing model that work in the current industry and make them work for you. Then maybe someone will someday pay thousands of dollars for the privilege of driving you home from Indiana to present you to his wife and finally get out of a 20-year exile in the doghouse!

FIVE PRODUCING MODELS

1. The No-Budget Model

For the first time in history, filmmaking has been democratized. Sure, I just spent a whole paragraph telling you why your movie might never see the light of day, but that's a question of distribution. When it comes to actually picking up a camera and making a movie, things have never been so easy! When cars were invented, you had to be a millionaire to own one. In fact, back then, a car cost around the equivalent of $500K, which is how much it cost Pat and me to make *Poultrygeist*. But along came a guy named Henry Ford, and the rest is history. All of a sudden, Joe the Plumber could own a car without selling his children on the black market. The same has happened with filmmaking. Whereas only giant studios could once afford the equipment it took to make a feature film, now the medium has opened up to everyone. It doesn't take your life savings to swing by Best Buy and pick up a digital video camera and some DV tapes.

With the no-budget producing model, the goal is to get a movie made. If it looks good, great! If not, that's fine, too. What matters is getting it done. To do this, all you really need is a great script, some actors, a camera, and a few accessories. You can produce a feature-length no-budget movie for less than $10K—even for as little as a few hundred dollars.

2. The Credit Card Model

This model closely resembles the no-budget model, but with a few ideological differences. Primarily, your goal is not only to get the movie made, but also to make it look good. To do this, you might spend a little more money on equipment, maybe pay your actors and crew a small sum (I emphasize the word "small,"[5] as it's a word I am very familiar with), and spend a little cash on props or location rentals. You may end up borrowing some money from family or friends, but this will all be on an unofficial basis, and you will retain all the rights to the finished film. The actual budget can be higher or lower than the figures in the No Budget Model, while elements from each model can be applied to any of the other models. I don't think it makes sense to spend more than $50K on this model.

3. The Troma Model

In this model, everyone hates you. Other than that, it has some very useful elements. At this stage, your budget will be high enough

---

[5] A NOTE FROM YOUR FRIENDLY FOOTNOTE GUY: Did someone say small?! Hey Lloyd, remember me? I've been getting so much fan mail from my appearance in your last book, *Direct Your Own Damn Movie!*, that your editor asked me to come back and do the footnotes for this book! I am so excited!!

that you have an opportunity to create quality on the screen to the point where you can compete with the major studios. Most of the time you will still lose this competition, but at least you can enter the race. Your film can play in independent theatres with a little effort, but without any guarantees of whether it will continue to play from week to week. Troma films are financed entirely through our company, either through investors, or—more often—with our own money, using limited partnerships, LLCs, and so on. The Troma movie probably won't have any stars[6] and is not sold to investors based on a package.[7] The budgets are usually around $500K.

FIGURE 1.1 *LK "produces" a beard to celebrate Kabukiman and Dora the Explorer's new child, pictured on the poster.*

[6]Well, folks like Lemmy from Motörhead, Ron Jeremy, and Trey Parker have acted in my films (for free), but they are not used in films as stars; that is, people do not buy tickets because these celebs have cameos. Some of the young leads in Troma movies have gone on to become stars, which later adds value to our films when they are reissued—Vincent D'Onofrio, Samuel L. Jackson and Jorge Garcia are a few examples.

[7]Mostly because I have a very small package that I can't even give away to people, never mind sell.

4. The Presale/Cross-National Model

Another option is to sell a film before it's even made, based on the "package"—this is basically the combination of director, stars, script, and so on. If you line up Steven Spielberg to direct the film you're producing and Julia Roberts to star in it, chances are pretty good that someone will see a moneymaking opportunity and give you all the money you need to do the film. What they will receive in return are the rights to your film, whether for a particular country or for television, and so on.

As with the Credit Card Model, don't let the budget here fool you. If you know Julia Roberts through your cousin's best friend's babysitter's sister and you can somehow convince her to star in your film based on your amazing script, your budget could be as little as 200 bucks. But the *Lord of the Rings* films were produced under this model, and they each had a budget exceeding $200 million. What distinguishes these models is not the budget as much as the way you raise that budget and what you use it for. So budgets under this model usually range from under $500K to $10 million. Sometimes they're a lot more.

FIGURE 1.2 *In addition to producing no-budget documentaries, LK is also accumulating footage of long-haired men for his personal collection.*

5. The Big Hollywood Movie Model

In this model, a giant studio puts up all the money to produce a film. The studio retains all the rights, and the producer is in many cases expendable. If you have reached a point in your career where you are making these types of films, stop reading this book right now and give me a call. I'd love to work with you!

FIGURE 1.3 *LK at his desk in the Troma building, getting affection any way he can.*

ATTEMPT #2 TO DEFINE "EXECUTIVE PRODUCER"

BY AVI LERNER

WHO IS AVI LERNER?

Avi Lerner is an independent film producer; throughout his career, he has graduated from producing B movies to A movies, although he does not like it when Lloyd makes jokes about him being a "fast lerner." Recent projects include Major Movie Star, Thick as Thieves, Brooklyn's Finest, Vampire in Vegas, *and* Rambo IV. *Avi also built his own studio in Louisiana to take advantage of the wonderful tax incentives available to filmmakers in that state.*[8]

As an Executive Producer, I am the person who says this is your time frame, this is your budget, and you cannot get out of your time frame or go over your budget. This is the number of days you get the movie, this is the number of extra days we've built in as a contingency, this is the number of cameras you can use every day, and this is the number of hours you are allowed to shoot per day.

[8]More on these tax incentives in Chapter 7 . . . I hope.

So now you may have a slightly better idea of what a producer does. Or you may still bc scratching your head wondering why there are 20 producers in the credits of *Martian Child*. Actually, I wondered that myself. So you see? You and I are on the same page. And speaking of pages, let's turn to the next one and talk a little more about me.[9]

[9]A NOTE FROM YOUR FIERY INDEX GYNO:* Hey, Lloyd, *big boy*. Since we're talking about being on the same page, I wanted to go ahead and introduce myself to your readers. I have a B.S. in Categorization from the Micronesia College of Fine Print, and I'll be preparing the index for your book. Elinor, your editor, called me last night and asked me to get an early start. She said something about your coming up short on pages last time and wanted to be sure we had a lengthy and comprehensive index prepared. The index is that enormously helpful and important reference material at the end of a book that no one ever pays attention to, unless it's a book about showbiz, in which case people want to see whether their names appear in the book!**

*"Gyno" is the politically correct term we at Troma use to refer to a member of the female sex. "Girl" is taboo and "woman" has the word "man" in it . . . you get the idea.

**FOOTNOTE GUY: Hi, Index Gyno! Nice to see you! You have a nice set of colons! I'm so happy we'll be working together. I'm really enjoying Lloyd's book so far, aren't you?

Nervous in Naples Asks Lloyd

Dear Lloyd,

As a producer, how many chances should you give an actor who is unbelievably talented, but also unbelievably unreliable (at best) or a complete psycho (at worst), before you fire them?

Help,
Nervous in Naples

Dear Nervous,

Depending on the situation, sometimes I get rid of talented, dedicated people because they disagree with me and sometimes I get rid of talented, dedicated people because I am an idiot. This happened to Vincent D'Onofrio during *The Toxic Avenger.* I sometimes get rid of people even before they have become a major problem; sometimes I keep someone who should have gone a long time ago.

The best way to avoid a bad situation entirely is to weed out the troublemakers during the casting process. I make auditions so horrible that anyone who makes it through without wanting to kill themselves (or me) has a good chance of making it through the shoot, which is equally as horrible.

I always go with the less-talented-but-more-reliable-and-loyal actor over the super-talented diva. However, sometimes bad apples do slip through. In these cases, I say: if it isn't ruining the film, keep Wacky around until you can fire him in front of everyone and make an example out of him. Of course, then he may want to come back and make an example out of you with his brass knuckles, so proceed with caution!

Good luck! And please review this book on Amazon while you're in that full-body cast. Thanks!

xoxo,
Lloyd

Chapter | two

How I Got a Rabbi to Hate Jews *or* How I Let Oliver Stone Beat the Crap Out of Me to Hone His Producer Skills

CO-EXECUTIVE PRODUCER: I know I said I would provide scientific definitions, but I really have no idea what the fuck these people do. Using my Yale-provided education regarding Latin prefixes, I am assuming they share head-honcho producing duties with the other Executive Producer. If anyone has a better idea, please e-mail me at lloyd@troma.com.

Synonyms: The Other Executive Producer, Co-Money Guy

Example: "I got a call from the Co-Executive Producer today about the budget."

"You mean Gary?"

"No, the other guy."

SPEAKING OF YALE. . .

Once upon a time, there was a young boy who graduated from Yale. Full of Boola Boola Eli Yale Optimism from the experience of producing *Rappacini* and directing *The Girl Who Returned*[1] while still a naïve young thing[2] in school, he dusted the moths off his bar mitzvah suit and decided to go and make a movie with sync sound for fun with friends to create a piece of art, rake in some money, and have a good time. Just call me "Candide."

Hear ye, hear ye, all movie makers and producers with stars in your eyes: I am going to let you in on a little-known secret that myself, my producing buddy Oliver Stone[3] (a childhood friend) and Garrard L. Glenn (a Yale friend) were lucky enough to discover early on as we set out to raise the money for *Sugar Cookies* (budget: $100K smackers). Your dentist is filthy fucking rich and dying to be part of the creative business of making movies.

Just think about it. Dentistry is ranked as being a profession with one of the highest rates of suicide. Patient after patient, cavity after cavity,[4] day after day, old women and old men recline in a chair with their mouths wide open[5] and have havoc wreaked upon[6]

---

[1]*Rappacini* and *The Girl Who Returned* are some of my earliest movies, which did not have direct synchronized sound. See my books *Make Your Own Damn Movie!* and *Direct Your Own Damn Movie!* for details.

[2]"Naïve young thing" is producer code for not yet ass-raped.

[3]Oliver Stone is a well-known* American film producer, director, and screenwriter who first rose to prominence as a young boy for beating me up and making me cry. He later came of age with his series of films about the Vietnam War.

*FOOTNOTE GUY: Lloyd, I know this wasn't intentional, but it's a little silly when you mention in a footnote that someone is "well-known." In the biz, we call that FU—Footnote Useless. It belittles your subject and belittles** the guy doing your footnotes, too, so if you could curb this behavior in the future, I'd really appreciate it, okay?

INDEX GYNO: Yeah, he's little enough!*

FOOTNOTE GUY: Thanks!*

****INDEX GYNO: I now need to index Oliver Stone on this page as well as in the footnote. We call that a WIN—a Wasted Index Notation, or, as we professionals call it, a "Windex." Shit! I just realized that I referenced Oliver Stone again in this footnote, so I'll need to add that in now, too.

[4]FOOTNOTE GUY: I'd like the small pleasure of filling someone's tiny cavity.

[5]Actually, this is starting to sound really good.

[6]I know, I know. Where is the fucking misery in any of this?! I'm getting to it.

one of the most sensitive areas of their entire bodies[7] as gums are rubbed and teeth are yanked all for that goal of attaining that million-watt smile. Being that no conversation or exchange beyond "'At ertz" and "Feeeeeez stahp dat" and "Moh vutah" are possible, just where is your dentist to get his/her necessary dose of human interaction and artistic fulfillment that feeds the soul?

PRODUCING LESSON #127: Don't be afraid to talk to everybody and anybody who will listen about your idea for the awesome movie you want to make. You never know who's going to cough up some cash for your production.

Your dentist is going to get that artistic soul fulfillment by investing a portion of that hard-earned cash in a movie. In particular, an X-rated[8] voyeuristic movie with lesbian sex and a couple of precisely placed handguns. For those of you who don't keep up with your recommended bi-annual dental checkup visits, you're fucking screwed.[9]

BUT ENOUGH ABOUT HALITOSIS

Returning to our original topic—me—if it makes you feel any better, I didn't know shit about making movies when I graduated from Yale. I knew I loved them and I knew they got me excited like nothing else.[10] All I knew is that I had made two of them (feature-length) already, without sound (and no one really wanted to see those), and I still wanted to make more.[11]

---

[7]Still sounds pretty fucking good.

[8]X-rated according to the MPAA (Motion Picture Association of America), those incredibly qualified censorship-anointing members of Hollywood studios I love so much who advance their own self-interests through a "voluntary" film rating system. Believe me, what was considered X-rated in the '70s would be PG by today's standards.

[9]My editrix Elinor is telling me not to be so discouraging* in the book so early on and reminding me that "fucking screwed" is repetitive.**

*EDITOR'S NOTE: The *New York Times* liked *Sugar Cookies*! Ha ha!

**ANOTHER EDITOR'S NOTE: Actually, Lloyd, "fucking screwed" is how I felt when they told me I was editing yet another one of your books, but that's beside the point here, as the more pressing question is *where* exactly are you headed with all this dentist talk? Your readers need practical advice.

[10]Nothing else legal, anyway.

[11]It may be worthwhile to point out the value in the producer being slightly sadomasochistic, as producing a film involves many elements of incredible, intense, joyful, satisfying pleasure coupled with excruciating pain. I'm getting a little feverish just thinking about it.

After Yale, I made *The Battle of Love's Return* fresh out of school for $8K with Garrard, Frankie, and Oliver. Not wildly popular (though in the film I do look awfully handsome dodging elevator doors and prancing around in my tighty-whities), but it did get people interested enough to give us more money to make our next feature film. I even once sent a copy of *Battle of Love's Return* to the venerable Herr Fritz Lang[12] and received this prized letter in response:

Dear Mr. Kaufman:

Thank you for sending me The Battle of Love's Return.

I watched it.

Sincerely.

Fritz Lang

That letter remains, to this day, one of my greatest treasures and contains one of the nicest things anyone has ever said about one of my movies.

Getting back to those lesbians and handguns I touched upon[13] earlier, I, along with the other producers on *Sugar Cookies*, thought we had our golden ticket—just like *American Idol*. I had written a pretty decent rough draft of a script that was, in a nutshell, an X-rated combo homage to Hitchcock's *Vertigo*[14] and MacKendrick's

---

[12]Fritz Lang (1890–1976) was an Austrian-German-American genius film producer, director, and screenwriter dubbed the "Master of Darkness" by the British Film Institute. His film *Metropolis* was the most expensive silent fivlm ever made at the time of its release and his 1957 film *Beyond a Reasonable Doubt* was just remade by Mark Damon, (whom you'll meet later in this book), starring Michael Douglas. *The Big Heat* is one of my favorite films. You'll learn more about producing from watching *The Big Heat* than from 25 years of USC film school.

[13]The only lesbians that let me touch upon them were my pet hamsters Stacey and Lacey. When I was in the sixth grade, I would watch the little rodents pleasure each other while slapping one off myself.

[14]*Vertigo* is the condition my mother-in-law experienced when watching *Terror Firmer*. It is also the title of a thriller directed by Alfred Hitchcock (1899–1980), a well-known revolutionary producer and filmmaker who was a master of psychological suspense.*

*INDEX GYNO: You're doing the "well-known" thing again. A big FU from you to FG. I know we have something special, but it doesn't make it okay, Lloyd.**

**FOOTNOTE GUY: Thanks for sticking up for me!

Sweet Smell of Success.[15] Only this "fromage" to Hitch had lesbians and handguns—a surefire recipe for success. We were going to make so much money that we would be able finance our next five movies from the net proceeds on this baby. But you know what? Even with the boobs and the beavers and a whole lot of stuff that's not so bad to look at, it ended up being a snore of a movie! Oliver tried to get me to dump the "older, more experienced director" early on and direct *Sugar Cookies* myself when he saw the way things were going, but I didn't listen to him.

FIGURE 2.1 *LK does his famous Quasimodo imitation as he directs rare Siamese twins attached at the tongue.*

Instead, we decided to let the older, wiser, more experienced Theodore Gershuny (who rewrote the script and made it even more boring) direct it. As part of digging ourselves into an even deeper hole, Gershuny's wife Mary Woronov played the lead—and this was a mistake. Mary is a wonderful and talented person, but she did not perform to her highest ability under the direction of her husband, nor did he include enough erotic material in the film to entice the audience . . . or us horny young bastards.

[15]*Sweet Smell of Success* is a classic 1957 American noir film starring Burt Lancaster, Tony Curtis, Susan Harrison, and Martin Milner, directed by Scottish-American director Alexander MacKendrick (1912–1993).

In my gut, I knew this movie wasn't reaching the potential it had on the page that made us all want to produce it in the first place. I knew the fact that the only thing the lovely, talented Mary and Lynn Lowry were stirring within me was the desire to take a nap with my sock, which is never a good sign. But I didn't listen to my gut. I just kept going.

Sugar Cookies did end up contributing to film history, however. It is the only X-rated movie in history to lose money! One positive result of *Sugar Cookies* was that Garrard L. Glenn, Jeffrey Kappelman (the Associate Producer for *Sugar Cookies*), and Oliver Stone formed an alliance, brought in fundraisers and ended up raising the money for Oliver Stone's first directorial effort, *Seizure*.[16] Mary Woronov and Tom Sturges, the *Sugar Cookies* Art Director, also joined the *Seizure* team. Oliver's amazing career was in bloom! Oliver had also invited me to start a movie company with him and to join him in his venture, but I politely declined and clung to my own producing dreams,[17] moving forward to make another shitty movie called *Big Gus, What's the Fuss*? and perpetuate my lifelong streak of fortuitous, genius career moves.

The Kaufman Curse strikes again.

But listen up, dear reader: you can use my shit as an example of what *not* to do. Sit up straight and listen, because this is Produce Your Own Damn Movie Lesson #852 and it's the most important. Trust your gut. PRODUCE WHAT YOU BELIEVE IN (and you will make a piece of art you believe in). DON'T COMPROMISE. If your heart is singing and your passion is flaring,[18] then follow it and don't give in, no matter what, no matter how tough.

---

[16]Oliver Stone later went on to direct the best movie in the history of cinema, *Alexander*, starring two of the homeliest individuals ever to walk the face of the earth, Angelina Jolie and Colin Farrell.

[17]And thus began my trajectory of wildly innovative, career-advancing instincts, which further manifested themselves when we turned down Madonna for a lead role in Troma's *First Turn-On* nearly 10 years later. And by "we" I mean Michael Herz, my Tromatic producing partner of 35 years.

[18]FOOTNOTE GUY: In fact, if any of these things are happening right now, call me! It sounds very interesting. Maybe I can be of some assistance? I may be little, but I have a lot of energy. You can reach me at 718-391-0110. Weeknights after 7:00 p.m. work best for me.

MARK HARRIS FINDS ART IN THE PASSION, NOT NECESSARILY THE DEAL

WHO IS MARK HARRIS?

Mark Harris is one of the few Oscar-winning producers who has poured his blood, sweat and tears into producing such movies as Gods and Monsters, Crash,[19] *and* Million Dollar Baby.

I can only produce movies I feel very strongly about.

The biggest mistake producers make is to make deals, not art with passion. If you just make the deals, you may be successful, but you won't be satisfied.

A POSSIBLE REVERSAL OF FORTUNE?

You want to know the truth, though? I will bet you *any given Sunday* that had *Sugar Cookies* been one of the *natural-born killers* it was meant to be and given a *payout* at the box office as fat as a 1999 bonus on *Wall Street*, it may not have opened *the doors* for Oliver Stone to move ahead with his own *platoon*.[20] So in some sense, everything does happen for a reason, even if we can't quite see the big picture while we're in the middle of it.[21] You're welcome, Oliver Stone!

---

[19]The Oscar winning one by Paul Haggis,* not the masterpiece by David Cronenberg.

*INDEX GYNO: He badmouthed *Poultrygeist* in *Entertainment Weekly*, didn't he?**

**LLOYD'S RESPONSE: Yup.

[20]FOOTNOTE GUY: I counted 5, IG, 5. You?*

*EDITOR'S NOTE: Lloyd, this is very funny, but maybe your readers need some clarification.**

INDEX GYNO: Actually, FG, there are 6 total.*

*** Oliver Stone did go on to make such box office hits as *Any Given Sunday*, *Natural Born Killers*, *Payout*, *Wall Street*, *The Doors*, and *Platoon*.

[21]FOOTNOTE GUY: This is some deep philosophical stuff, Lloyd. You've really grown a lot as a human being since we last spent time together. I have to say, I'm really digging it! Have you been reading any Marianne Williamson*?

*INDEX GYNO: Marianne Williamson is a spiritual activist, author, and lecturer. In other words, she is Lloyd's guru and self-help "bitch." He calls her "TroMarianne."**

**EDITOR'S NOTE TO INDEX GYNO: Ms. Gyno, would you please be so kind as to include this reference to Marianne Williamson in the index? I don't want her lawyers to be upset if we don't include her.

DON'T BELIEVE IN THE TOP 100, TOP 10 OR TOP ANYTHING LISTS

The American Film Institute (AFI) publishes a list of the top 100 films every year. How this list is compiled, no one can be sure. But here are my top five reasons not to believe in this piece of shit:

1. Art is not meant to be rated.
2. Don't trust lists heavily weighted toward George Lucas.
3. Don't trust lists possibly generated by individuals who think film history started with Leonardo DiCaprio and Kate Winslet on the deck of the *Titanic*.
4. If Ben Affleck and I are both left off of this list, how accurate can it really be?
5. Why should you listen to what other people decide are the best films?! Produce your own damn list!

Instead, think about how many people had to bend over in order to be included in this list.

JUST LIKE *JFK* AND *NIXON*

Oliver Stone and I had many sleepovers as young lads growing up in New York City. I would bound over to his house, sleeping bag in hand, eager for the fun, sleepless nights, baseball cards, girl-bashing, and rough-housing[22] ahead of me. Inevitably, at some point in the evening, Oliver would find something I said or did that would piss him off or throw him into a rage and he would beat me up. This behavior was very helpful in honing the strong decision-making/occasional artistic-bullying skills he would later need as a film producer. Oliver owes me! I'd flee, crying, in the middle of the night, and run back home. This continued well on into the seventh grade. Speaking of the seventh grade. . .

---

[22]INDEX GYNO: "Rough-housing"? Was it Oliver Stone who turned you into the "gay married man" described on your MySpace profile?

HOW STEVEN PAUL GOT STARTED AT THE RIPE OLD AGE OF 12

WHO IS STEVEN PAUL?

Steven Paul started as a 12-year-old child actor in Mark Robson's movie, Happy Birthday, Wanda June, *penned by Kurt Vonnegut, Jr. He eventually branched off into directing and producing his own damn movies, most recently* Ghost Rider, *starring yet another actor no one has ever heard of, Nicholas Cage. Steven Paul also manages such talent as Jon Voight and Gene Wilder. Currently, he is working with Steven Spielberg on producing* Ghost in the Shell, *a remake of a huge Japanese movie. Steven first met me when he was a student in my filmmaking class at the School of Visual Arts in New York City.*

When I was a kid, I bought some video tape equipment. I carried a backpack and a battery pack and schlepped it everywhere. I was 12 years old. At that time, people did not have video. So there I was, this 12-year-old kid, making movies. It was extraordinary. And when I was acting in a movie called *Happy Birthday, Wanda June*, the director, Mark Robson, turned to me and said, "Steven, can I see some of the stuff you're filming with the actors? I'd like to see how the rehearsals have been going."

It was really one of the first "Behind the Scenes" that was ever done. I did it with my own little video camera. I started doing all these interviews and learned how to do stuff with my video camera. It doesn't make a difference what format you work in—you've got to get the experience. In order to be a producer, you've got to learn how to direct, you've got to learn how to move the camera, you've got to learn how to move people around.

So that's what I did. From the time I was 12 to around age 16, I learned so much just by seeing the camera movement, seeing what was in the background. I began to realize that you need to pay attention to details in the background. What about the lighting? What about the sound? I started doing the same thing with headphones. I edited my own damn films—I was writing, I was producing, I was directing, I was editing, I was doing the special effects. There wasn't anything I didn't do. I was becoming a complete and total filmmaker.

And then when I was ready to make my first film, I ran around to all the studios. No one wanted to finance me. They were all sitting around and they all claimed they were going to finance me, but nobody would. I was having meeting after meeting after meeting. And finally, at 18 I was fed up and I realized that I had to make my own damn movie.[23] I set a date and started putting it all

[23]FOOTNOTE GUY: Hey, Steven, this is good stuff! Don't tell Lloyd, but I think it's too bad you're not writing this book. You have a lot of interesting things to say and I don't think there's a single fart joke in your entire sidebar so far!

together. Before I knew it, I had raised a little money from doctors. One guy gave me $10K. He introduced me to another guy. That guy gave me $5 K. Another guy gave me $7 K, and before I knew it I had put together $300K, $400K, in cash.

Then I went around to all of the equipment houses and I said you've got to give me a little credit. I went around to all the laboratories and said you've got to give me a little credit, too. Everybody I spoke to decided to help me because I had nice energy. I was talking to these people and saying, "Listen, you are going to be part of my future movie career."

FIGURE 2.2 Steven Paul with Jerry Lewis on the set of *Slapstick (Of Another Kind)* circa 1982.

FIGURE 2.3 Producer Steven Paul on set of *Baby Geniuses* starring Kathleen Turner (pictured left).

Anyhoo, in my efforts to forge ahead in my own producing career, I moved to the opposite end of the spectrum. Not making slam dunks in an X-rated feature? Why not try a children's classic for the whole family? A G-rated film adventure! And if the English language isn't working for me, why not try shooting in Hebrew?! And thus I set out to produce *Ha Balash Ha'Amitz Shvartz (Big Gus, What's the Fuss?)*. Pioneers far ahead of our time, we arranged a $200K co-production between the American and Israeli film industries, wherein each country was responsible for raising $100K. Michael Herz[24] and his wife Maris also invested in this soon-to-be abomination.

We were told that Israelis see every movie eight times, so we were bound to become their next national phenomenon. There would be two versions in two languages (which meant two negatives of the film). The movie would be shot in English and Hebrew ("Genius!" I thought. "Brilliance personified!") and have all the hot Israeli stars of the day—heck, Menahem Golan[25] was producing! He would raise half of the money with the Israelis and we would raise the other half and together we'd have a mitzvah.[26]

Yet had there been a tag line for Big Ol' Gus, it would have included the words *Sheer Fucking Twisted as Your Mother Lunacy*. Every bad decision I could possibly make, I made, in full and unabashed earnestness. Andy Lack, my co-producer, kept telling me I was crazy and to back out—he saw the writing on the wall, but I plunged onward, determined and stubborn, even though my guts were puking green goo.

---

[24]Michael Herz, the Jesus-like forgiving soul he is, did fuck up what could have been a productive post–law school life by becoming my partner at Troma Entertainment. His beautiful wife Maris has never forgiven me.

[25]Menahem Golan is an Israeli director/producer who was the pioneer of the pre-sell. (For more information on what the pre-sell is, see Chapter 6. To curb your curiosity and allay your confusion in the meantime: no, I am not referring to the part of the definition that describes what I sometimes do with my body on West 39th Street in order to finance my movies, but to the concept of actually raising production funds by selling a movie before it even exists.) I once spoke to Menahem about producing a movie based on a book Michael and I had optioned called *The Yale Murders*, and before I knew it, there were full-page advertisements pre-selling *The Yale Murders* in *Variety*, even though we hadn't signed a thing!

[26]I must be thinking about the mitzvah van outside the Barnes & Noble on 86th Street. I went in there for Channukah and oy, what I saw, what I felt . . . who knew?

Mr. Shabbat Shalom (Menahem Golan) dropped out for no apparent logical reason.[27] Our half of the money was already safely stowed[28] in an Israeli bank. The only fly in the ointment was that there was no money from Israel to match our cash. The Israelis contributed "services" such as film developing and processing, valued at about 50 times what they actually were worth. So we were fucked, or *schtupped*, as they say in Gaza.

Andy and I flew across the Atlantic to check up on our baby. As we arrived on the set, where all business was conducted in Hebrew, there was a lot of passion and intense gesticulation among the actors. Oh, I thought to myself, maybe Menahem dropping out wasn't such a bad thing after all—things seem to be moving along quite nicely. They seem very dedicated to the material, very committed. And then I got closer:

HOT ISRAELI ACTOR (MOISHE): When is the goddamn fucking lunch break?! We have been on this set all day and not done one fucking thing. My ass is tired and these bitches better feed us soon."
And then, turning to me, Moishe said: "I want more money, Mr. Producer!"

HOT ISRAELI ACTRESS (TOVAH): Shove your worthless piece of driveling shit back up your ass and then when it comes back out again, serve it on a plate to your mother.
And then, turning to me, Tovah said: "I want more money, Mr. Producer!"

This nonstop shrieking tower of Hebrew babble went on for what seemed like 42 hours every day. Panicked, I checked up on our money that was oh-so-safely stashed in that Israeli bank account only to find that the checks had been flowing forth to finance[29]

---

[27]And for this he did not pass "go." Nor will he have 72 Virginians in his afterlife.*

*EDITOR'S NOTE: Wrong religion, Lloyd.**

LLOYD'S RESPONSE: You're right! It's like the Pope said. There was no holocaust.*

***EDITOR'S RESPONSE: The Pope did not say that, Lloyd. Please don't get us in trouble with the Catholic Church. *Please.*

[28]I really wish all those English teachers had told me how foolishly fucking fishy alliteration is.

[29]INDEX GYNO: Lloyd, I hope you appreciate how hard FONT GYNO had to work in stressing the right letters for emphasis in this section. She is only part-time, you know, and the publisher hasn't really been paying her what she's worth.

JOE DANTE EXPLAINS THE IDEAL RELATIONSHIP

WHO IS JOE DANTE?

Joe Dante is a top-drawer producer and director of horror and science fiction films. Some of his most notable works include The Howling, *the soon-to-be-released* The Hole, *and the movies that brought the meaning of "cute" to a whole new level,* Gremlins *and* Gremlins 2: The New Batch. *Lloyd still owns them both on laser disc, and pops them in for a back-to-back marathon when he's feeling gloomy.*

As a director, if you find a producer who understands you and vice versa, you would be crazy to lose him/her, because every time you make a movie and put a new budget together there has to be a period of adjustment where you try to figure everybody out. Who's a phony? Who's not a phony? Who knows what they are talking about and who doesn't? You can cut through all that after you've made a couple movies by sort of hand-picking people in all the different areas and saying "I like to work with this guy and this guy" and "I don't particularly like to work with this guy. I don't want to work with him again." After you've made a couple of pvictures, you'll find that you have put together this band of regulars in front of the camera and behind the camera who are all on the same wavelength and can even communicate in a nonverbal way. You don't have to have long arguments about "Why did you do it this way?" or "What if we did it this way?" or "What should the ending be?" It's very important that it's a very personal relationship between a producer and a director. You must be on the same side; you can't have one guy on the studio side and the other one on the creative side. It must be a union.

the nightmare unfolding in front of me. Apparently, Andy and I were thought of as the "rich Americans." For the first time on foreign soil, I thought about blowing my fucking brains out.

BACK TO THE BIG FUSS

Big Gus, what's the fuss?! First of all, they were *dubbing* the lines into English. Even the version shot in the English language itself was so unintelligible, it had to be dubbed from English into English,[30]

[30] I later went on to repeat this same mistake when shooting *The Toxic Avenger II* in Japan, wherein the scenes shot with non-English-speaking Japanese actors trying to speak English were so unintelligible they also had to be dubbed from English into English.

just like *Trainspotting*. Michael Herz, Andy Lack, Pat, and I dubbed almost all of the voices. In fact, Michael Herz was so good at dubbing that he could have turned it into a career far more lucrative than continuously getting fucked in the ass by Troma for the past 35 years.

The whole ~~mess~~ fuss didn't really do much for my friendship with our associate producer/fundraiser Andy Lack, who was encouraging me to follow my gut. But I denied it. What had I done? Against my much better judgment, I COMPROMISED. I PRODUCED SOMETHING I DIDN'T BELIEVE IN. And I paid the price.

Big Gus, What's the Fuss? was released in Israel, but never in the United States. Someone did most certainly make money on it over there, but we never saw one fucking kosher cent. Our "partner," the lab, ignored us when we wrote to them. The Israeli distributor ignored us when we wrote to them. I tried to transfer the negative to New York City, but the Israelis kept it. I never saw or had it in my possession again. If I had had it, Troma could have potentially made money distributing this film during the video boom of the 1980s, as we contractually held all worldwide rights (except for Israel). Video stores back then needed to fill their shelves. You could sell anything that moves—even bowel movements like *Big Gus*! But without the negative and the ability to make release prints, we were powerless to license the film to distributors.

Actually, somehow, someway, I did, however, eventually manage to get my hands on a 16mm print of the movie. (Where this print has since gone to, I've no idea. It probably burned itself in an act of making the world a better place.) We wrote to temple congregations all over the United States to gauge their interest in renting *Big Gus*. Only one of them took us up on the offer. A rabbi at a synagogue in Cincinnati wrote us back after hosting such a screening:

Dear Lloyd Kaufman and Troma Entertainment:

Your movie, Big Gus, What's the Fuss? *was screened as part of the adult/youth interaction program for our congregation yesterday evening.*

This movie is an absolute abomination of which you should be ashamed. No torah-carrying self-respecting Jewish man would ever produce this piece of drek you call art. Give us our money back! I am sorry Hitler didn't incinerate you!

Regards,
Rabbi A. G.

P.S. What would your mother say if she saw this film?

Leave it to a rabbi to intuit that I have very little self-respect. The *Big Gus*, "What's the Mess?" mess, along with Rabbi A.G.'s guilt-trip-inducing letter, can be directly attributed to the origins of my becoming a self-hating Jew and later defiantly marrying a Methodist. I vowed that I would keep control over my negatives at least until the second coming. I learned that if you control the negative of your film, you control the rights to your movie and your movies will always take care of you.[31] Remember this, yet another cautionary tale, when you produce your own damn movie!

FIGURE 2.4 *To make meaningful films, you need to have meaningful experiences. LK had a powerful experience as the only Jew in Yemen.*

But heck, if *Big Gus* has been released in the United States and become a sensation, it may have been a sort of modern-day Hannah Montana. However, had Andy Lack not escaped from my madness, he probably would not have gone on to run CBS News, then NBC News, and then SONY Music. As you can see, Andy Lack has been acronymically[32] at the apex of his game in a long career. Andy Lack certainly does not *lack* (except for having to remember a nightmare production known as *Big Gus What's the Fuss?*).

First Oliver Stone, then Andy Lack. At least the Kaufman Curse is not contagious. There is only one target of its wrath and that target's name is *moi*! Everything does indeed happen for a reason, even if you can't always see it right away.[33]

The irony in all of this? The day after the movie was set for release in Israel, the Seven-Day War broke out. The theatre screening *Big Gus* closed down and all filmgoing in Israel came to a halt. While bombs were going off outside the cinema, the mother of all bombs was being projected *inside* the theatre.

In the spirit of that twist of fate or act of God, here is my first set of rules for producing your own damn movie:

1. Don't forget that when you're hard up for cash to make your movie, anyone is an approachable ATM.
2. What is it that makes your movie so damn special? It doesn't have to be X-rated like *Sugar Cookies*, but it has to have something compelling that makes it really unique and specific to you, the producer—not to mention the audience.
3. Get involved only in movies you feel truly passionate about. If it comes from the heart, it'll show and it'll work.

---

[31]Just like Chino at the Man Hole Club II just outside the Holland Tunnel in Jersey City takes care of me.

[32]FOOTNOTE GUY: Hey, Lloyd, what do you think of my word? I stuck it in when no one was looking.*

*INDEX GYNO: Hey, idiot, NBC and CBS are acronyms, but SONY is not!

[33]I can't help myself. I like Marianne Williamson. I'm also kind of getting into Deepak Chopra now. He's good, he really knows his stuff.

4. Trust your gut. If something nags at you, listen to it.[34]
5. Producing films in Israel can be ass, unless you have a good local producer.
6. As with Oliver Stone and Andy Lack and Steven Paul, remember who you meet in this world and who you work with, as you never know where they are going or where they'll end up. Always do your best to honor your professional relationships.[35]
7. Everything happens for a reason. (Reader, I encourage you to think about The. Power. Of. Now.[36])
8. **A**lliteration is **A**lso **A**ss.
9. Finally, forget what I said earlier about not listening to top ten lists. This top nine list is awesome!

Once upon a time a man lived through all of this. And he still. Wanted. MORE.

MICK GARRIS DISTINGUISHES THE MASTERS OF HORRORS

WHO IS MICK GARRIS?

Mick Garris is a producer, filmmaker, and screenwriter known for his adaptations of Stephen King stories. He is also the mastermind creator behind Showtime's Masters of Horror.

Whenever I've had a bad experience with producers, it's because they just want to save money, or they just want to pull the plug, or they just want to

[34]Particularly if she is your wife or significant other.**

And by significant other I mean your gay lover who lives on West 27th Street, Apt. 4G, double green awnings, south side of the street, between 10th and 11th Avenues.*

***FOOTNOTE GUY: Footnotes within footnotes? Have I told you that this is very innovative and edgy? This is why I love you, Lloyd!

[35]EDITOR'S NOTE: Lloyd, I am really moved by this moving spiritual side to you. I appreciate your making yourself vulnerable to your fans and aspiring producers.

[36]EDITOR'S NOTE: Lloyd, we finally have something in common! I love Eckhart Tolle, too! Every time he's on Oprah, I DVR it. And then I watch it on replay again and again!**

**INDEX GYNO: An Eckhart Tolle reference? Sweet! I'm not sure how to index it, but I'll figure something out. I'm starting to like you, Mr. Kaufman.

swing their dicks and show you how powerful they are. A good producer loves movies, loves what he's doing, and helps you do what you're doing. A bad producer is a guy who's just in it to get chicks, to make money, and has no respect for the movie being made. A bad producer counts pennies rather than help you figure out how to save the money—for example, finding a way to collapse a few scenes into one location because you're there for a day and then you're out. Not all producers are creative producers and that's fine, but they should be your partner, not your enemy.

Believe in what you are doing, but realize that if you're going to take a stand, you may lose. I'm very proud of the first two years of my baby, *Masters of Horror*, but it was adopted and abused in its third year and I didn't want to be a part of that. I understand why it had to change, but I didn't feel that I needed to be involved in it. I've been in the business for a while now, so that's easier to say. If it were my first show, I'd eat shit, I would take it. But I'm at the point now, thankfully, where I don't have to eat shit all the time—though occasionally I still have to chew on a turd or two.

A good producer is a confidante, a cheerleader, someone who doesn't say "no," but rather, "What about if we did this or this?" Again, a good producer acts as my partner and not my teacher or my boss. He or she helps me find a way to do the things I need to do to make a great movie. For instance, maybe it's not in the budget to have a crane or Steadicam everyday, but a good producer will come up with a way to help me do it. A good producer is as committed to the film as I am. We all share the same vision, enthusiasm, and excitement.

So Close in So. Cal Asks Lloyd

Dear Lloyd,

I want to know how to raise a film budget without having to work for someone else for 20 years. That is what I really want to know, because a few thousand dollars is the only thing holding me back now that I'm not in film school anymore.

Truly,

So Close in So. Cal.

Dear So Close,

I think you need to be a little more honest with yourself. If you want to make a film and you are not currently making a film, money isn't the thing holding you back.

You say that you went to film school. This leads me to believe that there is money floating around somewhere in your life. After all, film school isn't free. Uncle Lloyd thinks that one of the following may be true:

1. You don't really want to make a film, but you don't want to get a real job either.
2. You do want to make a film, but you haven't invested the time in coming up with an idea and actually writing a script. A script may be your best gateway into producing—much like pot being the best gateway into crystal meth.
3. You have some good ideas, but you are afraid to begin because you are afraid of failing.
4. You invested all of your money with Bernie Madoff and you are telling the truth about being destitute.

If any of the first three are true, then you need to examine whether filmmaking is truly what you have a passion for, or whether it was the only major where you didn't have to take Calculus with Dr. Pulaski at 7:00 a.m. And if the fourth option is true, I apologize for calling you a liar.

The fact remains—if you really want to make a movie, you can make a movie. It doesn't matter if the budget is the $13.57 it cost to buy 3 gallons of Karo Syrup and some red food coloring. Beg, borrow, and steal the rest.

And if you need to work for someone else for 20 years, do that and make movies in your free time. If you're doing what you love, you'll die a happy man.

And please review this book on Amazon. I'm really sorry I called you a liar.

XOXO,
Lloyd

Chapter | three

Film School or Porno? Taint No Difference or My Dinner with Louis Su

PRODUCER: If I, Lloyd Kaufman, president of Troma Entertainment and creator of *The Toxic Avenger*, am the producer, I'm the all-knowing, all-powerful one. If I'm directing, it's the guy listening to me. In any case, the producer is the one (or ones) who supervise(s) all production aspects from initial conception to final exhibition.[1] I, as producer, make some of the big artistic decisions—developing the script, choosing the actors, director, and so on. Some producers will take a stronger hand in all the artistic decisions; others will produce only what the director wants.

Synonyms: Go-To Guy, Answer Man

Example: "*I heard Mel Gibson has 23 children!*"

"*Yep, Mel Gibson is quite a producer.*"

[1]Not unlike what goes on at the Manhole Club, where I am known as Roy.*

*FOOTNOTE GUY: I'll go with you to the Manhole Club, if you want! I've been really lonely.

Let's recap. In the early 1970s I made a few movies that showed some promise (well, at least *Battle of Love's Return* got good reviews and Brian De Palma[2] liked it). I was learning from my mistakes and still wanting much more than just a taste—I wanted to eat a bigger piece of the moviemaking pie.[3]

I continued to further my informal Film Producer School education by taking on production roles in little known movies such as *Saturday Night Fever* and *Rocky*, supervising productions and lining up locations. *Rocky*, incidentally, was almost made without any Philadelphia location footage. This turned out to be rather insignificant in the end anyhow, as no one remembers the scene where Rocky runs up the steps of the Philadelphia Art Museum[4] and the museum staff to this day still wonder why people run up all of their steps at high speed and then pump their fists in the air when they've triumphantly completed their one-man race. The producers decided to obtain this footage using non-union crew members working under the radar in Philadelphia before principal photography began in Los Angeles. I was put in charge of this.

In order not to draw the attention of the Philadelphia teamsters, we had to keep a low profile. So, handling these under-the-radar location logistics such as parking permits, dressing and holding rooms for the actors (instead of big trailers and honey wagons), places in stores or neighboring houses to defecate (instead of visible port-a-potties[5]), put me in touch with the producing nuts and bolts I needed as a foundation for my career.[6]

---

[2]Brian De Palma is a major American director. He started with low-budget movies like Troma's *The Wedding Party* and graduated to mainstream movies like *Snake Eyes* and *Body Double*.

[3]EDITOR'S NOTE: Don't go there, Lloyd.

[4]Least of all the union crew members in Los Angeles who thought they were making a movie shot entirely on the West Coast and were unaware the non-union Troma team was setting up a *Rocky* location shoot in Philly.

[5]Again, we had to be very careful not to draw attention to the non-union production. Port-a-potties have an aroma that immediately says, "There is a movie being made here; break their non-union asses."

[6]There will be more on producing on location in Chapter 7. I hope.

SAGE ADVICE FROM ROGER CORMAN—ALSO SOME OREGANO ADVICE

WHO IS ROGER CORMAN?

Roger Corman is a prolific and legendary producer and director. He is the godfather—the Big Kahunah—of independent film. I was especially influenced by his excellent low-budget films based on the tales of Edgar Allan Poe and 1963's Man with the X-Ray Eyes. *It is not at all outrageous to suggest that every major actor and director in Hollywood today has gotten his start in a Roger Corman production—Martin Scorsese, Peter Bogdanovich, Jonathan Demme and Jack Nicholson, to name a few. Roger Corman may be the only person on IMDB with more producing credits than moi.*

There is still room to start as a personal assistant or an intern in the mailroom at the William Morris Agency[7] or as a gopher on a movie. Learn from the producer and/or learn on the set. People who work hard will rise. There are so many people who aren't good and don't work hard that almost anyone who does work hard will get that promotion.

FIGURE 3.1 *Roger Corman directing John Hurt in the 1990 film Frankenstein Unbound.*

We hold Roger Corman's truths stated here as self-evident. But it is a fact too often ignored by the "quality of life" people who feel that going home to your mother's funeral is far more important than serving pizza on the set of *Tromeo & Juliet*.

[7]Headquarters for the International Church of Satan. William Morris Agency recently merged with Endeavor Agency.

CUT TO:

Ho Tse Toh Tse Chinese Restaurant, somewhere deep in the heart of Chinatown, New York.

Louis Su and Lloyd Kaufman sit in a corner booth. A plate of Peking duck, a Canon VIXIA digital camera, a cheap Chinese knock-off of a BlackBerry, and a Chinese bootleg copy of *Class of Nuke 'Em High* DVD lay on the table between them.

LOUIS SU: Ni Hao[8], my friends, Ni Hao. My name Louis Su. I famous Chinese director.

WHO IS LOUIS SU?

Louis Su is the legendary but unknown Chinese film producer and member of the Chinese Cultural Revolution. A forefather in the champion of student rights, in response to the Little Red Book, he produced the Blue Balls Book, which led to the 1,000 blooming flowers renaissance period of China. As Lloyd Kaufman majored in Chinese Studies at Yale University, he is an especially appropriate and logical choice to record Su Syansheng's[9] musings. Some believe the name Louis Su is a pseudonym Lloyd used to direct porno films. But that's absurd, as Lloyd has never even seen a porno film. Louis Su is not Lloyd. He is Asian and infinitely more attractive, in a spicy hot, sweet-and-sour sort of way.

BACK TO:

Shot of Louis Su, elbows propped on table, chopsticks pointed at the camera, bowtie slightly loose.

LOUIS SU: Please forgive me, my English not so good. My good friend Lloyd ask me write chapter for his produce book. I say for sure, anything for my good friend Lloyd.[10] Plus, now he take me Chinatown for Hunan all-you-eat

---

[8]NI HAO: "Hello" in Chinese.

[9]SYANSHENG: "Mr." in Chinese.

[10]Plus, I won raffle for evening with next Tromette of the Month on http://www.troma.com. Until then, I go Chinese massage parlor and work it out.

buffet lunch. Sorry interrupt, Lloyd, but you forget we met around same time. I was big important American pornography director and you just little piece of Yale shit hoping to grow big making turd movie in Israel. I took you under my Peking duck wing.

LLOYD: Heh-heh, that's right Louis Su! Remind me again just how we, um, met?

LOUIS SU: I big famous American pornography director in 1970s, decade beautiful fashion and pinnacle of porno chic. I in same class as good dead friend Gerard Damiano, may he R.I.P.[11] now.

Louis Su erupts into a series of small but violent sneezes.

LLOYD: Louis! Louis? Are you okay?

LOUIS SU: I fine, I fine. Sum Yong Dong lodged in deep throat[12] last night. Sorry. We begin again. In order for you understand me, I must speak of rise of pornography chic in 1970s. Consider grand new art form.

LLOYD: Oh, really, Louis Su? I had, uh, I had no idea. I thought you were in this country on a sort of, uh, cultural exchange.

LOUIS SU: What's matter, you now old fuck? You remember, Lloyd, when we met first time I was producing, directing, editing, lighting my own porno movie musical call *The Newcomers* in 1973. Heh, heh. That title still make me pudding fart. It star Harry Reams, Jamie Gillis, Georgina Spelvin, and Tina Russel.

LLOYD: My, my, Louis Su! What, what—

Intense coughing fit from Lloyd Kaufman. Waitress brings over a pot of Chinese tea and some water and pours Lloyd a cup and glass of each, respectively. Lloyd takes a big gulp and clears his throat. Louis Su exhibits zen-like patience throughout this episode.

---

[11]According to *Merriam's Webster Dictionary*, "R.I.P." is defined as (1) standing for "rest in peace" or (2) the extraordinary ability one's nether regions possess when extremely relaxed.

[12]INDEX GYNO: *Deep Throat* is a movie, bitches. A big fucking famous porno made in the 1970s when porno was en vogue, hot, and very, very risqué. It cost less than $25,000 to make, made over $50,000,000, and was busted approximately 60,000,000 times by cops raiding the theatres screening it. But if you're reading this book, I think you might already know that.

LLOYD: Sorry, excuse me. Tell our readers, Louis, um, what made you decide to produce a porno?

LOUIS SU: Decision big, how you say? No brainer. It cost hardly any money to make and I write, produce, edit my own damn movie on 35MM film, and uh . . . heh-heh . . . also get to watch all action and learn on my feet all producing parts . . . and not just producing parts, but also other lovely female parts were bonus. Big. Bonus. Harry Reams had really big bonus! HAHAHAHAHA!!

LLOYD: Wow! You made a musical with naked people dancing. Naked gynos bouncing up and down!

Lloyd pulls a wad of crumpled tissues from his pocket and sets them in his lap.

LLOYD: It *is* sort of coming back to me now. It was very inspiring. You know, today in America, the Vivid and Wicked production companies practically have a monopoly on pornographic movies and everything is so . . . well, clinical—the story is reduced to videotape of people fucking and sucking. But in the 1970s, it was almost an art form, you know? Everyone in Europe and the United States, even respected directors with vision, were making pornos like *Behind the Green Door*, *Divine Obsession*, and *The Devil in Miss Jones.*[13] You were really able to say something with your story, go somewhere with your characters! I mean, that's what I have heard.

LOUIS SU: Dwei, dwei,[14] it's true, Lloyd man. Very true. ABC Channel 7 even reviewed *The Newcomers* when it uh, heh-heh, come out. This not happen, how you say? Nowadays. American Katie Couric won't talk about my porno piece of art on television. She hairy cunt.[15]

---

[13]Directed by the Mitchell Brothers, *Behind the Green Door* (1973) told the story of Gloria Saunders, a damsel abducted to a sex theatre and forced to perform various sexual acts with multiple partners in front of a masked audience (according to Wikipedia). Containing the legendary "post-ejaculation semen flying through the air for a full seven minutes scene," *Behind the Green Door* and Gerard Damiano's *The Devil in Miss Jones* (1972) were among the first 35mm pornos to be reviewed by mainstream media and widely released in the United States. *The Devil in Miss Jones* was later remade as *Forrest Gump.*

[14]DWEI, DWEI: "That's right" (in Chinese.)

[15]EDITOR'S NOTE: Oh, Katie, this is terrible. Louis Su is not from here, so he doesn't have good manners. Please forgive him. If you are reading this, I adore you.

LLOYD: Well, I remember you saying how much you . . . um, learned from the whole experience![16] How it inspired you to produce your own epic movies in Shanghai, such as *The Good Woman from Szechuan*.[17] See, I went to an all-boys school and spent one year in Africa, so I ~~was~~ am pretty retarded about the opposite sex. I mean, I thought fellatio was a gelato flavor. Now I know it's what you can do with farm animals. I took production jobs on blockbuster films as my training, while you, *you*, Louis Su, as a *newcomer* to the field, just immersed yourself in the world of pornography! I wish I had had the ~~foreskin~~ foresight to think about expanding my ~~penis~~ horizons by getting my own, sort of film school experience and training in working on the exciting films you got to work on! Porno can be a great film school. Sye sye,[18] Louis Su.

A loud crash emits from somewhere in the dining room behind Lloyd. He cranes his neck to follow the commotion and, much to his surprise, sees the familiar face of David Chien, aspiring young filmmaker and loyal, devoted Troma fan who occasionally assists Lloyd on projects in Los Angeles. David recognizes Lloyd and saunters over.

DAVID CHIEN: Hey, Lloyd, what's up?

Lloyd points his video camera at David.

LLOYD: David! Hi! I was just having, um, a late lunch with my friend Louis Su.

---

[16]INDEX GYNO: Daddy Lloyd, don't you think it's time you give up this façade and admit that you, in fact, are Louis Su?*

*EDITOR'S NOTE: Lloyd, is what Ms. Gyno says true? Because if it is, I'm not sure we can print this interview out of fairness to your readers. Also, I'm really not sure that the questionable "educational" tone of this chapter is in line with the goals of Focal Press. Let's talk.

[17]EDITOR'S NOTE: Lloyd, I do have to brush up on some of my dramatic references here, but are you sure Louis Su did *The Good Woman from Szechuan*? That's Bertolt Brecht, no? Yes. Yes, it is. Bertolt Brecht.*

*LLOYD'S RESPONSE TO EDITOR: Gesundheit! Bless you, Elinor!

[18]SYE SYE: "Thank you" in Chinese.

Camera pans to the lunch remains and place setting for one. David gives Lloyd a puzzled look but smiles back.

DAVID: Cool. Good to see you.

LLOYD: Yes, yes, good to see you, too. You know, I'm working on my next book, *Produce Your Own Damn Movie!*, and I was um, just talking to Louis Su . . . ohhhhhh . . . .

Camera again pans back to the empty lunch setting.

LLOYD: He's um, all finished . . . quick eater, and he's . . . he's in the restroom right now! Yes, the restroom. I was talking to Louis Su about how I did not want to go to or to pay for film school, so I used my production jobs as my own damn film school. Maybe you can tell me about your own film school experience—I know you have some opinions about that.

DAVID: Oh, yeah, well, there's this big delusion that after graduating from college with a degree in film, you will produce your first feature, it'll be accepted into Sundance, and you'll get a deal with a major independent film company. And then your career will take off with a three-picture contract from Sony Classics[19] that will send you into your very next production.

LLOYD: Yes, well, tell me how you see it.

DAVID: Well, I attended film school at the University of Southern California and graduated in 2005. I then spent some time assisting friends on their film projects and learned more by being a part of a crew than I ever did sitting in a classroom reading Film Theory. I met you during one of your *Make Your Own Damn Movie* master classes—

LLOYD: I remember! It was what, 2006?

DAVID: Yeah. You let me help you out with a variety of things like shooting B-camera for interviews and Troma events. I learned a lot just by doing that. I got to meet Eli Roth, Joe Dante, Stuart Gordon, Penelope Spheeris, James Gunn, and many, many more! And for all of this I've received a whopping $100 plus an Associate Producer credit on your *Direct Your Own Damn Movie!* DVD boxed set. I've loved working with a guy like yourself who has made a ton of

---

[19]SONY CLASSICS: A division of Sony Columbia that produces hardcore pornography, exclusively.*

*EDITOR'S NOTE: You are going to get us sued, gosh darn it! Sony Classics is consistently responsible for some of the best independent movies and discovering new producing and filmmaking talent.

films over many decades, as opposed to some of the professors I had who were failed and bitter screenwriters and directors. You know, the reality is that most people will struggle for years before they have the opportunity to make a movie, if they even produce it at all. Then, once they produce it, there is a high possibility they will likely never see their film distributed commercially. That's why so many of them have to go on to teach, becoming film professors and movie critics! Boy, are they jealous of you, Lloyd, and your independent body of work—

There is a low murmur in the dining room. Having been interrupted, Lloyd and David turn their heads in the direction of the din. A second gyno walks into the Ho Tse Toh Tse Chinese Restaurant and removes her sunglasses.

LLOYD: Who's that?

DAVID: That's Reed Morano.

LLOYD: Reed Morano, as in the cinematographer who just shot the Oscar-nominated *Frozen River* Reed Morano?

DAVID: Yup, that's her!

LLOYD: Wow, it looks like this hole-in-the-wall Chinese restaurant sure does attract a lot of film people who just happen to be very useful to the chapter I'm working on now for my book!

Lloyd rushes up to Reed.

LLOYD: Ms. Morano? Hi, hi! I'm Lloyd Kaufman from Troma Entertainment, creator of *The Toxic Avenger*.

Reed smiles pleasantly and stares blankly back at Lloyd.

REED: Who? Creator of what?

Lloyd blushes furiously.

LLOYD: Er, never mind. I'm writing a book and making a DVD boxed set called *Produce Your Own Damn Movie!* right now. It is very nice to meet you. Congratulations on all of the recent nominations and awards for your film *Frozen River*.

REED: How nice of you! Many thanks! But, I'm sorry, I didn't quite catch your name, who are you again?

David joins them.

LLOYD: And this is David Chien.

DAVID: Nice to meet you, Reed! Big fan.

LLOYD: And, uh, well my companion Louis Su is um, also here, but he's busy in the . . . restroom. The scallion pancakes didn't sit so well with him.

Reed's forehead creases briefly as she darts a look at David. He shrugs.

LLOYD: Well, David was just telling us about how he thinks you don't necessarily have to go to film school to make it in this business. Didn't you go to NYU?

REED: Yes! I graduated from Tisch in 2000.

DAVID: Did you like it?

REED: You know, I loved it, but I think film school is what you make of it.

DAVID: Do you think it's a waste?

REED: Not if you use it properly.

LLOYD: What do you mean?

REED: Well, I originally wanted to direct, but from the first set I worked on, where I saw the DP's[20] job, I knew I wanted *that* job. I wanted to know what the light meter was, where to put all the lights, how to use the camera to tell a story. I wanted to be sure I would be the one who got to see the story first—the one looking through the viewfinder, you know? Another older student told me to take every single technical class, no matter how boring, to offer to shoot everyone's films and to work for as many other DPs as possible so I would learn everything I needed to learn in order to be indispensable by the time I graduated.

LLOYD: Those were student films, right?

REED: Oh, yeah. I mean, I shot a ton of student films that were crappy, but all of us were learning at that time. Stuff that was good enough ended up on my reel and got me shoots after I graduated.

---

[20]DP: Director of Photography in a film. This guy or gyno presides over the camera and lighting crews on a film, ensuring that the artistic and technical vision of the image matches what the director wants.

DAVID: So you also learned by doing.

REED: Yes, but a lot of it has to do with networking. No matter what your particular interest in filmmaking is, it's so important to keep talking to people, working with them on films, and making a name for yourself.

DAVID: Yeah, I think it's a good idea, if you don't go to film school, and I don't think you have to—

REED: Well, no, you certainly don't *have* to.

DAVID: I also think it's a good idea to contact local filmmakers and become an apprentice. Maybe lurk around college campuses and befriend students who have access to the equipment room. Do what you can to be near a movie set, figure out how to get your hands on any camera. I mean, tuition at a film school can cost more than $50K per year. The serious film festivals are tough to get into without knowing someone. A lot of movies are crap anyway . . . at least if yours is good it will definitely get some attention and rise to the top. It's crazy! Instead of wasting time and money on USC film school, you could spend the $50K per year making a feature, or several features! You know the story about Werner Herzog stealing a camera from the school he was working in? I mean, you can even borrow your parents' camcorder and find something interesting to do with it!

REED: Yes, you do have to spend time learning sound, how to grip or set up lights. I mean, if you want to produce . . . what is it again?

LLOYD: Your own damn movie.

REED: Yes, if you want to produce your own damn movie, it's important to be familiar with as many aspects of filmmaking as possible, because it will only help you do your job better. It will make you a better leader if you understand what everyone on your crew or team has to deal with.

LLOYD: That's true.

REED: A lot of producers or directors have never even worked on a set in any capacity.

DAVID: And that's a huge mistake. A huge problem.

REED: Yes, when you jump headfirst into a movie that costs a ton of money, you should have a lot of experience in seeing how different people do it. I mean, this business is all about collaboration.

DAVID: Absolutely.

A brief uncomfortable silence falls over them.

LLOYD: Gee, where *is* Louis Su? He sure is taking a long time in the men's room. I hope he's OK! Maybe I should go check on him?

Reed reaches her hand toward Lloyd in sympathy.

REED: I'm sure he's just *fine.*

David grins.

REED: Anyway, it's also important to spend that time on sets to learn the tangible producing skills you can use in the outside world when you finish film school. Sound guys, editors—they all make good money. If you want to direct feature films for a living, unless you are a trust fund baby, you are going to need a source of income. But most of all, film school surrounds you with other budding filmmakers. If you stay in touch with these people, you could find yourself later making successful feature films with them!

LLOYD: (mumbles to himself) Like Oliver Stone . . . or Madonna.

REED: What?

LLOYD: Oh, nothing. Just thinking about relationships coming full circle.

REED: (a pause and then) Well, anyway, I've worked with a ton of people I went to school with—some of them have really hooked me up.

DAVID: But no one is going to hire you because you went to a great film school.

REED: Right. People hire you because you either know someone or you have a great reel or resume that proves your skills. Film school, if used correctly, gives you all of these. Anyone who says you don't need film school probably wasted their time while they were there and they're bitter.

DAVID: Not bitter, just a lot of money to pay back . . . but I'm learning on my feet on different projects now.

REED: Good! Well, you are right. You don't need film school. The degree is not going to get you shit in this industry. But it can get you producing, directing, and shooting jobs faster if you know how to play the film school game.

Reed checks her watch.

REED: Oh, listen! I was just picking up some wonton soup to go. I have to go to a meeting down the street about my next project. It was so nice to meet you! I like your spirit, David Chien.

DAVID: Yeah, great to meet you. I'll walk out with you. I need to get going.

LLOYD: Well thank you, thanks guys, thanks so much for making time to chat with me!

REED: Sure, sure, my pleasure. Nice to meet you, too . . . er . . . Charlie Kaufman, was it? And uh, tell Louis Su I'm very sorry to have missed him.

Reed takes the soup and pays at the cash register. David walks over to the door and holds it open for Reed.

LLOYD: Well, bye, bye, kids! Djai jyan![21]

Lloyd smiles to himself, shakes his head, sits back down at the table and attempts to remove some soy sauce from the camera. In fiddling with it, the camera begins to play back tape from an earlier interview with Ernest Dickerson.

ERNEST DICKERSON DOES NOT DICKERSON AROUND

WHO IS ERNEST DICKERSON?

Ernest Dickerson is a writer, director and director of photography of independent films. He is Spike Lee's favorite DP. Ernest directed Juice, *as well as a lot of episodic television, such as* Medium, Law & Order, Dexter, Weeds, Heroes, The L Word, Criminal Minds, *and more.*

ERNEST DICKERSON: I am a strong believer that in order to know something about the craft, you have to understand the history of the craft. I'm upset when I see young filmmakers who have no idea about movies made before *Star Wars.* I actually worked with a couple of actors who were talented but had only a vague notion of Marlon Brando and had never even heard of *On the Waterfront.*[22] How can you consider yourself a filmmaker if you don't know the classics?

Formal training gives you a sense of history that helps you tell a better story. It's like musicians who are serious about their work. You hear they listen to classical musicians like Bach, Tchaikovsky, and Mozart in their spare time. They learn the technique. If you are a true film lover, movies are your homework. History gives you a reservoir of knowledge you can dip into. Understanding how and why different directors made decisions will help you grow stronger in developing your own aesthetic and way of working.

---

[21]DJAI JYAN: "Goodbye" in Chinese.

[22]*On the Waterfront* (1954) was a tale of American mob violence and corruption among longshoremen, starring Marlon Brando and directed by Elia Kazan. It won eight Oscars, including Best Picture, Best Actor and Best Director.

CUT TO:

The camera shuts itself off. Lloyd pulls another crumpled wad, this time of paper, from his other pocket. It is an excerpt of notes for his book. He reads it:

"Film school at NYU costs approximately $65K per year. This figure is the cost of tuition and materials for film projects students will make."

Lloyd shakes his head.

CUT TO:

Louis Su stumbling back to the table, making a reference to the uncanny resemblance of the waitress' breasts to his pork dumplings.

LOUIS SU: Lloyd, please pass soy sauce. Soy sauce make my dumpling more, how you say? Succulent.

LLOYD: Louis Su! So glad you've decided to join me again. I was getting worried. How wonderful your American sense of humor is! Soy sauce always makes dumplings even more tasty. Anyhow, do you think we could please get back to the topic at hand?

LOUIS SU: You must be patient like warrior, Lloyd. Great Wall of China not built in one day. Pornography like lotus. Slow blooming to beautiful climax.[23]

LLOYD: I just couldn't agree with you more. This is what Eckhart Tolle tells me to focus on, in his book *Stillness Speaks.*[24]

LOUIS SU: As I saying, we do pornography in 1970s America not only because very titillating—

LLOYD: Wow, your vocabulary has gotten so much better since we first met.

LOUIS SU: But also we take risks with *The Newcomers.* We mix cum shots with singing and dancing. We experiment with camera lenses and filters. Porno then had real script, not just sex. Today, no can do, President Bush made bush sleazy, unacceptable. Back in 1972, you *could*[25] learn and work your way from porno to legitimate.

LLOYD: That's right, Louis Su. Though I had absolutely nothing whatsoever to do with your movies, and by nothing, I mean nothing, beyond referring you to some friends interested in the uh, industry.

---

[23]EDITOR'S NOTE: Lloyd, I'm very concerned we are getting off topic. Then again, I'm not sure what the topic is in the first place.

[24]INDEX GYNO: Normally I don't like to agree with the establishment, but I think Elinor's right—where is this self-help streak coming from? Where's the Daddy Lloyd we all know and love?

[25]FONT GYNO: Lloyd, the work on this project is getting really complicated what with all of the italics, underlining, bolding, and strikethroughs. Can you please talk to your publisher about a raise? My rent is going up, even for my teeny tiny studio apartment down here between two parentheses.

LOUIS SU: Heh-heh. That's right.

LLOYD: My Trinity school classmate was finishing up law school at Columbia, and he wrote the music for you. One of ~~our~~ your investors was a big investment banker involved in pizza franchise.[26] Also, a close friend had a father who was a furrier and had a factory in midtown where ~~we~~ you filmed everything—that one location was the origin of everything for the project, right? For *The Fur Trap*, your next adventure after *The Newcomers*? The location added such high production value. And then, then . . . came your Pulitzer Prize–winning script!

LOUIS SU: Heh-heh. Yes. The factory even had some, uh, beaver furs!

LLOYD: Louis Su! I am moo goo gai panning that pun! This location you used actually leads to a good lesson for our young producers! Here, let me show you.

Lloyd fast-forwards the camera to an excerpt from a Roger Corman interview. Roger Corman speaks to the camera.

THE CORE OF MORE FROM CORMAN

ROGER CORMAN: There are really no secrets about producing, but one of the ways I have been able to get more production value than bigger productions is by shooting in the biggest location I could find. Also, if you are able to use an old set already constructed on a studio lot or on location, it is a great way to save money.

Lloyd turns the camera off again and turns to Louis Su as they get up from the table and get ready to leave.

LLOYD: You know, you really do have to take advantage of those interesting locations, like a fur factory, that you already have access to and save money by filming in them. Make the best and most of your pre-existing relationships, whether from film, college, the Manhole Club, whatever! You just never know where they are going to take you.[27]

---

[26]FOOTNOTE GUY: Speaking of pizza, can you send down some page fresheners? Someone just cut a big cheese down here in the margins. Personally, I suspect the chick in charge of the index.*

*INDEX GYNO: What, did you think I wouldn't see this, asshole? If anything stinks worse in this book so far, it's you.

[27]FOOTNOTE GUY: Your love is taking me higher, Lloyd. Higher than I've ever been lifted before. Which is significant for a little guy like me way down here!

CUT TO:

Louis Su smoking a cigarette, watching a young woman straddle a bicycle loaded with fresh vegetables.

LOUIS SU: Man, you still got it, Lloyd. You still shake your mojo. I overheard that Reed Morano when I was taking big Chinese dump and she very, very smart almond cookie. Troma always does well when paired with gyno power.

LLOYD: Speaking of the gyno power in *The Newcomers*, do you remember how it was on the front page of *the New York Times*?

LOUIS SU: Yes, there was massive raid of porno theatres in Big Apple and *Newcomers* was mentioned front page, *New York Times. Newcomers* busted by cops! HA HA HA HA HA!

LLOYD: Boy! You guys just had all the luck! Kind of like when those bombs dropped in Israel during *Big Gus* premiere. Like the universe is trying to tell you something, like it was supporting ~~my~~ your thinking ~~I~~ you might just be a big fat failure. I mean, Rhonda[28] tells us change our thoughts, change our lives. We *attract* what we *think*.

In those ancient celluloid days, porno was a way in, economically and educationally, but you could go to jail for transporting a 35mm print of pornography across state lines. It was scandalous, scary, and illegal. Nowadays, I'm not sure the pornography route will take you very far or teach you very much. First of all, pornos these days are no longer interested in developing an actual story line or plot. I mean, they can hardly be called films. There is no artistic purpose in making porno today.

LOUIS SU: That's right. Besides, according to *Hustler*'s Larry Flynt, they need bailout. They, too, are failing in bad American economy.

LLOYD: No, no, Louis Su, I don't think the porno business needs a bailout. I think what our young producers need to know, in addition to the fact that they don't necessarily need to go to film school (this is a personal decision[29]), that they can gain practical real-world experience working on other projects in various crew capacities. For about 10 percent of what it cost to make a 35mm porno film in 1970, you can go out and make, direct, and produce your own

---

[28]INDEX GYNO: Rhonda Byrne, who wrote that piece of shit called *The Secret*, which millions of people have forked over money to buy into her "magical ways of thinking."*

*EDITOR'S NOTE: What happens if I start "magically thinking" that you've *already finished* writing this book, Lloyd and that it is *actually useful* to budding movie producers?**

**LLOYD'S RESPONSE: See?! I told you it's shit! XOXO

[29]FOOTNOTE GUY: Lloyd, I am really impressed at how much more open you are to other perspectives. This gives me hope for our relationship.

damn movie for next to nothing these days, what with all of the cheap cameras out there that provide broadcast quality

Look at Giuseppe Andrews! He's an actor in successful movies made by those megaconglomerates.[30] But he's a brilliant producer of independent movie masterpieces. He produces, writes, directs, shoots, edits, and composes his own music on all of his own damn movies. His complete budgets for Troma releases like *Trailer Town* and *Touch Me in the Morning* come in around $2K.[31] No crew; he's just a one-man show! His movies have some graphic adult material, but they sure ain't porno!

LOUIS SU: Yes, yes, very true, Lloyd. Nothing to stand in way of young people today who want to produce movie.

LLOYD: Nothing except yourself.

The cheap Chinese BlackBerry knock-off on the table vibrates. Lloyd picks it up and reads an incoming e-mail.

A NOTE FROM MARIANNE WILLIAMSON

-----------------------Original Message-----------------------

From: marianne@mariannewilliamson.com
Sent: January 31, 2009 1:13PM
To: Lloyd Kaufman <lloyd@troma.com>
Subject: Your course in miracles

Dear Lloyd:

I am so pleased with the progress you are making in your own self-development. You are so attractive. And super hot, too! I want to worship at your big throbbing love shrine.

Best,
Marianne[32]

------------------------End Message---------------------------

[30] *Independence Day*, *Detroit Rock City*, and so on.

[31] His movie *Dribble* was in the Tromadance Film Festival and got a standing ovation. I have a producer credit on one of his recent movies. Andrew's movies contain more old naked men with droopy ball sacs than you will ever see in your lifetime.*

*FOOTNOTE GUY: I feel like I haven't seen much of, well, anything in my lifetime. It's hard being small.

[32] EDITORS'S NOTE: Lloyd, I got a call from our fact-checking department and they have no evidence whatsoever that Marianne Williamson has ever returned any of your 37 e-mails

Moved at Marianne's acknowledgement of his progress, a teeny, tiny, nearly imperceptible tear forms in the corner of Lloyd's eye. He blinks it away and puts the phone back on the table.

LLOYD: I think the important thing is, once again, to start with material that speaks to your heart.[33] For you, Louis Su, it was the 1,000-flowers-bloom pornography in the 1970s. For me, as of late, it's the dastardly evils of the fast food industry and hypocritical billionaire limousine liberals.[34]

A waiter in the restaurant uses a remote control to turn on the overhead fan. This remote control also somehow turns on Lloyd's camera. We now see Trent Haaga talking to the camera.

IN THE TRENT-CHES WITH TRENT HAAGA

WHO IS TRENT HAAGA?

Trent Haaga is an actor, screenwriter, and filmmaker of low-budget horror films rapidly moving up the film food chain. In a true exhibition of sadomasochism, years ago, he co-starred in Terror Firmer *and assistant-directed, co-wrote, and acted in* Citizen Toxie. *He later went on to co-author* Make Your Own Damn Movie *with Lloyd. Recent projects include a producer credit on* Easter Bunny, Kill! Kill!, *writing credits on* Deadgirl, *and acting credits in* Killer Bike Chicks *and* Defective Man!

TRENT HAAGA: Hi, I'm Trent Haaga and I'm reporting live from *Troma's Edge TV.*[35] No, I'm not, I'm actually not. This is flashing me back to the *Troma's Edge TV* days. I'm here to talk to you, Lloyd Kaufman, about producing movies. Use me how you need to use me, Lloyd. Just like you always have.

LLOYD: Let's talk about *Easter Bunny, Kill! Kill!* You were the producer.

---

to her. Also, I have serious reservations about using real people, especially real living people who have millions of dollars and access to a bevy of lawyers, as fodder for your jokes. Even if the rest of this email is real, I *know* that the last part is not.

[33] INDEX GYNO: Other organs are included, too.

[34] INDEX GYNO: And hard-bodied lesbian monkey love, obviously.

[35] *Troma's Edge TV* was a comedy sketch show that Trent helped me produce for Channel 4 in the UK. Trent and Tiffany Shepis served as narrators for this show. *Troma's Edge TV* ran for two years on British TV, but has never been seen on American television.

TRENT: Yes, and as producer, the one thing I didn't do, which is an executive producer thing, is use my own money, except for a few hundred dollars. A lot of people think the producer is the guy who whips out his checkbook and gives all the money to the director.

LLOYD: How much was the budget?

TRENT: *Easter Bunny* was about $8 K, give or take a couple of hundred bucks. We had a crew of about six people. I was the producer, I was also acting as an AD [Assistant Director], I did a little acting in it, but fundamentally we had to make the plan. We had to take the script and break it down. We had to find the locations. We also needed to cast our movie and make sure that the actors would work for free. We had to find our sound guy, find our DP [Director of Photography], we had to make sure everybody was fed, we had to make sure the costumes were together. A bigger film would have a wardrobe person, and so on, and as a producer, I would have to make sure that those departments have everything and that they stay within budget. But on *Easter Bunny* I had to have everything there standing by, everything at arm's length, and ready to go. That's how a producer functions on an $8 K movie.

LLOYD: So, on a lower budget film, actors are providing some of their own costumes?

TRENT: Yeah, basically, a lot of it had to deal with my going to the actors' houses and looking in their closets, picking out clothes that they didn't mind either losing, or getting bloody. We had to break down the script to how many script days there were and what costumes they needed. Basically, it's all the fundamental building blocks of having everything ready. There's tapes, there's cameras and there's a sound guy, and there's food. You've got to know when lunch is going to be served. Each day, you need to know what needs to be shot and how much time there is to shoot that.

You have to know when you're going to move into the next scene and whether or not you feel like you finished the current scene. You are kind of like the overlord and taskmaster. I had a great relationship with Chad Ferrin, the director of *Easter Bunny, Kill Kill!*—I could say "Chad, you've got to lock down this scene and get it done. We have ten minutes. If you could do one, two, three, or four setups in ten minutes, then it would be great. I would recommend you do everything that you need from the beginning to the end of the scene in one setup, and if there's time we have left over, we can shoot other angles." You're spending a lot of money, so you have to watch every dime.

The best way to become a producer is to understand every aspect of filmmaking. Write some movies, assistant-direct some movies, make some breakdowns, and make some schedules. Work for Troma, be a PA (Production Assistant), pick up a second meal for people, and understand what it will cost you to wrap earlier in the day. Will it be more cost-effective to let people go home after two hours or to keep them, even though they're grumpy and they're not getting good work done and they need to be fed? There is a series of checks and balances.

LLOYD: Talk a bit about how Troma produces both good and bad.

TRENT: Well, what's good about Troma is that you, Lloyd, really instill the value of a dollar in all of us. I remember coming to you in your office and you said, "Trent, this is going to be the biggest *Toxic Avenger* yet. Write me the script. *Citizen Toxie*'s going to be $3 million dollars."[36] I wrote you a script with multiple characters in full makeup, car chases, an exploding school, time travel, and M60 machine guns. When the numbers came down, we had a small fraction of that budget, but you never said, "Hey, take out the car chase." You never asked to cut anything out. We'd been given a lower budget and we had to figure out how to do everything—the car chase, the school explosion, everything! Certainly in Hollywood, they would build a big model and get some TNT and an explosives expert and blow it up, but as you and I and those of you who watched the *Citizen Toxie* documentary[37] know we took a picture of the school and put it in a wooden box, filled it up with gasoline and firecrackers, put it on a C-stand, and did a forced perspective shot.[38] For ten dollars, we did a shot that Michael Bay would do for $250K.

As far as Troma-bad goes, I think that it's part of the Kaufman magic and it's part of the frustration. We'll set up a scene, but we don't know how it's going to be shot, or even where we are going to set it up. The great artistic experiment comes from thinking on the fly, but it costs time, money, and effort. Sometimes we know where the scene is, but we don't know where we are going to put the camera. Lloyd sees someone in the background doing something interesting and then we have to pick up the camera and film that and it drags things out. You play around a lot, you don't have a shot list,[39] like

---

[36] *Citizen Toxie* ended up being made for $400,000.

[37] *Apocalypse Soon* is the documentary on the making of *Citizen Toxie*. It is available on the *Make Your Own Damn Movie*! DVD boxed set, available from http://www.troma.com: BUY TROMA!

[38] A forced perspective shot uses the camera to create an optical illusion that an object is further, closer, smaller, or larger than it actually is. It manipulates the view through use of scaled objects and the correlation between these scaled objects and the vantage point of the spectator or camera.*

*FOOTNOTE GUY: I think that was the first informative footnote in this book! Thanks, Trent! Can I call you sometime?

[39] INDEX GYNO: My personal shot list while working on this book has been the following: Tequila, Tequila, Irish Car Bomb, Lemon Drop, Tequila.

other people do on other movies. But you film for 18 hours a day—and *Citizen Toxie* had about 30 days total of filming.

When you're doing a movie in eight days, like *Easter Bunny, Kill Kill!*, it's as simple as, "Here are the shots. This is what we have to do to get from here to there in the scene, because we have to get out of that scene in a half hour." Sometimes, on *Citizen Toxie*, you said it would be a half hour, but it would often take us a lot longer.

LLOYD: Great! Any other advice that you would care to give to young producers?

TRENT: They need a guy like you, who is willing to take someone who is untested and lump as much responsibility on their back as possible. As you can see in the documentary about the making of *Citizen Toxie*, I made a lot of novice mistakes. But I was able to learn from them and also learn how to save money.

The best thing about Troma is that through my having acted, having written, having done PA work, craft (food) services, and so on, I gained great knowledge of every aspect of filmmaking. So now, when someone says, "This stinger is going to cost you X amount," I can say "Fuck you, I'll buy the stinger at Home Depot," because I know what a stinger is.

LLOYD: Of course. A stinger is an after-dinner drink with brandy and crème de menthe. Talk about the Troma cast, how they're not in the Screen Actors Guild.[40]

TRENT: Don't go SAG with the Troma movies. Troma movies are very rambunctious and high-spirited and if you went SAG and had the large cast that you did, it would end up costing you too much. I've never been in SAG, so I think in my opinion, you're doing the right thing when it comes to that. Acting cannot be taught and it doesn't come with a SAG card. If you go to a bar or restaurant here in L.A., every waiter and bartender has a SAG card. Does that mean that they are more talented than a huge Troma fan?[41] I don't think so. They cost you a daily minimum plus all sorts of union add-ons.

---

[40]The Screen Actors Guild (SAG) was a union founded in 1933 to support film and television actors.

[41]Such as huge Troma fan, 500-pound Joe Fleishaker! Joe is not in SAG, nor is he even an actor, but he has appeared in at least a dozen Troma movies. Trent first came to Troma as a fan as well. He had a good job as a computer nerd. He kept showing up at *Terror Firmer* cast auditions, even though he had never acted, making at least six separate trips to our offices. Eventually, he confessed he wanted a part in *Terror Firmer* more than anything in the world. I could see he was talented and his Troma-love was obvious. Instead of a small part for an avid fan, I gave Trent one of the leads in *Terror Firmer*!

LLOYD: What do you think of Troma crews?

TRENT: There are usually way too many crew on Troma movies. You have to feed them and have bathrooms and places for them to sleep. There's an emotional baggage and drama that goes with them as well. Many fans who work for free suck. But your crews are okay. I like the way you'll have two or sometimes even three units filming different scenes at the same time! You also understand how important it is to have a Plan B.

LLOYD: Yes, well, producing the Troma way means being ready with a Plan B.[42] This means backup actors, backup locations, contingency plans. One of the biggest advantages in my doing double duty[43] as the producer and director is the fact that I direct like a producer, in that I'm always juggling the balancing act among time, money, and the art itself. Most directors do not have to think about time or money at all, which sometimes results in their becoming a producer's nightmare in going over budget and hurting the ultimate final product.

Having this Plan B is vital to the success of the movie. I shoot the nude scenes first, because even if an actor promises to bare his skanky hi-lo for the sake of the movie, you can't be really sure he's going to do it until it's all already done. And in case he negs and decides on-camera nudity will forever

FIGURE 3.2 Producer, actor, writer, and director Trent retires for the night in Troma's lavish sleeping accommodations.

[42]INDEX GYNO: It does not refer to the pill I had to take after my walk of shame this morning following last night's unprotected back book action.

[43]Not to be confused with the double doody that happens after eating a typical Troma lunch on set.

tarnish his image, you should have another actor waiting in the wings to take his place. Same goes with back-up locations.[44]

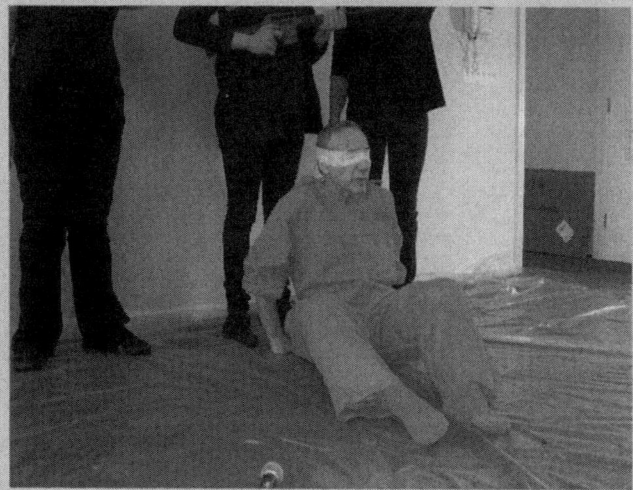

FIGURE 3.3 Confusion arose on set of *Citizen Toxie* when line producer said, "It's time to shoot Lloyd." A full day of filming was lost.

FIGURE 3.4 Producer LK and crew can't understand why leading actors won't come out of the boxes (pictured center).

[44]There will be more on back-up locations in Chapter 7. I hope.

FIGURE 3.5 Typical crew of a Troma Production seen here on the set of *Terror Firmer.* The head in the foreground belongs to a character that blew his fucking brains out, played by LK.

CUT TO:

Lloyd's camera shuts itself off again. He and Louis Su are now on the Canal Street uptown subway platform. The train pulls into the station and they get on.

LOUIS SU: You remember when you sold Troma Building in Hell's Kitchen? Real estate agent was fat guy, suspenders wearing. Why American men think suspenders okay?

LLOYD: I agree. I prefer bow ties.

LOUIS SU: Anyway, that guy, that guy, heh-heh, he was in *The Newcomers*! Remember Lloyd? Now he sell real estate.

LLOYD: What you put in, you get back out, Louis Su.[45]

LOUIS SU: Yes, yes. I got out pornos because business was oligopoly.

LLOYD: Which rhymes with monopoly. Which rhymes with endoscopy.[46]

LOUIS SU: Lloyd, where you go with this?

LLOYD: Everything really does come full circle. You ~~I~~ do ~~my~~ your first musical movie as a porn and then some 30 years later you do musical with chicken zombies. ~~My~~, uh, your entrance in the pornography world was a crash course in producing movies and ~~my~~ an opportunity to discover that the heretofore frowned upon combination of sex and humor was something that came naturally and really worked. This inspired me and was influential as I went on

[45]INDEX GYNO: Just like my many experiences with young muscular index guys pleasuring me with exclamation points.

[46]A sort of unpleasant medical ass-fucking.

to make the raunchy R-rated sexy baseball women's liberation satire comedy *Squeeze Play*. Of course, making pornos may not be the exact way to go in this day and age—you don't need to make a porno (maybe just an adult film with graphic sex, if that speaks to you), but of course, I do not know for sure, as I have never even seen one, much less produced one.

Look at Trent, I am so proud of him. Do you know he was all set and "green-lit" to start shooting a big movie that he wrote? It was going to star Lindsay Lohan, Olympia Dukakis, and Shirley MacLaine?[47] And then, like the day before the cameras were set to roll, Lindsay got brought up on drug charges or something and had to go to rehab. That movie never got made. Trent survived that and he survived the Troma experience and still continues to get his own damn movies produced. He is living in L.A. and I know he will make it big!

CUT TO:

Louis Su emerges from the underground subway, disappearing into the last remaining sex shop on 8th Avenue and 37th Street, never to be seen again.

[47]Trent's original script featured three "old" women. Lindsay Lohan came on board as a replacement for one of the original three characters once the producers discovered through tracking (i.e., surveying) that a movie centering on a story about three old women would not sell enough tickets to merit a budget. The entire production was, of course, aborted once Lohan ran into troubles with the law. Meanwhile, a movie featuring old men, *Wild Hogs* (2007), starring spring chickens Tim Allen, John Travolta, Martin Lawrence and William H. Macy, proceeded to gross well over $40 million dollars in the beginning of its release, on their "tracking."

Losing It in Las Vegas Asks Lloyd

Dear Lloyd,

What do you do when you're over budget, over schedule and one of your actors walks off the set?

Love,

Losing It in Las Vegas

Dear Losing It,

You have just described every Troma film ever made.

The answer is to buckle down and get your fucking movie made. No excuses. You don't have the money you need to rent your location? Take over a friend's garage and turn it into your location. You're running out of time? Start cutting pages out of the script! That's what we had to do on *Poultrygeist*, and I think it ended up as a much tighter film.

Your lead actor walks off the set? You have two choices. Either get on your hands and knees and do whatever you need to do to get him back. Or, throw in a joke about plastic surgery and finish the film with a different actor. Just for kicks, why not choose someone who looks nothing like the actor who quit? I did this on *Tromeo & Juliet*.

All of these situations are unfortunate, but unless a tornado swept through your set (which you could still use to your advantage, as it will add a shit-ton of production value to your

[1]Having a real tornado in your film, complete with real death and destruction, will lead viewers to believe that you have used expensive computer graphic effects and they will be very, very impressed.

film[1]), it's a pretty good bet that all of your problems could have been avoided with a little extra preparation. At this point, you can either abandon your movie, or you can finish it and learn from your mistakes. As my friend Captain Planet likes to say, the power is yours.

xoxo,
Lloyd

P.S. Because you live in Vegas, another option would be to take what's left of the budget and go to the roulette table. I'd put my money on red 17. Good Luck!

P.P.S. Please review this book on Amazon. Thanks!

Chapter | four

Producing Movies Inevitably Gets You Stoned (And Is Really, Really Hard)* *or* A Union Dose of Some Shirley Jackson Optimism Goes a Long Way

*And so am I.

CO-PRODUCER: Sometimes connotes an involvement in financing the film. At other times, it can be defined as a producer with less power than those under the plain ol' "Producer" credit. In other words, more of a *catcher* than a *pitcher.*

Synonyms: One of the other producers

Example: "If the job of co-producer is anything like the job of co-author, it must suck ass."[2]

A NOTE FROM MY EDITRIX

-----------------------Original Message-----------------------

From: elinor@repress.com
Sent: January 9, 2009 4:58 PM
To: Lloyd Kaufman <lloyd@troma.com>
Subject: Louis Su

Dear Lloyd,

I like how you set the book up with your talk about the 1969 Mustang, the different producing models and then segue into your early directing/producing career. You also present an informative myriad of ways to obtain your producing skills—via school, working on movies, etc. I'm not really clear where Louis Su fits into the whole picture, but anything to deter our young producers from considering pornographic filmmaking as a viable gateway to a producing career in this modern age!

Perhaps in this chapter you could talk about some of the challenges that producers face?

Can't wait to see more pages from you soon!

Best,
Elinor

Sent via BlackBerry by AT&T

------------------------End Message---------------------------

I scrolled through this message on my BlackBerry as I waited for my luggage to plop itself onto the carousel at JFK. Pattie and I had been visiting our daughter Charlotte in Yemen, which is, yes, as

[2]Imagine this phrase being spoken by James Gunn, Trent Haaga, Adam Jahnke, Sara Antill, Kurly Tlapoyawa, Ashley Wren Collins or any other sucker who has ever attempted to co-author a book with Lloyd.

I recently learned, a real country. While watching the hypnotic spin of other people's suitcases, I thought about what Toxie would do if he were in Yemen. And then I was jarred by a loud buzz from my BlackBerry again.

----------------------Original Message------------------------

From: bigfriggindeal@aol.com
Sent: January 9, 2009 5:01 PM
To: Lloyd Kaufman <lloyd@troma.com>
Subject: Re: Interview with John Carpenter

Dear Lloyd:

We got your interview request and while John is flattered you thought of him, unfortunately he will be unavailable to participate. Best of luck with the book!

-Max

Assistant to John Carpenter

------------------------End Message---------------------------

WHO IS JOHN CARPENTER?

John Carpenter is a major independent film producer/director/screenwriter/composer/director who works primarily within the sci-fi and horror genres. Most notably, he directed the original *The Fog, Halloween* and *Escape from New York.* He's kind of a big deal.

Pattie jabbed me with her elbow and told me to stop exhaling so noisily. I two-finger typed a quick response to Max:

----------------------Original Message------------------------

From: lloyd@troma.com
Sent: January 9, 2009 5:04 PM
To: John Carpenter <bigfriggindeal@aol.com>
Subject: Re: Re: Interview with John Carpenter

Thanks, Max. I do come to LA at least once a month on business. Is there a chance Mr. Carpenter might be available to be interviewed for my book on another date?

This book, my fourth, is a very important project for educating young filmmakers about being true to their own selves . . . . Thanks!

This message was sent from Lloyd's phone.

Please forgive typos!

-------------------------End Message---------------------------

---

By this point, my luggage was doing laps on the carousel in front of me. I heaved it off and bundled myself up to brace myself against the heartless NYC winter cold ahead of me on the other side of customs. My pants started buzzing again. I got a little excited, then smiled and breathed a sigh of relief as I realized it was just my BlackBerry. I pulled off a glove and took it out again to find an instantaneous message from Mr. Carpenter!

-----------------------Original Message-------------------------

From: bigfriggindeal@aol.com
Sent: January 9, 2009 5:07PM
To: Lloyd Kaufman <lloyd@troma.com>
Subject: Re: Re: Re: Interview with John Carpenter

Hey Lloyd,

John's schedule is pretty packed for the foreseeable future, so it looks like it won't work out. Sorry about that. But again, best of luck with the book! And feel free to let me know when it's heading to press -- I'd love to read it!

-Max

Assistant to John Carpenter

-------------------------End Message---------------------------

---

Oh, yeah, like I was going to send a copy of this book (for which my publishers will make me shell out $19.95) to John Carpenter's handler because he'd "love to read it." You'd think that someone who's been alive and thriving in the business for nearly four full decades running his own independent film studio would occasionally get to pull some big "muckety-muck" *Halloween* strings, but alas, alack, such is not the case. After 40 years of producing movies, it's never too late to be insulted—remember that, dear reader.

I started thinking about *The Lottery,* that short story by Shirley Jackson that they make you read in grammar school. If you've never been subjected to it, consider yourself lucky. It starts off great. It's a small town, a beautiful hot summer day in June—it's obviously a place where everyone knows everyone else. While reading it, you might picture red-checkered picnic tablecloths, ice cream, hot dogs, friendly greetings at the local store, beautiful nebulous hairless boys. Then you realize it's the day of the annual town lottery. Wow! The lottery! Someone's gonna win big today! What'll they win?!

FIGURE 4.1 *LK uses telescope to look at hairless man with hands on hips.*

There's a dramatic, suspenseful buildup as every Tom, Dick, and Harry waits to see whether his or her number is going to be called. Finally, a winner is chosen. Lucky Tessie Hutchinson. And what does she win? She wins the opportunity to be stoned to death—literally stoned to death with rocks by her fellow town residents. This beautiful story ends with Tessie's neighbors, all sexes, ages, and sizes, slowly but surely pelting her to death, bit by bit, stone by stone.

Ouch.

THE ULTIMATE SELF-STONING JOB, OR THERE'S A HOLE IN MY BEGEL ~~BAGEL~~, MAN: A SHORT HISTORY OF DAVID BEGELMAN

Some people do anything to climb to the top of the producing food chain, only to be stoned to death. Take David Begelman, the infamous Hollywood producer who, in 1960, co-founded the Creative Artists Agency (CAA), a talent agency that represented completely unknown actors and directors such as Woody Allen, Marilyn Monroe, Peter Sellers and Richard Burton, to name a few. After 13 years of agent-ing, he left CAA to take over Columbia Studios, where he produced such movies as *Close Encounters of the Third Kind* (a movie that can't even begin to surpass Troma's *Invasion of the Space Preachers* in its level of importance and sheer number of fans).

At the top of his game, Begelman—the virtually and ultimately unheard-of success story of man-turned-agent-turned-studio-mogul—suddenly found himself at the heart of several embezzlement and check forgery scandals. One of his first victims included his client Judy Garland (while he was at CAA), with whom he may or may not have had an affair.[3] He allegedly titled a 1963 Cadillac convertible that had been given to her as part of her compensation for appearances on Jack Paar's[4] television show to himself and then also claimed that Judy had blackmailers demanding $50K for naked photos of her getting her stomach pumped after a drug overdose. Although the story about the photos and money were totally fabricated, her drug problem was not. Rather than let the world potentially see incriminating photos of "Dorothy Gone Wild,"[5] Judy paid up and Begelman walked away with $50K.[6]

Nearly 15 years later, actor Cliff Robertson[7] received a letter from the IRS stating that he had received $10K from Columbia

---

[3]And bravo if he did. That gal was a belter!

[4]Jack Paar was an above-par American radio and television talk show host who hosted *The Tonight Show* from 1957 to 1962.

[5]Of all her roles, singer/actress Judy Garland is perhaps most famous for playing Dorothy in *The Wizard of Oz*.

[6]Now, if he had used that $50K to go produce his own damn movie, he'd be a hero in my book. And by "my book," I of course mean this one that you are holding in your sweaty hands. However, he probably just bought a boat or something. Yawn.

[7]Cliff Robertson is an Oscar (for *Charly*, in 1968), Emmy and Lifetime Achievement Award–winning actor with his own star on the Hollywood Walk of Fame, now best known for playing "Uncle" Ben Parker in the *Spider-Man* movies.

Pictures. Robertson had never received the money. Upon investigation, a check forgery for $10K was traced to Begelman. Robertson shared the honest story of his victimization and was silently blackmailed and stoned by the Hollywood community for revealing the truth about Begelman. He spent most of the 1980s getting a tan rather than working on movies.

To add insult to injury, Begelman lied on his resume and said he was a Yale alum. Imagine! Trying to pass himself off as a student of my alma mater! Next thing you know, George W. Bush[8] will say he graduated from Yale![9] Begelman even went on to run MGM and Gladden Entertainment, but was never able to repeat the success he enjoyed while at Columbia. By 1995, Begelman declared bankruptcy and committed suicide in a hotel room in Century City, Los Angeles.[10]

A LOTTERY TICKET WITH A BIG "?" ON THE PRIZE

Now, let me tell you—because I feel it is my duty to be frank and honest with you—producing movies is a lot like winning a fucking Shirley Jackson lottery in which you may not want to participate. Begelman's downward career spiral was self-inflicted, but often—no matter how experienced you are or what level you are at—obstacles are going to arise. The producers who make it in this world are the ones who realize there is a hell of a lot of sacrifice involved. And, as Reed Morano emphasized at that star-packed Chinese restaurant in Chapter 3, this is an enormously collaborative business where you have to rely on and work with others—people, equipment, companies. As a successful producer, you think you've won big; you've made your dream come to life, but you might just end up getting completely stoned[11]. . . in fact, it's pretty much *guaranteed* that

---

[8]George W. Bush, arguably the greatest U.S. president since Abraham Lincoln, coined the phrases "Mission accomplished!" and "Bring it on!"

[9]EDITOR'S NOTE: Bush did graduate from Yale, Lloyd, and he was in your class! Don't you remember?*

*LLOYD'S RESPONSE: I was probably too busy getting stoned. For my film work, I mean.

[10]I blame Judy Garland.

[11]FOOTNOTE GUY: I'm stoned right now.*

*INDEX GYNO: I'd like to get Oliver Stoned!**

**FOOTNOTE GUY: I don't get it.

you will get stoned. Let's just hope it's not. . . to death. In fact, my assistant Matt Lawrence can tell you that I consistently get stoned on a regular basis. And I'm definitely not talking about the herbal kind of trip.

HOW SHANLEY GAVE LLOYD THE SHAFT . . . LEY

BY MATT LAWRENCE, RESIDENT TROMA BITCH

WHO IS MATT LAWRENCE?

My name is Matt, and I am Lloyd's assistant here at Troma. Lloyd is currently asleep at his desk, some partly masticated Twizzler drooling out of his lips, with an empty bottle of Popov and some Judy Garland songs playing on his iPod. With a comatose Kaufman here and a book deadline looming, I suppose it might be Good Samaritan–ly of me to continue where Lord Kaufman left off (or passed out). How about a story?

Recently, Lloyd was given the opportunity to interview John Patrick Shanley for his (i.e., *this*) book. Yes, you heard right: John Patrick Shanley, famed playwright, screenwriter and filmmaker of *Doubt*. Award-winning, respected, brilliant—an artist in every sense of the word. Recipient of an Oscar, some Tonys, the WGA Lifetime Achievement Award and oh, the uh, Pulitzer Prize for Drama. So many awards that the man needs his mantelpiece reinforced.

On a chilly, snowy, flurry-filled Friday afternoon, Shanley greeted and ushered us into his spacious, airy apartment, the entire second floor of a beautiful building not far from Union Square. Immaculate and pristine, the walls of each room were painted a different striking, vibrant color. The smell of the apartment was intoxicating. *This* is how success lives, I thought. In awe, I knew that it's not everyday one gets to share the same room with an Oscar winner. Of course, I had already met Yacov Levi, who wrote and directed the Troma release *The Killer Bra*, a true honor in itself, but Shanley had worked with the likes of Tom Hanks, Meryl Streep and Philip Seymour Hoffman. And here he was, agreeing to be interviewed by Lloyd for *Produce Your Own Damn Movie*, the book and DVD box set!

I quickly set up the camera and audio as Lloyd made (awkward) conversation with Shanley. About five minutes before shooting, Lloyd proffered hard copies of the interview and personal releases[12] (which had been

[12]PRODUCING LESSON #155: Always get releases and contracts signed *before* you begin filming. Logical enough, right? But you'd be surprised how often films, both big

e-mailed ahead of time to Shanley). Lloyd also presented Shanley with a DVD of his (i.e., Lloyd's) newest film, *Poultrygeist: Night of the Chicken Dead*, as a token of his gratitude. Shanley perused the release for a few seconds, then eyed the *Poultrygeist* DVD cover of its skeleton head with a protruding ax, a protruding chicken monster and a protruding eyeball for a quiet five seconds before saying, "You know, I don't know if this is a good idea . . . I think . . . maybe—I need to speak with my agent."

The sound of the air was sucked out of the room. I was shell-shocked. I immediately looked over at Lloyd, our fearless leader, a pioneer in the business for the past 40 years. Poor Lloyd—poor charming, brilliant, generous and handsome[13] Lloyd. The president of Troma Entertainment's mouth was agape and his ass lay in his arms, courtesy of Mr. Shanley. Shanley kindly ushered us out, elaborating, "You know, when I see a DVD cover with an eyeball popping out, I start to wonder. . . ." Fair enough, Mr. Shanley.[14]

Lloyd whined, considering the possibility (i.e., the reality) that Shanley did not know who he or Troma was before sitting down for the interview. It dawned on me that this opportunity had been both Lloyd's and my very own lottery. I had thought working for Troma had finally paid off, as I would now be hobnobbing with the artistic elite. Instead, I found myself packing the camera (i.e., paper) bag with the equipment that we never even used to almost interview a famous director who had no idea who we were. And for Lloyd, a man who has influenced some of today's biggest filmmakers and been imitated by countless others, it was a private stoning as the result of one lousy DVD cover. Shanley hath casteth-ed a pretty heavy stone. Together, Lloyd and I returned to the Troma offices that afternoon, our tails between our legs.[15]

I can tell, weeks later, that Lloyd is still bothered by the events that transpired that unfortunate afternoon. Sadly, his neck and back are still tense as

---

and small, begin shooting with contracts not yet signed. In fact, on the megabudget picture *The Sorcerer's Apprentice* (a Bruckheimer production), filming is currently going on and—according to sources—even the script has not yet been completed. As a result of this insanity, departments apparently are laying off people until the "producers" see where the script is going.

[13]EDITOR'S NOTE: Lloyd, stop it! Matt's original adjectives read "nebbishy, often smelly and dumpy."

[14]Although, as many Tromites know, the *Poultrygeist* DVD cover is actually quite benign by today's standards. But maybe the Shanmeister is straight-up old school?

[15]And, to add insult to injury, Lloyd forgot his hat at Shanley's apartment. Whether this was a ploy to get back into the Shanley compound or Lloyd is truly senile is up for debate.

I give him his daily full body massage. Who says that working at Troma doesn't have its perks?

P.S. Dear Mr. Shanley,

If you are reading this sidebar, Lloyd made me write it. I think you have great hair and I loved the way your apartment smelled of fresh apricots. I wish I were there now. If you're looking for a personal assistant, assistant director (*Doubt 2: Doubt Harder*), driver, whatever—I'm your man!

Please get me out of Tromaville.

P.P.S. Dear Lloyd,

If you read my postscript to Mr. Shanley, it's all a lie. However, as a young filmmaker, I can't afford to burn any bridges, regardless of how I truly feel. Working with you has been incredibly enlightening and I am forever grateful for the wisdom you have imparted to me. I love you.

P.P.P.S. Dear Mr. Shanley,

Ignore my last postscript. I need to cover my tracks and blow smoke up the old man's ass so he doesn't fire me.

P.P.P.S. Dear Lloyd,

I'm sorry you had to find out this way.

Now, you may be thinking to yourself, "Of *course* that would happen to you, Lloyd." But wait: Lloyd Kaufman getting kicked in the balls may not seem odd, but it happens to everyone. Even people who are actually respected in the industry. Read on:

GETTING STOOD UP BY OSCAR

LLOYD KAUFMAN: What was the third Oscar-winning movie you did, in addition to *Gods and Monsters* and *Crash*?

MARK HARRIS: Well, that was an interesting experience. It was called *Million Dollar Baby*. While I was doing *Crash*, it was given to Clint Eastwood as an actor, but he said he would only do it if he could direct. The production company approached Paul Haggis to ask if he would step aside as a director and let Clint come on and direct it. Paul acquiesced and gave the movie over and we made a lot of money out of it. It came out before *Crash*, though—we were halfway through it when that was being made. Everything has its own destiny.

LK: Today, I might give a Production Manager a producer credit, but I notice today regarding Hollywood movies, there are 1,400 producer credits on them. What is that about?

MH: They say "it takes a village to raise a child." Well, it takes a village of producers to produce a film. There are many different ways to get a cast—one of these is to make an actor a producer. A writer can direct, but you can also give a writer a producer credit!

LK: Is that what they do on television?

MH: Well, television is a different medium—the writers are the executive producers. The executive producers in film take that credit because they are the money-makers, or they brought in a piece of talent. We had a group of people on *Crash*. Bobby Moresco and Paul Haggis wrote the script and took very little money, so I was the only producer among the three of us, but we all decided to produce and then Cathy Schulman came on because she was part of Bob Yari's group[16] and then we got Don Cheadle as an actor to produce.

LK: So there were five or six producers? That's nothing.

MH: Yeah, for today that's nothing, but without one, none of the parts would fit.

LK: Many young people want to win Oscars; what do they have to do as producers to win an Academy Award?

MH: The folks who deal with the Oscars are a club called the Producer's Guild and the Academy of Arts and Motion Picture Sciences. They have their membership and this is not a public election. They make their own rules. They look at who qualifies most out of their freely flowing subjective criteria.

LK: Meaning that they choose whom of several producers gets to go on stage to accept an Oscar or other award in front of billions of TV viewers around the world?

MH: Yes, right. That doesn't mean the others don't deserve it. It just means this club made the decision.

LK: In your case, what happened?

MH: I was shut out of the opportunity to go up on stage, even though I was the one who said *Crash* shouldn't be a TV show—we needed to make it as a movie. I got it to all the financiers and was involved in the rewriting, budgeting, editing, and casting. Do I think I deserved to be acknowledged? Absolutely. Did I get to do it? No. That doesn't take away anything I did.

LK: Was there an explanation?

MH: Yeah, they didn't feel I did enough. They gave it to Cathy Schulman. She did more in the latter part of getting the crew and all that. She was a good Line Producer and they also gave one to Paul, because he was involved with everything. That's the way it went. There were many people in the Academy who were upset about how I was treated.

LK: Have they changed the rules?

MH: I don't know. I'm like Groucho Marx. If anybody wants me as a member, I don't want to join the club.

---

[16] I believe they brought on Mr. Money.

YOU DON'T HAVE TO BE A SHITHEAD TO BE A PRODUCER

Mark Harris is a pretty classy guy.[17] First of all, he's an Oscar winner and he agreed to be interviewed by me, whose highest award is the Franklin, Indiana "B Movie Celebration Lifetime Achievement Award." Second, I shot the first 20 minutes of the Mark Harris interview with my video camera in the "off" position, only to have David Chien point out my error. Mark kindly agreed to start the interview over again from the beginning. Third, once we finished the interview, I had offered to take Mark to dinner as a thank-you. I was worrying all day about coming up with money to pay for the valet parking for my rented Hyundai among the Bentleys and Rolls Royces at Mozza.[18] But Mark was generous and chose Froman's Deli down the road. The two of us dined royally for about $35 bucks and had fun bantering with Brenda, our waitress!

WHICH WAY WENT BLAIR WITCH?

So you see, winning the producer lottery—making a successful, award-winning movie—can be disturbing. Sweet, but it can turn sour quickly. Mark Harris continues to produce great movies. The people who made the hit mockumentary *The Blair Witch Project* have not been so fortunate.[19] These young folks came up with an absolutely brilliant marketing plan that sold the movie through websites, blogs and viral marketing techniques that left you wondering if the *Blair Witch* story was fact or fiction. They hit the lottery and became an overnight sensation! And then, they couldn't do it again—and, in my highly regarded opinion, the fault lies totally with their distribution

---

[17]INDEX GYNO: I give you shit all the time, but you're not so bad yourself, Lloyd. You have to admit. As much as we all want to, especially those who have had the misfortune to work with you for extended periods of time, I don't think anyone could *not* like you. In fact, you're a pretty darn loyal supporter and cheerleader for life. Elinor was totally wrong about you.*

*EDITOR'S NOTE: Index Gyno has contempt for you, Lloyd. How low can you go—even pretending to be the Index Gyno all the way down here?!

[18]Mozza is so trendy that they don't validate your parking ticket, so it costs a week's salary and your left testicle to park there.

[19]FOOTNOTE GUY: Actually, Lloyd, there was a *Blair Witch Project 2*, it's just that no one's really heard of it. Kind of like me. No one's really heard of me, because you keep trying to pretend I don't exist. But I do exist, Lloyd. I do. And I'm sooooo lonely.

company, which—as I gather—screwed them over by ignoring the strengths of the campaign on their first film. I believe that they were sucked dry, stoned to death—brilliant young guys and gynos who changed the face of filmmaking and marketing. They were brought down by a combination of mediocrity, incompetence, and greed in the upper echelons of the film business. As talented as they were, having won the producer lottery, their film careers were stoned, like an unfaithful Muslim woman under Taliban rule.

It's been a tough lesson that you cannot control everyone and everything around you as a producer. It's a lesson I stone myself with repeatedly. There are too many rules and too many unions that were supposedly formed to protect you but end up distracting you and sending you farther and farther away from the piece of art you are trying to create. What you can control is the awesomeness of the script that gives you the story you are going to tell, whether it is your own or that of someone you are collaborating with. Also, you need to control the people you select to work with as your creative team (from the actors down to the crew) and the standards by which your movie will operate.

CLIMBING HIGH UP AT IHOP: LESSONS FROM STAN LEE

As a producer, if you want to have a meeting, you need to hold the meeting in a location that will allow you to focus on the meeting. Stan Lee[20] introduced me to the beauty that is an IHOP.[21] At an IHOP establishment, there is no need to fuss with valet parking (like at Mozza) and worry that your car seat is going to get jacked too far forward so you won't be able to slide it back into its perfect spot for your legs or that some bored guy on the late night shift is going to swipe your last condom stashed away in the glove compartment for last-minute emergencies, or, in my case, just rare luck. Furthermore, no matter what time of day—be it morning, noon or night—the IHOP is serving exactly what you need.

---

[20]Stan Lee is an American comic book legend, icon, writer, editor, former president and chairman of Marvel Comics, and co-creator of *Spider-Man*, *Daredevil*, *The Hulk*, *The Fantastic Four* and *The X-Men*, to name a few.

[21]The International House of Pancakes or—in this case—**I H**ave **O**ptimal **P**roducing **P**ower!

When that hamburger with fries arrives, well, the ketchup bottle is already there, and it is always full. If, instead, those buttermilk pancakes with strawberries on top slide under your nose, well, the maple syrup is within an arm's reach, along with boysenberry and blueberry as well—more colors than a gay rights parade! The Sweet'N Low and the sugar, salt and pepper, cream, butter, whatever your condiment[22] needs are, they are met, and they are met immediately, within near nanoseconds. IHOP lets you concentrate on your movie script or meeting, because everything you need is at your fingertips.[23]

FIGURE 4.2 *Why are pop culture legend Stan Lee and brilliant musician and composer Dennis Dreith (right) ruining their reputations by being photographed with LK and a* Poultrygeist *poster?*

---

[22]INDIGNANT FOOTNOTE GUY SAYS: It's terrible how they're tearing down all of the landmark buildings and building condiments.

[23]This portion of the book has been sponsored by IHOP! Good food, good people, good marketing.*

*EDITOR'S RESPONSE: Neither Focal Press nor its parent company, Reed Elsevier, have received any compensation from IHOP for this thinly veiled advertisement. Why do you always put me in situations like this, Lloyd?

All of this exists to let your creativity flow forth effortlessly, beautifully, juicily, just like the sirloin steak for $6.99. Nothing can stop you and you can focus on what really counts. Yet, if you choose to meet at that "impressive" three-, four- or five-star restaurant offering a fine selection of "today's specials," you are bound to be interrupted countless times for your order of coffee, water and choice of dessert, not to mention the requisite "Are you still working on that?" (when your meal is still clearly only half-eaten) and then, before you can swallow a bite or muster an answer, the "Is there anything else I can get you?" and so on and so forth.

That is not how you should run your producer ship. Put all the people and elements in place and at arm's length to help you do the best possible job you can. Create your own damn cinematic IHOP!

Stan Lee taught me this, and for that, I am forever grateful to Stan the Man. "Excelsior!"[24]

TERRY JONES TELLS US WHY HIS PRODUCER WAS NOT THE MESSIAH, JUST A VERY NAUGHTY BOY!

WHO IS TERRY JONES?

Terry Jones, one of the members of the famed comedy group Monty Python, is a world-class director, screenwriter, actor and author, as well as a Chaucer scholar. His most renowned works are Monty Python and the Holy Grail,[25] Life of Brian, *and* The Meaning of Life. *Subsequent to his Monty Python films, he directed* Erik the Viking, Personal Services, *and* The Wind in the Willows.

En route to taking out the garbage, Terry Jones walks by the loo and hears the chain being pulled, the perfect moment to receive a phone call from me, cinema's ultimate proprietor of human waste and bodily fluids. The two of us then had a conversation about two different types of producers.

Jones divulged his personal experiences with producers, outlining the differences between what constitutes a "good" producer and what constitutes a "bad" producer. For Jones' directorial debut, *Monty Python and the Holy Grail*, Michael White, the film's financier, "foisted" a young producer named John Goldstone on the Pythons. However, the "foisted" Mr. Goldstone

[24]This is how Mr. Lee signs off on his work and IHOP deals. He's my (uncostumed superhuman) hero.

[25]Co-directed with Terry Gilliam.

turned out to be the "perfect" producer, effectively raising money and creating an efficient and practical structure for the production to follow. Goldstone always trusted the creativity of the director with whom he was working. For example, he would set up casting calls and make suggestions, but never make final casting decisions. Goldstone's producing style created the ideal environment for Jones and the Pythons. Goldstone would put together the nuts and bolts of the film, while trusting the Python's directors' aesthetic vision. The six Pythons had a "unified vision," remarks Jones. "So it would have been impossible for the producer to have the last word anyway." Goldstone stayed on to produce other Python movies. "Collaboration with a good producer who supports the director's aesthetic 100% is a great thing."

Unfortunately, the producer for a recent ill-fated project of Jones thought that he, as producer, would handle the nuts and bolts in addition to being a strong "creative" force. This led to trouble. The UK Film Council supported Jones and his co-writer Anna Söderström's vision,[26] while the producer only pretended to get behind it. Mr. Bad Producer told Jones that it was going to be a pleasure to work with him, yet continually undermined Jones. Most notably, the production designer was working from the producer's script and not Jones's and Anna's, causing Jones to say, "Producers have no business rewriting my material!"

The producer and his marketing team were also vying for Terry's main characters to be changed to teenagers. The *coup de grace* occurred when the producer meddled with a 30-second promo that Terry was preparing for the 2009 Cannes Film Festival. Terry quit and the film officially fell apart. The promo was going to be used to pre-sell[27] the film, so Terry wrote and organized the promo, but the producer began to retool, rework, tweak, adjust, or whatever other word the producer might have used to justify unwarranted changes. Jones stated, during our chat, "If this producer interferes with a simple Cannes Film Festival promo, imagine what it would be like if I were to direct the film? I was just lucky to get out before it was too late, because it was obvious the kind of producer I was dealing with up front."

---

[26]Terry and Anna did not originate the script. It was brought to Terry to direct, but the writer did not want Terry and his writing partner Anna to change it. A year later, the writer backed out of the project and it was up to Terry and Anna to do what they wanted with the script. The UK Film Council continued to provide script development funds to Terry and Anna as they continued to work. Unlike the United States, the UK and most other countries have government agencies that subsidize the indigenous and independent arts. However, the United States does have a series of laws, regulations and tax breaks that do help media mega-conglomerates continue their dominance, but nothing specifically allocated for indigenous, independent art.

[27]More about this in Chapter 6. I hope.

Is there a lesson to be learned from this? Yes! First, the troubled project didn't originate with Terry, so there was no way he could have final say. If you produce your own damn movie, you are less likely to get stoned to death because you can control the material. And second, if you want to be a strong, creative producer à la Irving Thalberg or David O. Selznick,[28] then be straightforward with your director and make sure that he realizes he is merely a "hired gun."

FIGURE 4.3 LK says that if you want respect from your cast and crew, you must always dress like Terry Jones when producing a movie. Terry Jones is pictured here directing on the set of *The Wind In The Willows*, circa 1996.

FIGURE 4.4 Terry Jones shows his feminine side as he directs *The Wind in the Willows.*

[28]Irving Thalberg (1899–1936) was an Academy Award–winning film producer during the early years of motion pictures; David O. Selznik (1902–1965) was the iconic Hollywood producer of the epic *Gone with the Wind* (1939), among others.

QUOTH THE DRAVEN, EVERMORE

WHO IS DANNY DRAVEN?

Danny Draven is a producer/director/cinematographer/editor who quickly moved up to the Production Manager/Assistant Director level to produce his own low-budget independent horror films, such as Crypts *and* Ghostmonth. *He is based in Las Vegas. Danny's book,* The Filmmaker's Book of the Dead, *will soon be released by Focal Press.*[29]

When you're producing low-budget films, you can call yourself a producer, but you're also doing the job of a line producer. So with my films, I was always not only the producer but also the line producer, as well as the director. But when you're producing the film, you have to deal with everything. You'll deal with everything from late actors (I've had a few drunk ones) to the cops showing up, the fire department showing up, people wanting to see permits (i.e., "What are you doing here, sir?") more times than you can count.

On my films, we've never been able to afford a production manager, so I end up doing most of the producing work myself. For one, I want to write every check—I want to know where every penny of that budget is going. On these lower-budget films, I don't trust the line producer enough, because of the circumstances we shoot under—we only have six or eight days to shoot, so I need to know where every $5 and $10 check is going at all times. I have to sign every one of them. And you have to do that, because you have to make sure that every penny you spend is on the screen. You don't want to be spending $50 or $60 on comforts such as a little refrigerator for your production office—you shouldn't even *have* a production office. All money should go on the screen, if you are working with limited means.

FIGURE 4.5 Danny Draven was excited when Lucio Pavarotti rose from the dead and sang an aria from *Madame Butterfly* on set.

[29]EDITOR'S NOTE: I am appreciative of your plug, Lloyd. I truly am. But it doesn't really make up for that disgraceful IHOP ad.

FIGURE 4.6 No CGI here! Danny Draven was pleasantly surprised when Willie Nelson stopped by the set.

WHY TAMAR SIMON HOFFS ALWAYS MAKES UP THREE DIFFERENT BUDGETS FOR THE SAME FILM

WHO IS TAMAR SIMON HOFFS?

Tamar Simon Hoffs is a producer/director/writer who rose to recognition with her short film The Haircut, *starring John Cassavetes, which appeared as an official selection of the Cannes Film Festival in 1983. Most recently, she directed, wrote, and produced* Red Roses and Petrol *and* Pound of Flesh, *both starring Malcolm McDowell.*

I've made three feature films that all had the same budget: $350K. One of these films was *Stony Island*, made in 1976. The other was *Red Roses and Petrol*, made in 2003. The last was *Pound of Flesh*, which wrapped in early 2009. As a producer on *Stony Island*, I worked with the director Andy Davis, who taught me my very own invaluable producing lesson #213: you need to have multiple budgets for the movie you want to make. For example, you have your $2 million version, complete with dream cast and union location shoot; the $1 million version of the budget, which calls for filming in far less time; and the $500K version, to be shot on an incredible HD camera. Each time, I've ended up with my lowest budget model. And each time, I've still been able to make a great movie with wonderful actors that have then gone on to win awards. If you have a good story to tell, you find people who want to work for nothing to tell that story and who are in it for the thrill of making movies. So I always have three budgets—just in case!

FIGURE 4.7 Malcolm McDowell, (left), cracks up at poultrygeistic pun, *CLUCKwork Orange*. He is pictured here with Tammy Hoffs.

THE MPAA LOTTERY

Once you've shot your movie, you've got to come up with a final cut that the producer and distributor (if you're lucky enough to be me, the producer and distributor can be the same person) will be happy with (as happy as the director[30]). Regarding your final cut, one of the challenges that will stand in your way as an independent producer is known as the Motion Picture Association of America, or the MPAA.

The MPAA is a group of fascist-loving, homophobic, gun-wielding child pornographers[31] in charge of rating movies. They are supposed to rate a movie from the point of view of the elements in it so that the public can learn how much sex and violence is contained therein.

---

[30]Which, again, if you're lucky enough, is the same person as the producer and distributor . . . moi!*

*FOOTNOTE GUY: You work so hard to be recognized, Lloyd. Just like me! Let's hear it for the little guy! Anyone?

[31]EDITOR'S NOTE: This is a false statement. I'm just going to start pointing them out. You have used up all of my patience.

The MPAA seem to think this grants them permission to evaluate a film's artistic contribution. They have a huge double standard, in that they allow movies produced by one of the megaconglomerates to pass through the ratings criteria much more swiftly, with as much of their sex, gore, and violence intact as possible whilst disemboweling an independent film with the same elements.

The movies Troma has made for our audiences have had to meet criteria to fit an R rating. The MPAA also won't even look at a film until it is finished, which too often proves very costly to the filmmaker. Once you've made a composite print[32] of a movie and then have to go back and recut it, it becomes extremely expensive. It is something that most low-budget independent films can't afford to do a second time. When you cut the composite film, you have to splice on the picture. The appropriate sync sound is several frames back, so you actually hear it on the projector—the picture and sound are not together. When you join the cut pieces together, the sound is all messed up. It jumps. To fix it, you have to remix the sound tracks, which costs thousands of dollars.

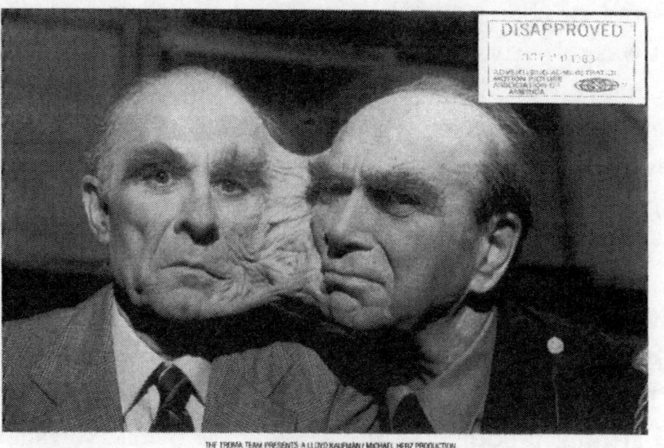

FIGURE 4.8 *Here is a publicity still that the MPAA banned, saying it was "too much" for the American public.*

[32]COMPOSITE PRINT: Film and sound "married" to each other on celluloid picture.

Take *Troma's War*, one of our masterpieces that was released right around the same time of *Die Hard. Die Hard*, which came out ahead of *Troma's War*, was allowed to keep its significant amounts of serious, realistic blood and violence, but *Troma's War* had to cut everything, including goofy slapstick punches and bullet hits—stuff you would see on early morning network news and cartoons[33] on television. This ripped the heat out of the movie, not to mention my own heart, and *Troma's War* was a flop. Our fans got mad and thought we had sold out. They showed up at our movie and there was no sex or violence. It was all about the contract with our video company: we had to deliver a movie that would get an "R" rating. If we didn't, they wouldn't pay us. In other words, we were royally screwed. I wanted to blow my fucking brains out. The president of the MPAA at the time told Michael Herz, in no uncertain terms, that our movie was a no-good piece of shit.[34] So on *Troma's* War, we ultimately decided not to listen to the MPAA and instead to deliver the movie as I had shot it and how our video company wanted, saving the pussy version for the theatrical release only.

Years earlier, Lee Hessel, Executive Producer of *Cry Uncle*, taught me the trick of obtaining MPAA approval and then putting the footage that was unfairly cut out back in, doing our best to come close to the original running length that the MPAA approved. We got caught with *Bloodsucking Freaks*, where we re-added 48 minutes to the 54 minutes that had been approved by the MPAA for an "R" rating. If you get caught, as we did, the MPAA can sue you for copyright infringement, that is, using the MPAA letters such as "R" without proper authorization. Our punishment on *Bloodsucking Freaks* was having to take out advertisements in *The Hollywood Reporter* admitting our wrongdoing. The MPAA would probably be shocked to see Troma's gentle, family-friendly movie, *Doggie Tails* (2003), a cute, charming talking-dog movie for little tikes. Nowadays, films can also be rated on tape, which is a far less expensive process, though we don't even bother to get our movies stoned (i.e., rated) anymore. We just don't care about the rating.

---

[33]There is an added advantage in that early morning news and cartoons on television are often interchangeable.

[34]The MPAA is never, ever supposed to comment on the aesthetics of a film. So this underscores the arrogance toward independent artists.

But the MPAA favors movies with mega-conglomerate budgets to plaster ads and billboards all over our highways, buildings, trains and buses. The MPAA and their double-standard "stoning" policy is one of the major reasons so many independent producers have gone out of business.[35] Through the rise of home video, Troma pioneered the strategy of having a home video version or even a "director's cut" version that is separate from the theatrical version. Luckily, Harvey Weinstein[36] also used our strategy, but he was powerful enough to really make this happen on a larger scale without getting paddle-spanked.

PAUL HERTZBERG ADVISES AGAINST FALLING IN LOVE WITH AN UN-COMMERCIAL PROJECT

WHO IS PAUL HERTZBERG?

Paul Hertzberg, founder of CineTel Films, is a very successful producer of science fiction and disaster movies, such as Icarus, Bone Eater, *and* Gargoyle. *He is currently developing a movie called* I Spit on Your Grave.[37]

The biggest mistake I see producers making is falling in love with a project, without regard to how commercial the film is and thereby having limited chances for financial success in recouping the money from investors. That hurts everybody, including the producer who might have gotten a fee out of it, and it makes it harder for him to go to the investors in the future. It's one thing to follow your vision, but you'd better make sure that there is a marketplace for your project.

[35]Also, the MPAA is currently lobbying in Washington, D.C., 24/7 to get the FCC to destroy the free, open, diverse and democratic Internet that currently exists. The MPAA has officially come out against "net neutrality." Please go to YouTube and type in "Lloyd Kaufman Defines Media Consolidation."

[36]Harvey Weinstein is an American film producer and studio chairman. He is a co-founder of Miramax Films, and today he runs the Weinstein Company with his brother Bob. He is the most beloved man in the film industry—he's just like Mother Teresa, if she had been large, bit people's heads off, and shat down their necks.

[37]It's a remake of Ingmar Bergman's sex and violence splatter classic, *Virgin Spring.*

FIGURE 4.9 Major independent film producer Paul Hertzberg looking quite Vice Chairman-ental of the IFTA (Independent Film & Television Alliance).[38]

I had to join the Director's Guild of America (DGA) after working on *Rocky* in order to continue working production jobs on DGA movies. And remember, I was working on *Rocky* to further my nontraditional film school knowledge and also to put money back into the company that Michael and I were building. However, when we produced a movie, Troma couldn't afford to hire the required staff under the Director's Guild of America rules.[39] So I directed under the name of Samuel Weil[40] and while in post-production for *Troma's War*, the DGA brought me up on charges, or, in other words, tried to kick me out for directing a non-union movie. The *New York Daily News* had visited the set and printed a huge Sunday feature

---

[38]More on the IFTA in Chapter 6. I hope.

[39]Because I was a DGA member, any movie on which I functioned in a DGA capacity was required to be a DGA signatory, which meant that the Production Mangers, Assistant Directors, Unit Managers, and so on would all have to be DGA members, which would have doubled our budget. Also, the DGA rules require all members to eat a baby once a year and sacrifice a 12-year-old virgin boy to the god Ra.

[40]EDITOR'S NOTE: Does Sammy know Louis Su?*

*Samuel Weil was Lloyd's maternal great-grandfather.

*INDEX GYNO: Yes, they are very similar. I found a reference to a mutually shared weekend in Haiti.

describing my supposed direction to actors on the set. Like I ever tell actors what to do.[41] Ha!

Stanley Ackerman, a turd at the DGA, seemed to enjoy calling our offices and threatening to kick me out and fine me $15K. I was summoned to the DGA New York headquarters and put on trial, DGA-style. Ackerman used the *New York Daily News* piece as evidence that I was director of *Troma's War*. The article described me telling a large, muscular guy with a pig nose to grunt; it then went on to report how I was dissatisfied by the orgasmic noises coming from a big-breasted gyno. I said to those gathered around the table in judgment, "Is this your evidence—your *Troma's War* smoking machine gun? If telling a pig-man to snort louder and telling a bimbo to groan is what you gentlemen consider to be directing—if that's what you believe is directing—then our profession is in deep trouble." Everyone except Ackerman laughed. I continued: "Michael Herz is one director and the other credited director, Samuel Weil, is not I, but a symbolic name for the Troma-team collaborative effort." I was, for our purposes, merely acting in my role as producer/director. "I am a strong producer. In the tradition of David O. Selznick, I need to tell the director and actors what to do." I was exonerated but later resigned from the union.

Years later I lit into a now very old Stanley Ackerman while I was on the dance floor of the annual DGA awards. I was on the arm of my wife Pat, and she almost killed me. The story of my getting pushed out of the union became legendary within the DGA.[42] The DGA has since improved its rules. Now young DGA members routinely take production jobs on other films to learn and advance their producing careers and DGA rules permit them to direct ultra low-budget movies.[43]

Any union that would do everything they can to stone its members for trying to create a piece of art is not a union that has its

[41]FOOTNOTE GUY: Lloyd is always barking orders to everyone, even me. I get no respect. When Lloyd steps all over the actors, it's only figuratively. But he steps on me because I'm so small that he can't see me.

[42]I like to believe that the DGA is embarrassed about this matter and the fact that I am a well-known director who is *not* a DGA member. Producers and directors are often surprised to discover that I am not a member of the DGA.

[43]The DGA rules, however, still require the annual eating of at least one baby.*

*EDITOR'S NOTE:—*Gasp*!

members best interests at heart. I understand that Oscar winner Jon Voight[44] went "SAG-Financial Core" (wherein you are allowed to be a member of the union and do nonunion work, yet are unable to vote) in order to do a film he really believed in, but one in which the filmmakers didn't have enough money for a union production. Because of his daring choice, SAG uninvited him from attending the SAG Awards, for which he was nominated for his performance in the TV show *The Five People You Meet in Heaven*. Even poor black-listed[45] Professor Irwin Corey was fined by the Screen Actor's Guild for acting in our non-union 1983 production of *Stuck on You*. As Trent Haaga said earlier, because I produce movies that call for very large casts, my films could never be made using SAG actors under a SAG contract. Our budget would quadruple!

Also, if we were to produce a union movie, SAG would get a gross percentage of the movie profits before anyone else involved in the film got any money whatsoever—not the people who wrote it, the people who directed and acted in it, or the people who invested money in it. SAG bureaucrats, the people who do the absolute least to create the engine of jobs a movie production creates and utilized zero artistic ingenuity—they get their money first. In other words, everyone who had absolutely nothing to do with the reason the movie exists in the first place gets a huge chunk off the top before anybody else. This is fundamentally wrong. The 92 percent of actors who never work may or may not agree with me.

AVI LERNER AND BUDDY GIOVINAZZO SAY UNIONS CAUSE AMERICA'S LOTTERY

WHO IS BUDDY GIOVINAZZO?

Buddy Giovinazzo is a director/writer who began his career with Troma's Combat Shock. *His most recent feature,* Life Is Hot in Cracktown *(based on a book he wrote of the same name), stars Kerry Washington, Lara Flynn Boyle, Illeana Douglas and Shannyn Sossamon.*

---

[44] Jon Voight is an American Oscar, Emmy, and BAFTA (British American Film and Television Alliance)–winning actor perhaps best known for his roles in *Midnight Cowboy* (1969), *Deliverance* (1972) and *Coming Home* (1978). He is also Angelina Jolie's father and thereby grandfather to hundreds of orphans worldwide.

[45] During the "Red Scare" of the 1950s.

AL: On an A-list film, we'll do a movie for anywhere from 40 million to 50 million dollars. It's all about the budget—you take as much money as you can based on how much you think you can sell. We do use the Screen Actors Guild, but I think one of the major problems with America and the economy are the unions—the unions are the reason why America is incapable of producing anything on the level of other countries—because of the way the unions treat their members and the companies that hire their members.

For example, if someone in our business is making $2.5 K a week, which is a great salary for anyone in the world, then the union will take 30 percent of that. They take 30 percent of the cost and use it for whatever reason they want. When you have five or six different unions, everyone takes his own share.

BG: Our budget for *Life is Hot in Cracktown* was $1 million dollars. We had a SAG cast, but a non-union crew. When you're a small film, like ours was, the unions will sometimes come and try to shut down your production. A union representative will approach the cameraman and say, "Hey, do you want to be a member of our union?" and that question is a crew member's dream. All crew people want to work on union films, because that's where the money is. The union rep will offer him direct union membership and shut down the rest of the production.

A lot of times, someone on the crew who wants to be in the union will call the union and complain that we aren't paying them overtime, and the union will come down and shut you down. We were lucky no one did that on our film, but if I were a bastard director, it would happen. If no one complains, and there's no money to be had, they don't shut you down.

AL: The most ridiculous union in the world is the teamster's union. Every 17-year-old has a driver's license and yet they need the union to protect them. Like you need a special education to drive a truck. A lawyer will study three years at a university; a doctor will study seven years at school and in residency in order to be a good doctor. A driver needs maybe one or two weeks to learn how to drive and yet a driver on a union movie in New York will cost you $6 K, $4 K a week, and then the unions will take $2 K. This is outrageous. You have to take a certain number of them and you have to have teamster captains—production coordination and a driver coordination. The way that America is forced to use unions . . . it's helping un-America. And that's the reason America is bankrupt.

FIGURE 4.10 Producer Avi Lerner gets in "Gere" on the set of *Brooklyn's Finest*.

MY PERFECT NIGHT IN

My taxi had pulled up outside the door of my domicile with the "I Love Tromaville" sticker peeping through the front-door window. This book was getting more and more depressing with each passing day. At least now, within the confines of my own home,[46] I could wallow in my stellar standards of sexual depravity coupled with my superior code of moviemaking ethics and watch our country stone itself in each documented nanosecond on CNN.

MAKING A MOVIE SUCKS "WHY ARE WE DOING THIS—WE HATE MAKING MOVIES!"

BY STONING VICTIMS TREY PARKER AND MATT STONE

WHO ARE TREY PARKER AND MATT STONE?

Trey Parker and Matt Stone first came to Troma with their brilliant musical movie masterpiece, Cannibal the Musical, *which has never once been seen on U.S.*

---

[46]INDEX GYNO: Lloyd, baby, you sound awfully lonely. Do you need a massage?*

*FOOTNOTE GUY: I do! I need a massage! You have no idea how much your muscles hurt when you're this small and constantly jumping up and down in the margins of book-land just to get noticed.

television, thanks to the MPAA and those mega-conglomerates, but has been distributed by Troma and has sold an estimated zillion videotapes and DVDs. Parker and Stone later went on to create South Park *(that show you may have seen on television in the middle of the night sandwiched between "Slanket" and "Life Alert" infomercials) and, most recently, the movie* Team America. *They are now working on a new movie—some kind of* Godzilla *satire, I believe.*

Trey Parker: Making a movie is just brutal. We forget that. Trying to remember back to those days where you were making a movie just because it's was fun—I can't imagine why we would have done that! We started making *Team America* and we got totally screwed in our deal. At one point, Paramount said "We're not making the movie unless you guys do it for free." So we're not making any money on this movie. We're basically making an independent film again, only this time it's with studio money. But then when you're here at two in the morning pulling your hair out because you can't figure out how this scene's going to go with that scene and you've been over it a million times and you're just like "*Why* are we doing this? We hate it. We hate making movies." There's a time where you really love it and that's right before shooting. You get this idea and you think "I think we're going to be able to do this, we'll put on a show and it'll be great!" and then the production goes on and on and you get kicked in the balls over and over and you compromise.

Matt Stone: It's all just a series of compromises from day to day and week to week. You have something in your mind—"OK, this is what the movie should be," and then every day it's just, "Well, we can't do that . . . there can't be five Korean soldiers, can we have three?" We can have two. Okay, two. "Well, their faces don't move for this puppet movie." OK. "Well, we want to shoot a car chase throughout LA." Well, we've got only one car . . . . It's every time you shoot a movie. You just compromise from the day you've got the idea until the day it's in the can.

THIS IS FUCKING DEPRESSING . . . ANYBODY ELSE WANT TO STOP READING AND GO OUT FOR A BEER?

So you see, part of this business is just about surviving the stoning that comes from everyone from wannabe investors to ratings boards, to the peons who make up the rules about who goes up on stage to accept an Oscar, to having your production shut down by a truck driver. No need to inflict this stoning upon yourself Begelman-style, because it's going to come at you, no matter how small or big you are, no matter whether you're a beginner or veteran. Producing a movie is the ultimate lottery ticket—actually, it's more like the "Mystery" scratch-and-play kind—and speaking of scratch-and-play, I think I'm going to do just that at this very moment, since I'm now at home and no one else is around.

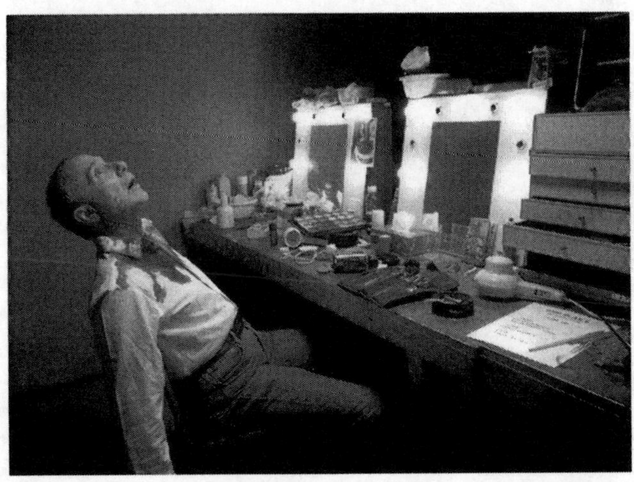

FIGURE 4.11 *LK re-enacts the much-beloved suicide of David Begelman.*

Eager in Erie Asks Lloyd

Dear Lloyd,

Although I have read all three of your filmmaking books, I would like to see more information on film financing.

Yes, I know Make Your Own Damn Movie *encourages us to contact doctors and dentists in our towns, but I would love to know more about the actual mechanics of creating a pitch and an investment memorandum.*

What are these investors hoping to hear from me? Should I expect to actually talk to the doctor or dentists when I call, or will I probably not get past the receptionist? How can I ensure that I will be taken seriously and not seen as some kind of fraud?

Film financing has absolutely got to be the hardest part of the process and your guidance would be invaluable. I look forward to your next book, plus the Direct Your Own Damn Movie! *DVD set, which will join the* Make Your Own Damn Movie *box set on my movie shelf.*

Sincerely and eternally yours,

Eager in Erie

Dear Eager,

Thanks for your question. It's great! In fact, it may be the best question I've read all week! Unfortunately, it is very long and I am dying for a Slurpee at the 7-Eleven. Please review this book and all the others on Amazon.

XOXO,
Lloyd

Chapter | five

Is There a Business Plan? Is IMDB Ass? *or* Secrets of Financing and Producing from the Pickled Brain of an Elaborate Non-pyramid Schemer*

*I still suck at chapter titles.

LINE PRODUCER: Produces "lines" for Robert Downey, Jr. and other strung-out talent.

Synonyms: Candy Man, Sugar Daddy, Lindsay Lohan's dad

Example: "Wow, I am feeling rough today, Dogg."

"Me, too. Let's call the Line Producer."

A NOTE FROM MY EDITRIX

-----------------------Original Message-------------------------

From: elinor@repress.com
Sent: February 13, 2009 7:52 AM
To: Lloyd Kaufman <lloyd@troma.com>
Subject: Definition of Line Producer

Dear Lloyd:

When we talked about defining producer terms, I thought we had an understanding that we would be imparting useful information through these definitions. We've given you a lot of leeway in this regard, but I really feel like I need to put my foot down.[1]

You know I love your sense of humor and will trade puns back and forth with you all day when this project is finished, but the reality is that this is a serious didactic book about film producing. It will be featured on shelves in the Film Production section of Barnes & Noble, not the humor section.

Lloyd, please keep this in mind. We have several more books planned in this series and I would hate to have to re-negotiate that deal.

I trust you'll make sure the rest of your producer vocabulary definitions are based on factual information.

Best,
Elinor

P.S. Was that you who called into Oprah's special on escort services asking for a companion for a gay married man?

Sent via BlackBerry by AT&T

-------------------------End Message---------------------------

LINE PRODUCER: Manages the budget of the movie and sometimes even takes on roles similar to a Unit Production Manager (the person responsible for managing all costs of the movie and delivering it on budget[2]). The Line Producer works

[1]FOOTNOTE GUY: Hey up there! Watch where you put that big foot down! We're trying to work down here.

[2]More on the definition of Unit Production Manager in Chapter 7. I hope.

on location and is often involved in hiring key crew members and negotiating deals with vendors.

Synonyms: None known

Example: "Hi, my name is Zelda and I'll be the Line Producer on the film."

A FEW WORDS VIA E-MAIL FROM MY CO-AUTHOR ASHLEY

------------------------Original Message------------------------

From: ashley@suckedintoworkingforlloyd.com
Sent: February 13, 2009 2:07 AM
To: Lloyd Kaufman <lloyd@troma.com>
Subject: **I**'m a **M**assively **D**ead **B**itch (IMDB)

Lloyd:

Hi! How are you! Happy Friday the 13th! Congratulations on the box office results of *Poultrygeist*! I hope you have a really great Valentine's Day with your Pattie-Pie tomorrow night. I wanted to let you now that you are the warmest and most sensitive filmmaker that I have ever met. I am so lucky to be working with you. OMG, you are soooo hot and soooooo brilliant.[3]

Anyhow, you're probably noticing that I'm writing this e-mail to you really, really late at night. And it's because I can't sleep. I have to say that ever since you totally wigged on me and called me 3 times in a row from the airport on your way to Yemen for New Year's (1 standard phone call, 1 follow-up to the phone call and 1 follow-up to the follow-up) and then sat down for three long interviews with me, I horrifyingly realized that you basically re-told me all these funny stories that you've already told in your other three books (which I've just finished reading). And now I'm really stuck, Lloyd, and I'm not sure that I'm going to be able to help you finish your book!

I mean, you've made it pretty clear you need a gazillion pages and I'm just not sure where they are all going to come from! There's another problem, too. I've been doing my best to completely immerse myself in everything Troma to prepare myself for co-authoring this book on producing. However, remember how I told

[3]EDITOR'S NOTE: This is **not** part of Ashley's e-mail, Lloyd.*

*LLOYD'S RESPONSE TO EDITOR: Don't font at me. I'll bet the Index Gyno wrote it. She wants to take me to the Nano World Con.**

**INDEX GYNO'S RESPONSE TO LLOYD: Not true. I hate Lloyd.

you I get sick on small planes and in the back of taxicabs? Well, the truth of the matter is that your movies also make me nauseous. Like, I want to puke up green vomit kind of nauseous. And it's the kind of puke that's not the good "I'm a little excited" kind of puke. I mean, it's really not pleasant. So I kind of have to watch all of your movies with only one eye. Half open. Without my contact lenses. Even though I'm as blind as Sarah in *The Toxic Avenger.*

Soooo, in preparation, I decided to really take to just *listening* to your movies and interviews while blindfolding myself and doing my best to draw your essence out, because I'm sensitive, you know, I feel I can really *hear* your story and help you communicate it to fledgling producers everywhere, but honestly, as I was transcribing our interview sessions where I went through all of your producing credits on IMDB (and there are boatloads of them), I noticed that you hardly remember anything about Troma anymore!

So what can I write about? That's why I'm writing about the fact that I'm having trouble writing about finding material to write about.[4]

I tried to approach your partner, Michael Herz, but he's always at the gym when I stop by and prefers not to have to think – much less talk – about you. Then I talked to your assistant Matthew, and he told me he's afraid of you. So then I asked Evan what he knows about you and he says he sticks around Troma only because you attract lots of chicks, and well, I don't know what to do! The worst of it is that you keep saying you don't know anything about producing because you've never really had to! So, I've cut and pasted some of my transcription notes from our sessions here that clearly illustrate my dilemma:

ASHLEY: So, Lloyd, what about *The Dark Side of Midnight*? Tell me about that one.

LLOYD: Did we do that? I don't think so. Maybe we bought it?

ASHLEY: Well, you are listed as Producer.

LLOYD: Huh. Yeah, I don't remember.... No, wait a minute. Wes Somebody made that flick, not me.

ASHLEY: Oh, okay. Well, let's move through the list. What about *Lust for Freedom*?[5]

LLOYD: You mean what those people who work at Disney World are thinking right now?

---

[4]INDEX GYNO: The repetition will get you to at least the 100 page mark, sweetheart.

[5]Re: *Lust for Freedom*, I wrote in some shit-disturbing narration and turned it into a women in prison film. Women's lib stuff was *hawt* then.

ASHLEY: No, Lloyd. I'm talking about the movie you produced in 1987.

LLOYD: Oh, uh, yeah. We put money into the film and re-wrote it. We probably added in some lesbians and footage of worms. You know. We were Executive Producers.

ASHLEY: Oh. Great! And then what?

LLOYD: Uh, we distributed it. Hey, where did you find this stuff?

ASHLEY: IMDB.[6]

LLOYD: IMDB is ass.

ASHLEY: Heh. Ummm, OK, sure. Whatever you say. What about *Combat Shock*?

LLOYD: *Combat Shock*! Great movie! Ahead of its time. We're just releasing it again on DVD right now.

ASHLEY: Cool! You and Michael invested in it and became Executive Producers, right? And Troma acquired the worldwide distribution rights before the film was completed and then distributed[7] it, right?

LLOYD: Yes! I also sort of…fucked it up. Maybe. That's debatable.[8]

ASHLEY: Wow! Cool. Well, what about *Girls School Screamers, Igor and the Lunatics* and *Dialing for Dingbats*?

LLOYD: Where did you find this stuff?

ASHLEY: IMDB.

LLOYD: IMDB is ass. We own *Igor and the Lunatics.* I know that much…and I do not remember anything on that film. It's a crazy-ass movie, however.

---

[6]IMDB is the Internet Movie DataBase found on the Internet that acts as a sort library of movies and actors. It's not always (okay it's not ever) entirely accurate or complete.

[7]INDEX GYNO: Various forms of the infinitive verb "to distribute," as in the "distribution" and "distributed" you use here will get you to at least page 102.

[8]Buddy Giovinazzo's *Combat Shock* originally came to us as a movie titled *American Nightmare*. It was definitely not a *Rambo*-style action film. In order to make the film seem more commercial, we purchased stock Vietnam war footage and used it to create a prologue (Spielberg later stole this technique when making *Saving Private Ryan*) that the director did not want. It was shot on 16mm. Troma blew it up to 35mm so it could be released in cinemas—even though it came out during the age of video cassettes—and this resulted in an unsuccessful but prestigious theatrical release complete with a review in the *New York Times*. The movie ultimately turned a profit (possibly due to the prologue we added and the misleading title of *Combat Shock* that we gave it) and is now being released as a 20th-anniversary DVD, which contains both Buddy's original *American Nightmare* version and the Troma *Combat Shock* version. http://www.troma.com: BUY TROMA!!!

ASHLEY: Uh, ok. What about *House of the Rising*?

LLOYD: You mean what Congress does when President Obama walks into the room?

ASHLEY: No, I mean *House of the Rising*, the movie you produced.

LLOYD: Really? Uh, Troma distributed it! Where did you find this stuff?

ASHLEY: IMDB.

LLOYD: IMDB is ass.

ASHLEY: Huh. Well, what about *Class of Nuke 'Em High II: Subhumanoid Meltdown* and *Class of Nuke 'Em High III: The Good, the Bad, and the Subhumanoid*?

LLOYD: Yeah, Michael Herz and I produced both of those at the same time. I had a hand in writing them – I also wrote the lyrics for the title song, "Class of Nuke 'Em High Part 2, It's a Subhumanoid Boogaloo Comin' At You!" I'm the Oscar Hammerstein of low-budget movies.

ASHLEY: Right. Totally, I see that. Well, there must be a producing lesson in the *Nuke 'Em High* sequels.

LLOYD: Hmmm. Yes, we planned to do both of those at the same time, but I wasn't ultimately happy with the results, even though they were profitable. We also made *The Toxic Avenger II* and *III* at the same time, too, only that was a total accident.

ASHLEY: Yes, yes, you talked about that already in one of your other books!

LLOYD: Oh! Good! Well, those other books are pretty good. Have you seen the reviews on Amazon? You know, maybe we should talk about Hollywood sequels.

ASHLEY: OK, OK, OK then. Yes! We will, at some point. Now, what about *Fortress of Amerikkka*?

LLOYD: We wrote and produced it in the late 1980s. It was about a futuristic society where everyone in the world hates America. What a preposterous idea that is! Who could ever hate the land of George W. Bush? I was originally supposed to direct it as well, but Michael thought I should focus instead on being the "face" of Troma.

ASHLEY: And what a beautiful, pristine, unblemished face it is![9] OK, so what about *Touch Me in the Morning*?

LLOYD: I really don't think Pattie-pie would approve.

ASHLEY: No! The movie! The movie you produced. *Touch Me in the Morning.*

---

[9]ASHLEY'S RESPONSE: I didn't say that, Lloyd.

LLOYD: No kidding. Where did you find this stuff?

ASHLEY: IMDB!

LLOYD: IMDB is ass. But *Touch Me in the Morning* is a masterpiece by Giuseppe Andrews and was produced for less than $2K.

ASHLEY: Well, IMDB has scores more of producing credits attributed to you!

So, Lloyd, perhaps now you understand my problem. Anyhow, this whole thing has me uncharacteristically traumatized to the point where I just keep playing "IMDB is ass, IMDB is ass, IMDB is ass" over and over and over again in my head like a broken record and I've now convinced myself that **I**'m a **M**assively **D**ead **B**itch if I don't help you finish your book in time to get it to your editor by the deadline!

Please help and please, please, please do not blame this on one of your 1960s LSD-induced Iron Maiden flashbacks. There must be something of value to share with the producing youth in this world. Something? Anything!!!

Thanks for listening, Lloyd. I appreciate your being so open!

Best,
Ashley

P.S. You also wanted me to remind you that Dr. Phil is doing his special on "in-ing"[10] gay married men next week.

Co-author Ashley Wren Collins

FIGURE 5.1 *EDITOR'S NOTE: Now you're forging autographs, Lloyd? You've sunk to a new low.*

-------------------------End Message---------------------------

[10]*In-ing*, the opposite of *outing*, refers to exposing a man for his secret heterosexuality.

COMPARE, CONTRAST, COAGULATE: LLOYD'S PRODUCING AND ACTING RESUMES ON WWW.LLOYDKAUFMAN.COM AND WWW.IMDB.COM

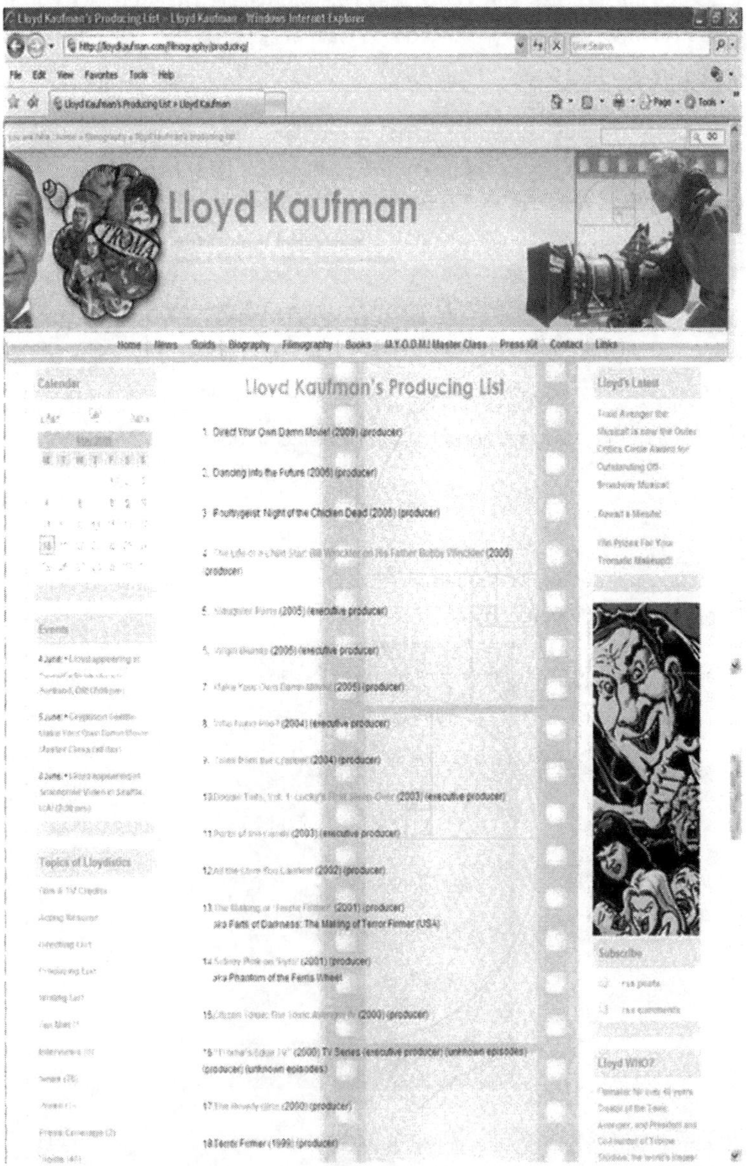

FIGURE 5.2a *Ashley hopes you will begin to recognize her dilemma and Lloyd's bad memory. Lloyd's producing credits on http://www.lloydkaufman.com.*

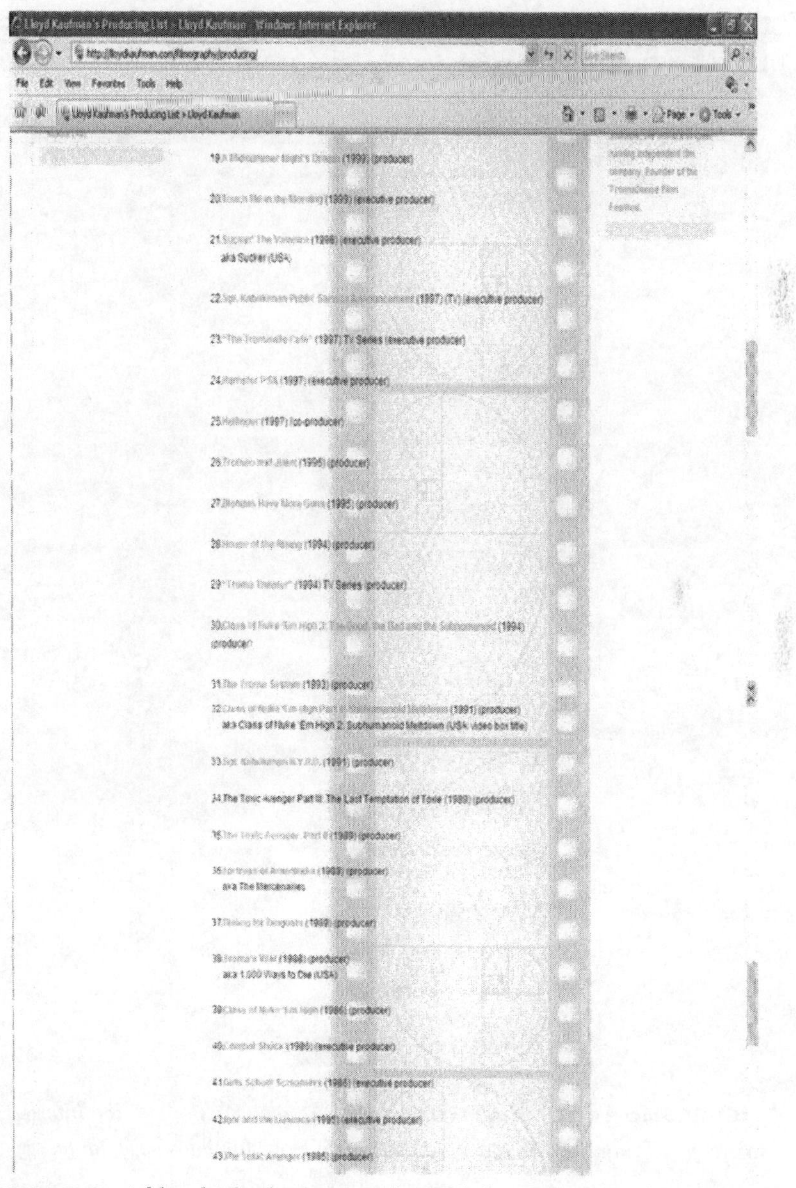

FIGURE 5.2b *Ashley thinks this list is really, really long. She wishes Lloyd would stop suffering from his Iron Maiden flashbacks that erase his memories.*

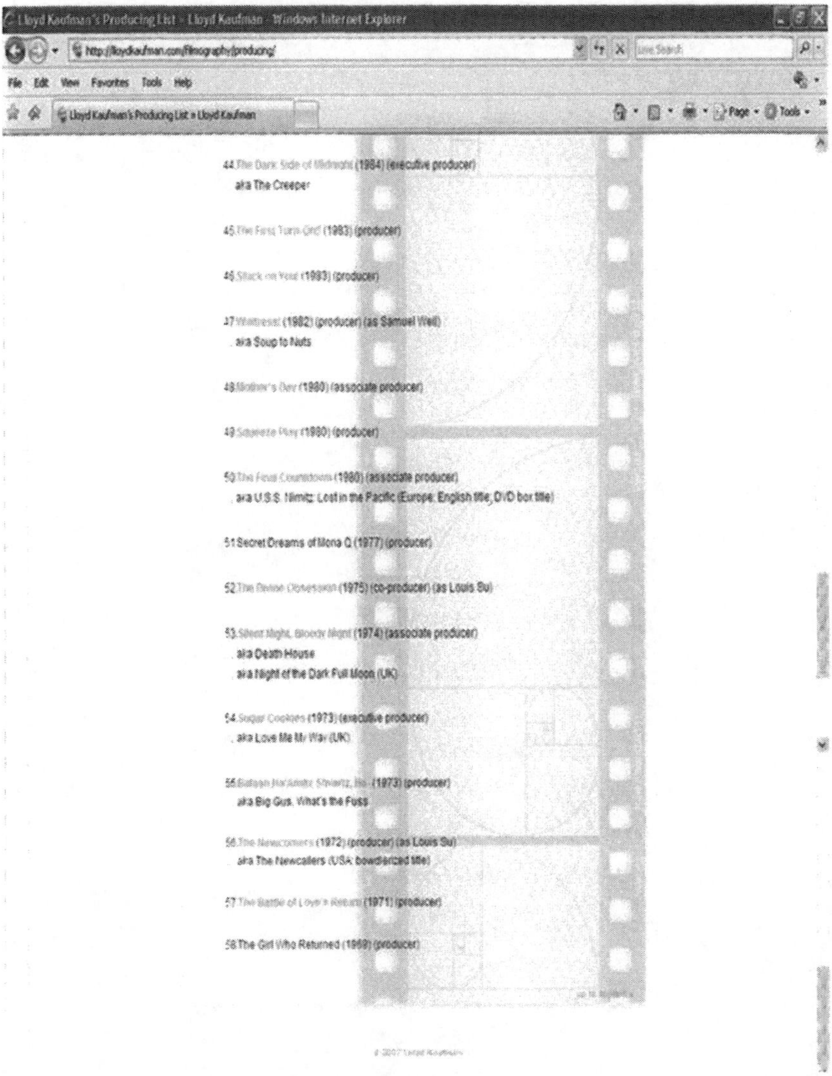

Lloyd Kaufman's Producing List - Lloyd Kaufman - Windows Internet Explorer

http://lloydkaufman.com/filmography/producing/

44. The Dark Side of Midnight (1984) (executive producer)
aka The Creeper

45. The First Turn-On! (1983) (producer)

46. Stuck on You! (1983) (producer)

47. Waitress! (1982) (producer) (as Samuel Weil)
aka Soup to Nuts

48. Mother's Day (1980) (associate producer)

49. Squeeze Play (1980) (producer)

50. The Final Countdown (1980) (associate producer)
aka U.S.S. Nimitz: Lost in the Pacific (Europe: English title, DVD box title)

51. Secret Dreams of Mona Q (1977) (producer)

52. The Divine Obsession (1975) (co-producer) (as Louis Su)

53. Silent Night, Bloody Night (1974) (associate producer)
aka Death House
aka Night of the Dark Full Moon (UK)

54. Sugar Cookies (1973) (executive producer)
aka Love Me My Way (UK)

55. [illegible] (1973) (producer)
aka Big Gus, What's the Fuss

56. The Newcomers (1972) (producer) (as Louis Su)
aka The Newcallers (USA: bowdlerized title)

57. The Battle of Love's Return (1971) (producer)

58. The Girl Who Returned (1969) (producer)

FIGURE 5.2c *Ashley is way psyched that these reproductions off the Internet are taking up so much space. Maybe she* can *help Lloyd fulfill his page quota!*

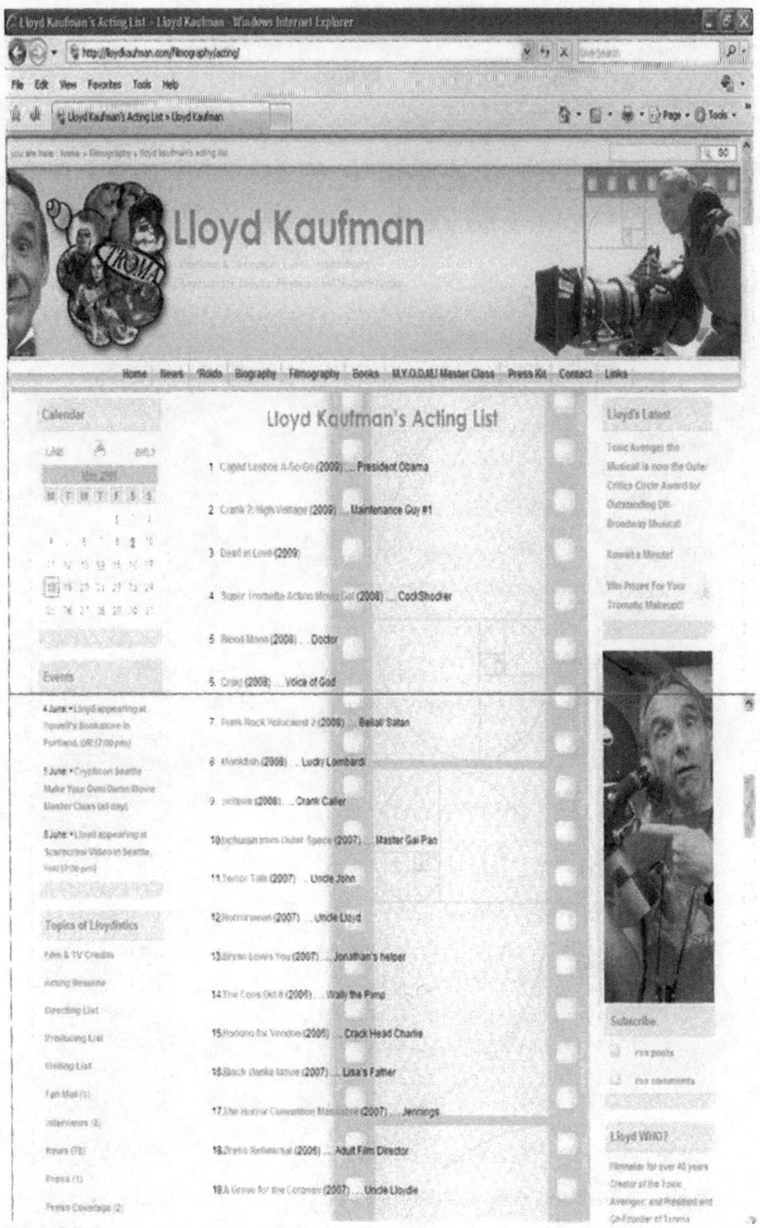

FIGURE 5.3a *Lloyd's acting credits on http://www.lloydkaufman.com.*

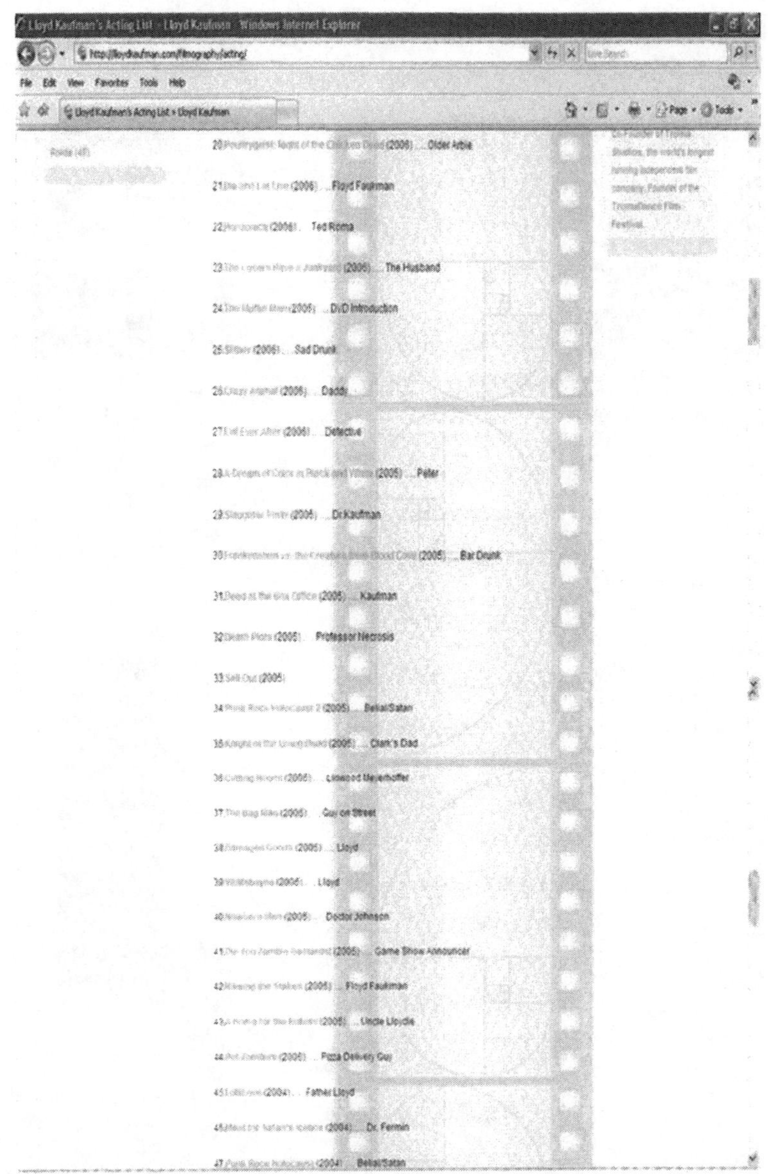

FIGURE 5.3b *Though she worries about Lloyd's memory loss, Ashley is proud of her brilliant thought to include these figures so Lloyd's readers can appreciate his illustrious career that he cannot remember.*

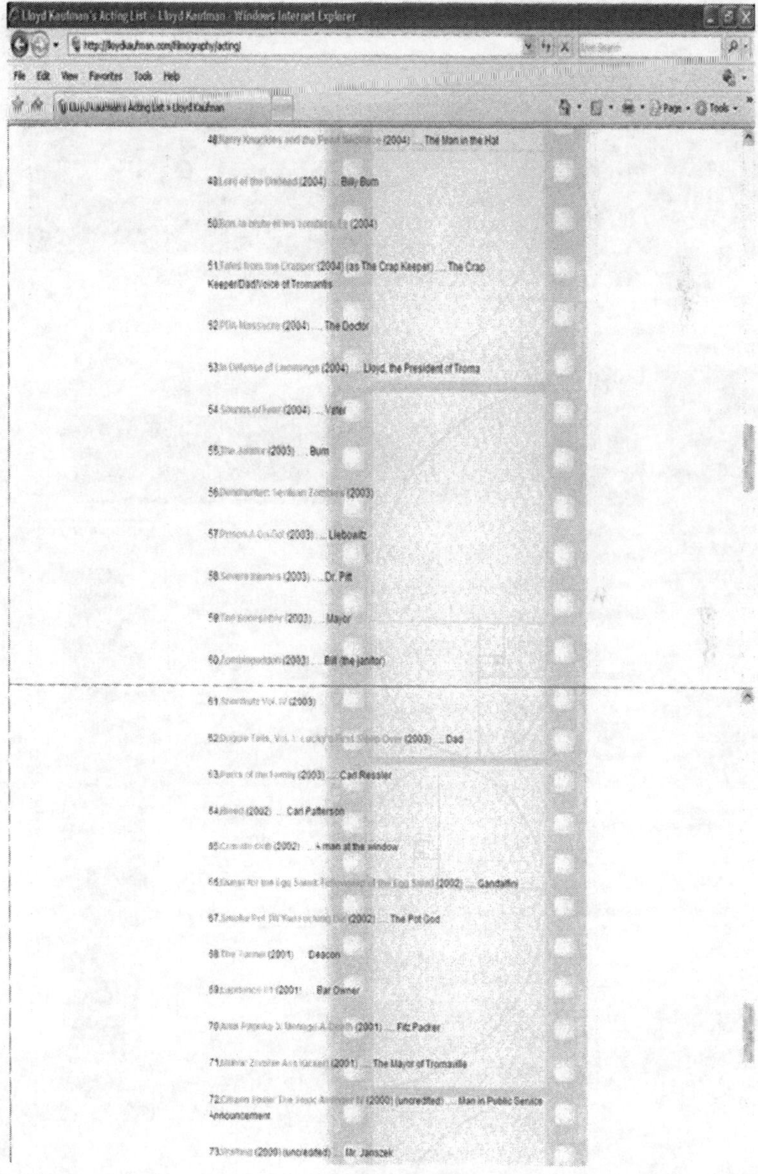

FIGURE 5.3c *EDITOR'S NOTE: Ashley, I'm going to have to encourage you and Lloyd to forge ahead with some actual text here … there must be more to share about producing, no?*

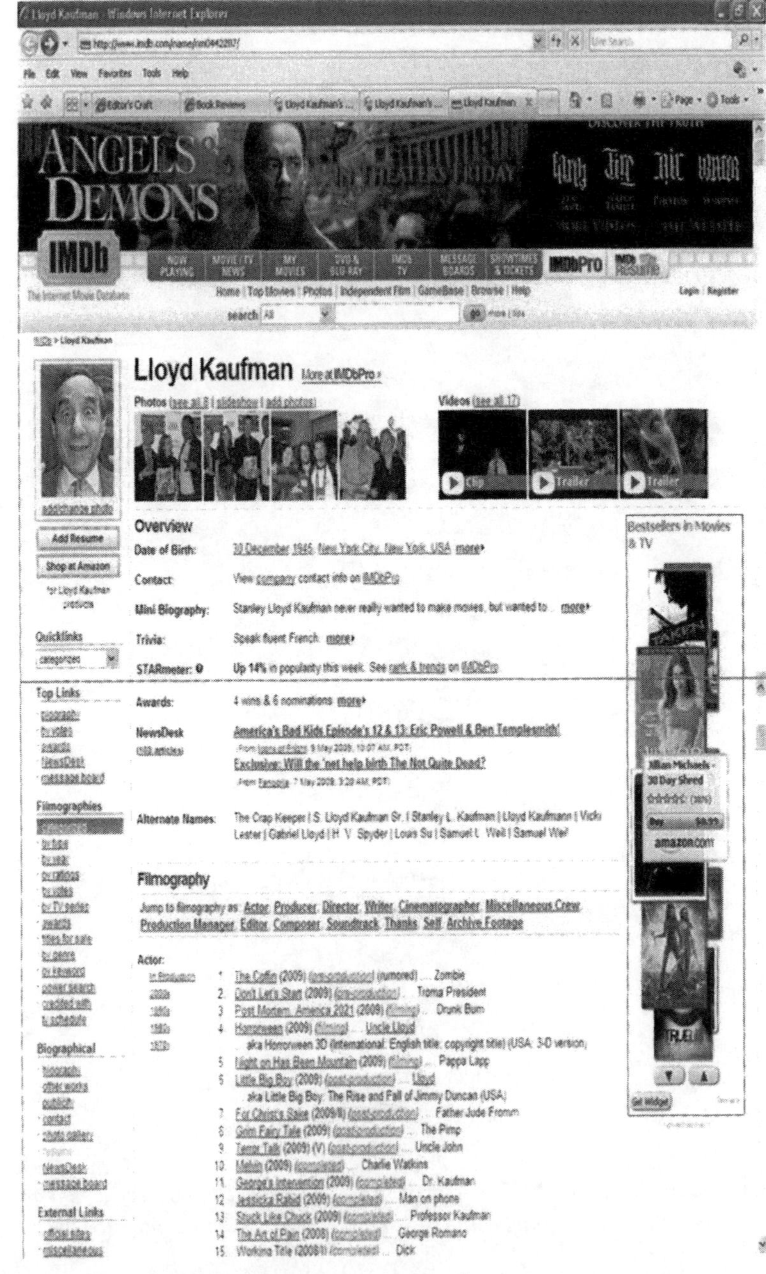

FIGURE 5.4a *Lloyd's credits on http://www.imdb.com.*

Miracle Diet Exposed

16. Bikini Bloodbath Christmas (2009) (V) .... Dr. O'Masterblaster
17. Caged Lesbos A-Go-Go (2009) .... President Obama
18. Crank: High Voltage (2009) .... Maintenance Guy #1
    ... aka Crank 2 (USA: alternative title)
19. Nun of That (2009) .... The Pope
20. Unholy Reunion (2009) .... Boris
21. HellBilly 58 (2009) .... Jack Kaufman
22. Hanger (2009) .... Melvina the Tranny
23. Dead in Love (2009)
24. Clown Dad (2008) .... Clown Grandad
25. Corpus Kristi (2008) .... Doctor
26. Psycho Sleepover (2008) .... Anchorman
27. Super Tromette Action Movie Go! (2008) (V) .... CockShocker
28. Blood Moon (2008) .... Doctor
29. Bryan Loves You (2008) .... Jonathan's helper
30. The Wimp Whose Woman Was a Werewolf (2008) (V) .... Brody
31. Bachelor Party in the Bungalow of the Damned (2008) (V)
32. Un cazador de zombis (2008) (V) .... Lloyd
    ... aka Zombie Apocalypse Now! (International: English title: DVD title)
33. Craig (2008) .... Voice of God
    ... aka Craig: The Movie (USA: informal title)
34. Punk Rock Holocaust 2 (2008) (V) .... Belial / Satan
35. A-Bo the Humonkey (2008) .... Ronald Weinberg
36. Monkfish (2008) .... Lucky Lombardy
37. Schism (2008/I) .... Crank Caller
38. Meat Weed America (2007) (V) .... Art Dealer
39. Zeppo: Sinners from Beyond the Moon! (2007) .... President Kaufman
40. Street Team Massacre (2007) .... Lewis Dickinson
41. Pretty (2007) .... Teacher
42. Uchuujin from Outer Space (2007) .... Master Gai Pan
43. The Horror Convention Massacre (2007) (V) .... Jennings
44. Misadventures in Space (2007) .... Lord Admiral Kaufman
45. Crazy Animal (2007) (V) .... Daddy

43. The Horror Convention Massacre (2007) (V) .... Jennings
44. Misadventures in Space (2007) .... Lord Admiral Kaufman
45. Crazy Animal (2007) (V) .... Daddy
46. The Devil's Muse (2007) .... Lisa's Father
47. Poultrygeist: Night of the Chicken Dead (2006) .... Mature Arbie
    ... aka Poultrygeist (USA: short title)
48. Die and Let Live (2006) .... Floyd Faukman
49. Shadows in the Woods (2006) (V) .... Steve Stonewall
50. The Cops Did It (2006) .... Wally the Pimp
51. No, My Other Possessed-Zombie Girlfriend (2006) (V) .... The Announcer
    ... aka N.M.O.P.Z.G. (USA: DVD box title)
52. Hoolgonica (2006) (V) .... Ted Roma
53. The Losers Have a Junkyard (2006) (V) .... The Husband
54. The Muffin Man (2006) (V) .... DVD Introduction
55. Meat Weed Madness (2006) (V)
56. Think Tank (2006) (uncredited) .... Drive-Thru Customer
57. Slither (2006) .... Sad Drunk
    ... aka Incisions (Canada: French title)
58. Dress Rehearsal (2006) .... Adult Film Director
59. Hoodoo for Voodoo (2006) .... Crack Head Charlie
60. Evil Ever After (2006) (V) .... Detective
61. A Dream of Color in Black and White (2005) .... Peter
62. Slaughter Party (2005) (V) .... Dr Kaufman
63. Frankenstein vs. the Creature from Blood Cove (2005) .... Bar Drunk
64. Dead at the Box Office (2005) .... Kaufman
65. Death Plots (2005) .... Professor Necrosis
66. Sell Out (2005)
67. Knight of the Living Dead (2005) (V) .... Clark's Dad
68. Cutting Room! (2005) .... Linwood Meyerhoffer
    ... aka The Cutting Room (USA: DVD box title)
69. The Bag Man (2005) .... Guy on Street
70. Damaged Goods (2005) .... Lloyd
71. Wolfsbayne (2005) .... Lloyd

FIGURE 5.4b *Ashley feels that by now, you are really feeling her pain. One man, one Iron Maiden flashback, so many credits!*

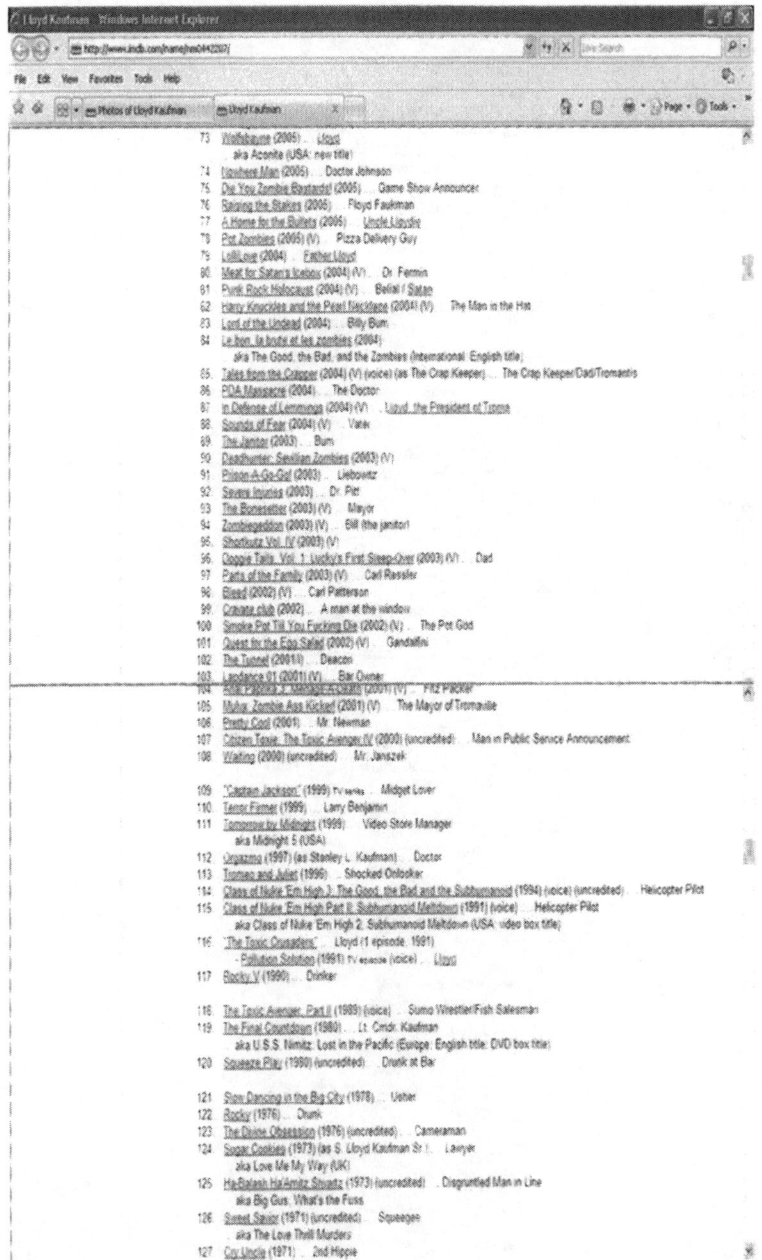

FIGURE 5.4c *Ashley wants to know if you are starting to lose track of all of Lloyd's credits, too.*

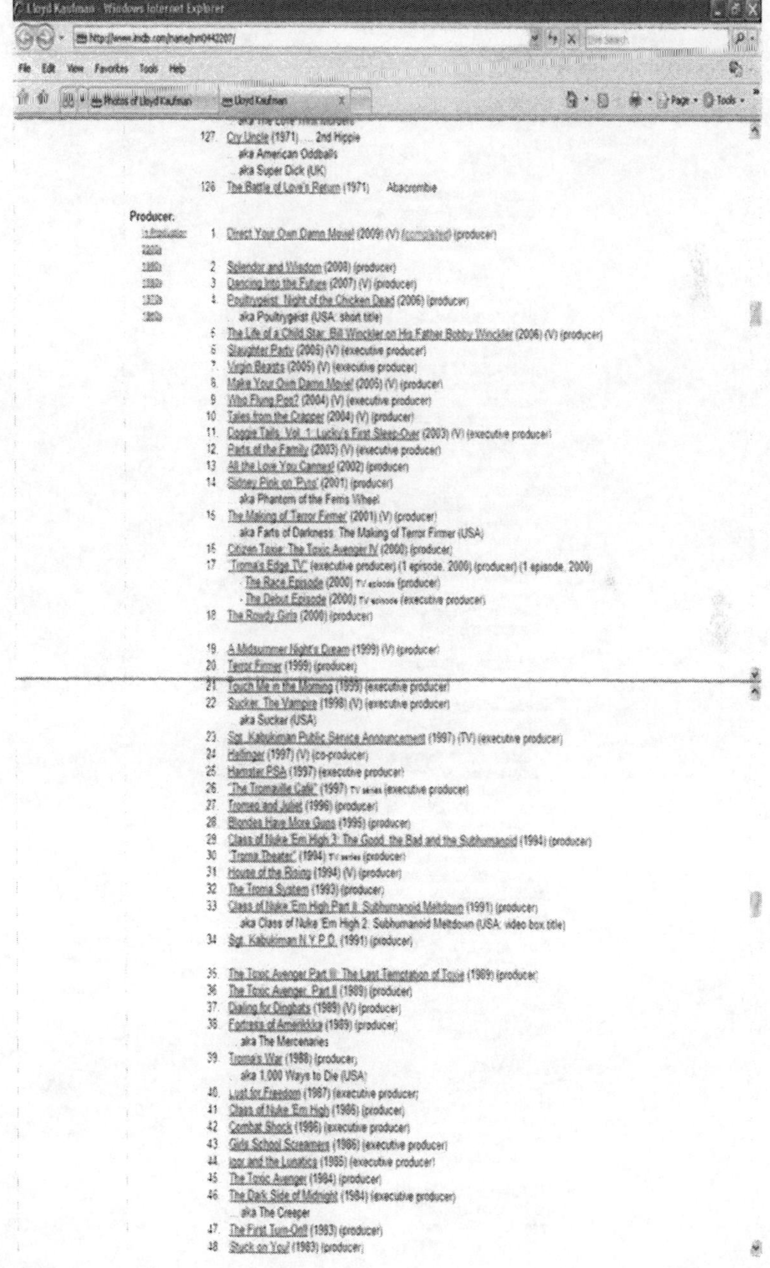

FIGURE 5.4d *EDITOR'S NOTE: Ashley, you and Lloyd really need to get back on track.*

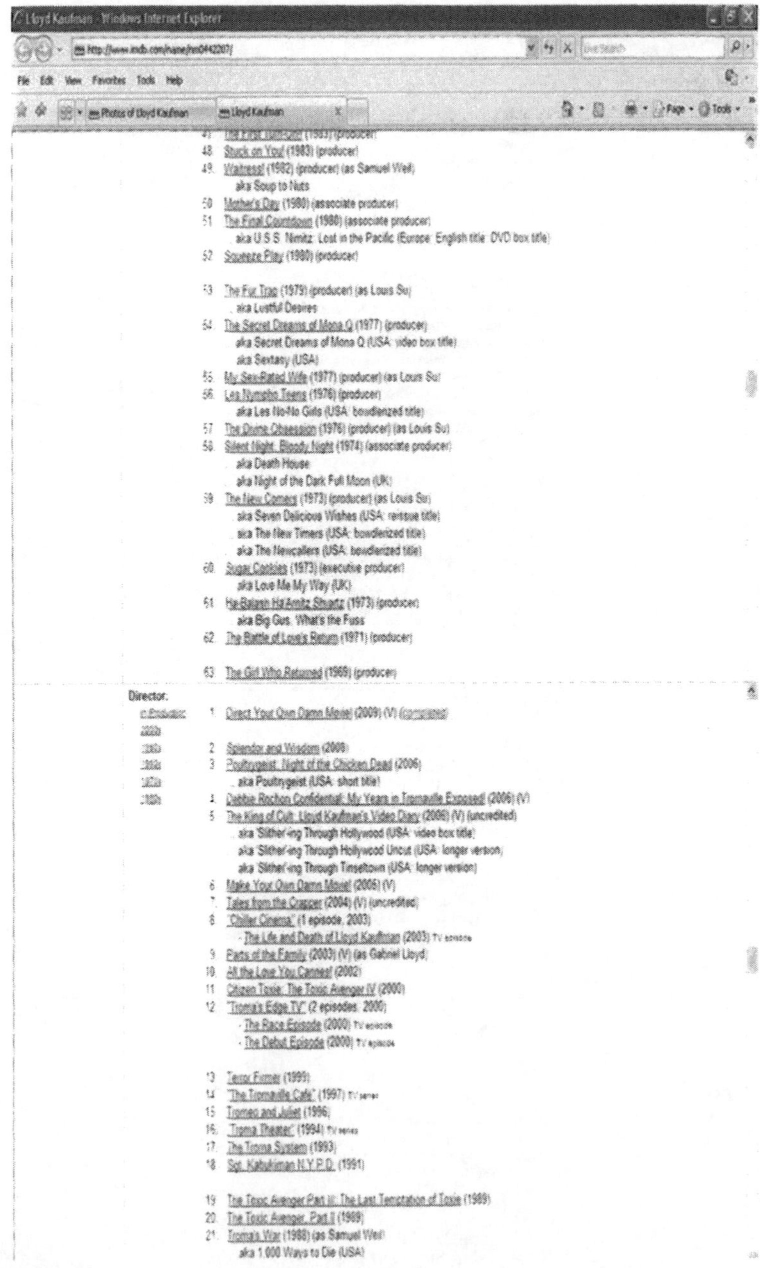

FIGURE 5.4e *INDEX GYNO: Genius. This will get you to at least page 120.*

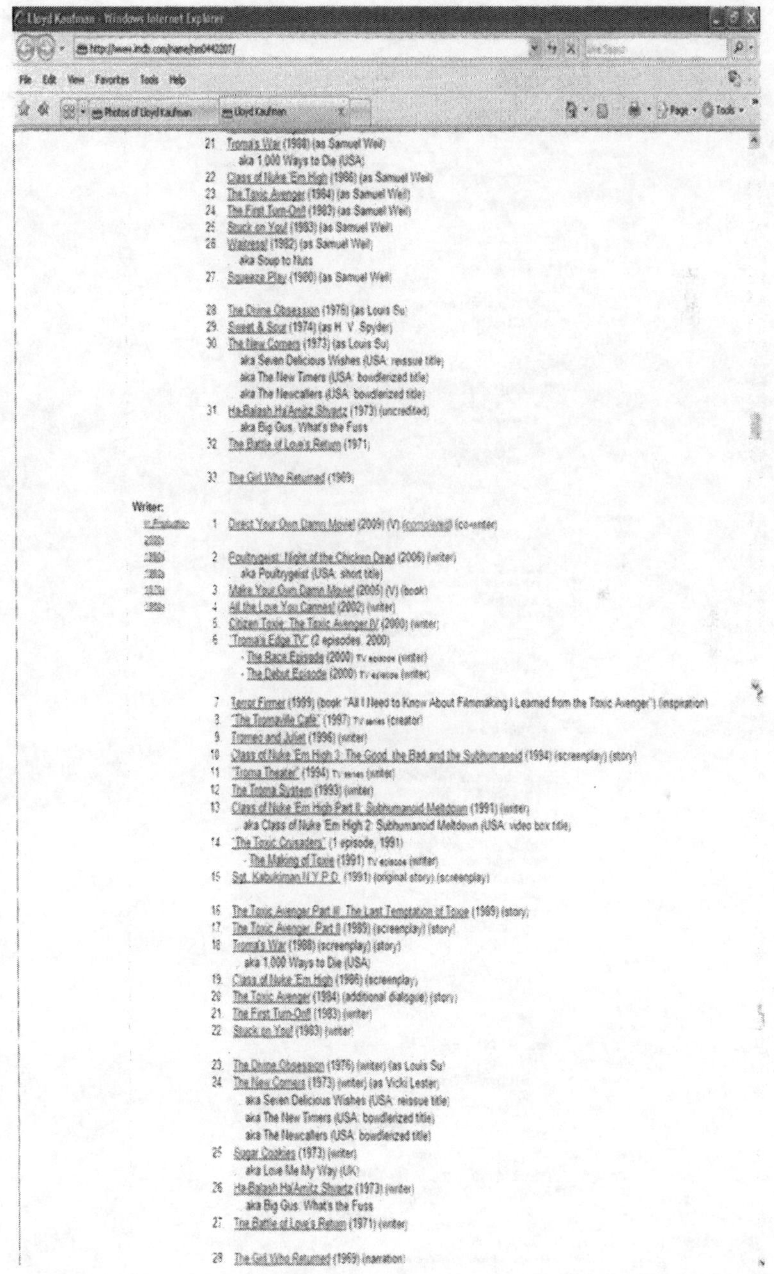

FIGURE 5.4f *FOOTNOTE GUY: Yikes! This is a footnote nightmare! Because these captions are at the bottom of all the pages, they fall under my department as well. Ack! Help!*

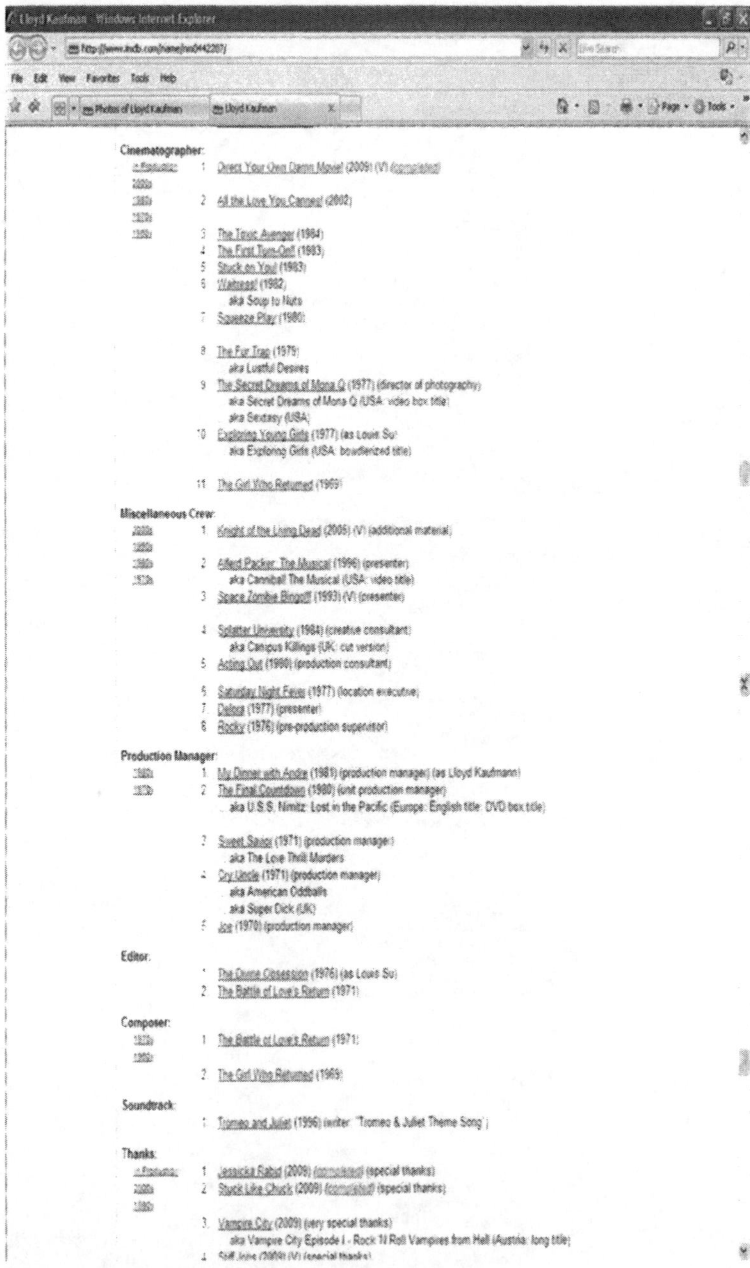

FIGURE 5.4g *EDITOR'S NOTE: Lloyd, Ashley is just the victim here. I am holding you responsible. We get the point. Please move on. Please.*

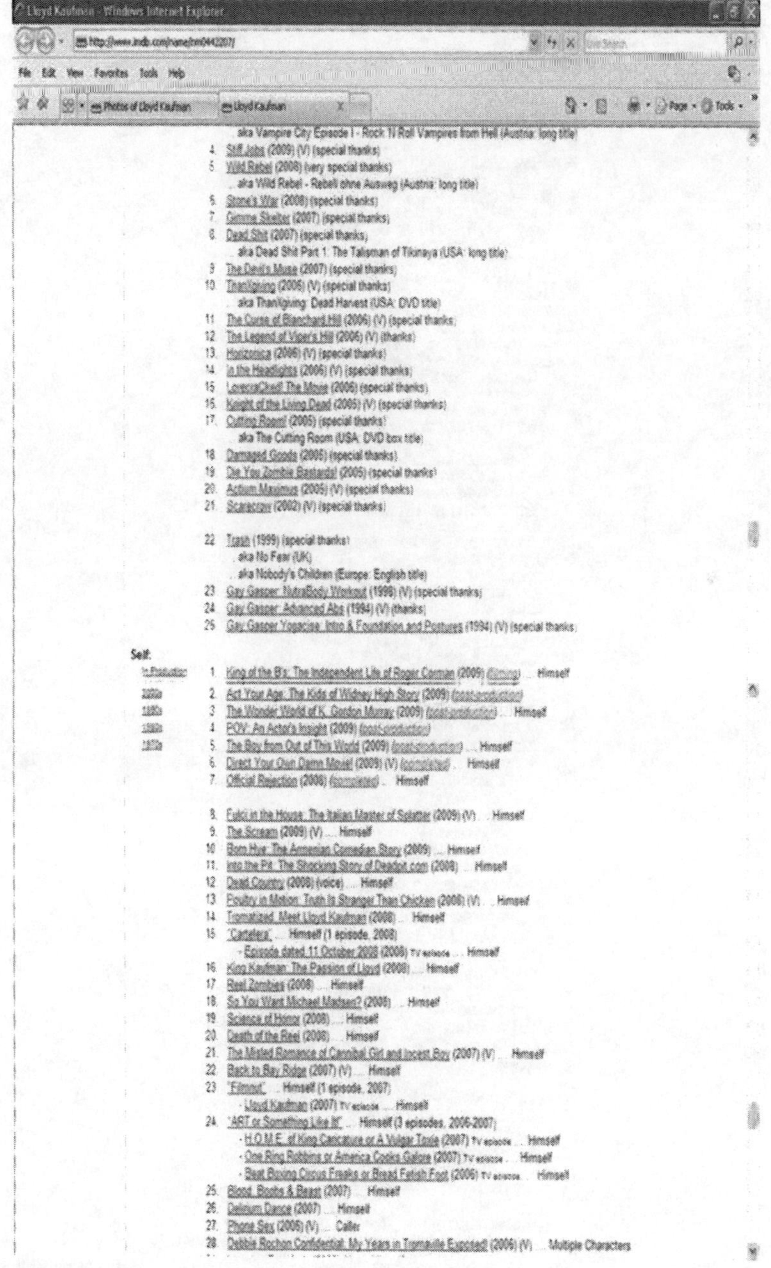

FIGURE 5.4h *INDEX GYNO: Lloyd, if I've said it before, I'll say it again…you've got a helluva lot of stamina.*

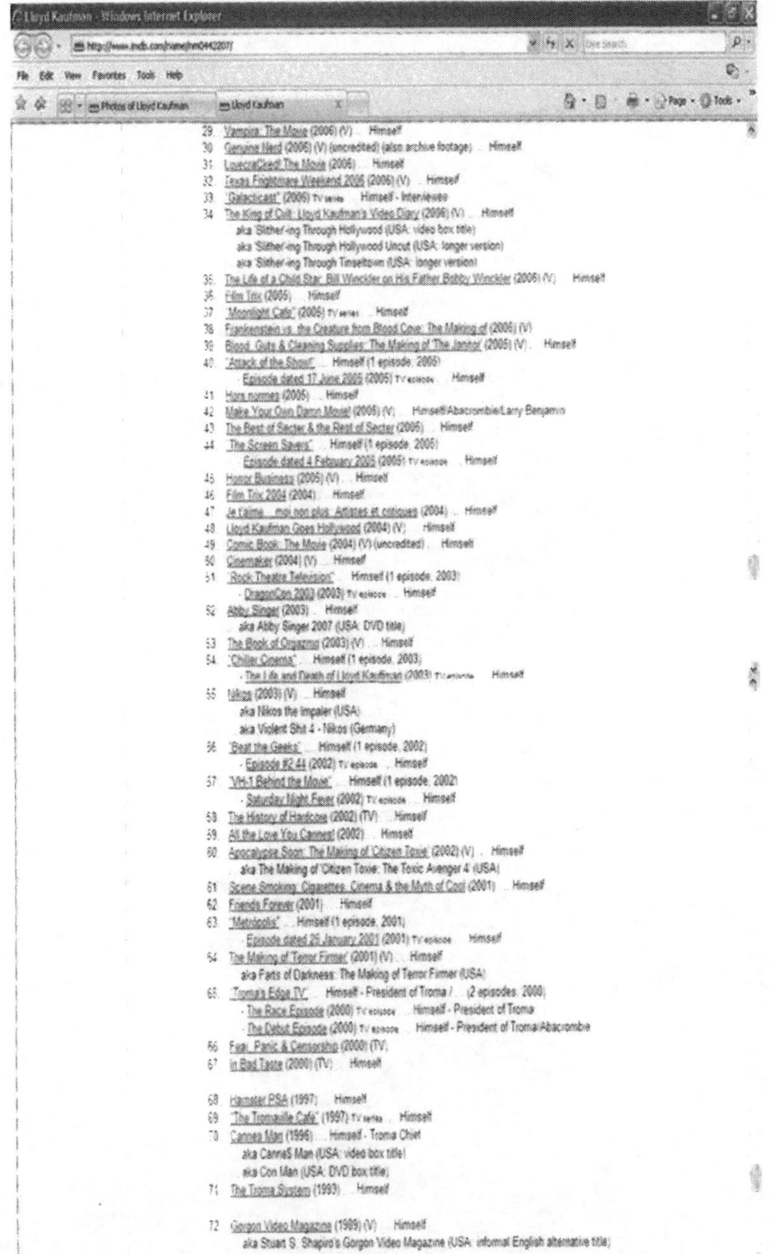

FIGURE 5.4i *EDITOR'S NOTE: Ok, that's it! Enough! Return to the story, please.*

THE ACCIDENTAL BUSINESS PLAN

I have to admit it: I was in shock. I had just returned from the Berlin Film Festival to find Ashley's e-mail in my inbox, buried among 318 offers to enlarge my penis and 57 messages from a bank manager in Lagos, Nigeria. Was it possible that I was becoming so old that I couldn't remember all the movies on which I was credited as Producer/Writer or Executive Producer or had fluffered and distributed? And did Evan really only stick around me for the potential to meet chicks? Apparently, both were true.

FIGURE 5.5 *LK bravely subdues extremely dangerous 60-pound woman on movie set in Berlin.*

But you know what? That doesn't really matter. I realized, while rereading Ashley's e-mail over and over and over again as I took the lovely N train from Manhattan out to the Troma Building in Long Island City, that there was at least a pattern in our conversation she had transcribed. And the pattern was that we at Troma actually had a business plan that we had adopted and followed over the years! We produced and subsequently distributed a lot of movies over several decades. Mind you, they were all movies we believed in and that had something unique—that special quality that speaks to you, for whatever reason. In doing this, I apparently racked up some more producing credits, at least according to that shit IMDB search engine.

It was, in fact, part of our whole business model, the brilliant thinking behind the pattern being, of course, that in addition to producing our own Tromasterpieces, we also acquire great films from aspiring filmmakers, who—for whatever reason—can't find the money or the right executive producer or distributor to believe in and support their production. Sometimes we give that last piece of money needed to finish shooting a film and then I add in some element to set it apart from the crowd. Like Toxie, Troma steps in to save the day! See *Monster in the Closet*, *Def by Temptation*, or *Cannibal the Musical*. No one would touch these great movies.

Then, in distributing, we get our investment back "off the top" (so we're not bending over, waiting in dreadful anticipation to make back our investment costs), and then we get a percentage of the profits following our initial investment. And then, that percentage of the profits goes toward financing our very own Troma movies à la the *Class of Nuke 'Em Highs*, *The Toxic Avengers*, *Tromeo & Juliet*, and so on and so forth. So we're furthering our personal mission and our business to make movies of the future by investing in *other* movies we believe in (again, that whole come from the heart, thing) and using the return on those investments and funneling it back into the business to grow our business. Pattie thinks I'd make a great guest on that Suze Orman[11] show.

One of the movies we took on in the early 1970s was called *The Incredible Torture Show*. When their original distributor got hold of the movie, he fucked the whole thing up by releasing it as an R-rated movie and cutting out all of the sex and violence that made it funny and "over the top" in the first place. As a result, the movie flopped. It had no stars in it, but it didn't need stars. If a movie doesn't have stars, it's got to have something else that is going to hold your attention. In the case of *The Incredible Torture Show*, that something else was sex, violence and misogyny.

Now, this was way back in the twentieth century, and it was sometime in the early 1970s when we invested in this movie. Newspapers were puritanical in that time and you couldn't place an advertisement with the word "torture" in it, let alone a picture of a bikini-clad woman, unless the bikini was altered and appropriately drawn over and transformed into a pair of Bermuda shorts.[12] So

---

[11]EDITOR'S NOTE: I *love* Suze Orman!

[12]Buffalo, 1977. Someone at the Buffalo News took a magic marker (now called a Sharpie, but back then it was a magic marker) and actually *drew* a pair of 1890s bloomers on our bikini-clad gynos in our newspaper ads for *Squeeze Play*. Make your own damn censoring of independent advertising!

we put all the so-called "bad of taste" footage from the "director's cut"[13] back in the movie, changed the title to *Bloodsucking Freaks*, distributed it, and it was a cult hit! Now, today, *Bloodsucking Freaks* is too politically incorrect, riddled with too much misogyny,[14] but back then, we didn't know any better. The point is that when you control the content (i.e., the distribution, as in the Troma Model for Producing Movies), you are able to make sure that the movie you are putting out there in the rest of the world is exactly the vision you want others to see, and not some "product" others have had the chance to disembowel[15].

ROGER CORMAN PUTS HIS FINGER ON THE MONEY QUESTION

LK: Do you as a producer put your own money into films?

RC: I finance all of my films myself, which is generally considered not a good plan, but if you are careful and you know what you're doing, it's a good investment, because frankly you keep 100% of the profit.[16]

LK: How would you describe your basic business model as a producer today? Certainly our $500K Troma formula is not so good anymore.

RC: In our business model, we first think, "What would we want to make that would give us pleasure?" Of course, someone in the stock market or in real estate who's investing money to make a movie wants his name on a movie that will be a commercial success. So he tries to predict whether it will first go to theatres, to DVD, or to cable and so on. However, I learned from the experience and there is a great quote from William Goldman: "Nobody knows anything." I think that is true. It isn't that nobody knows anything; it is that nobody knows everything. You have a good idea based upon your own ability and experience, but you never know for certain.

I come as close as I can to calculating what I think the market will be and what is a possible return on the investment, knowing that I can be way off in that guess

---

[13]The term "director's cut" did not exist back then. Troma invented it later.

[14]INDEX GYNO: I forgave you for your past a long time ago, baby...and *what* is that smell down here in margin-land?!

[15]FOOTNOTE GUY: Speaking of "disemboweling," I had Mexican food for lunch. I apologize. That may be what you are smelling, Index Gyno.

[16]Pattie-Pie and I put up about $500K of our nest egg* for *Poultrygeist*, so we will get 100%. . .of the loss! I told her she was investing in *Transformers VI*. Please don't tell her where her money went.

*INDEX GYNO: Great chicken pun, Lloyd!

and knowing how much I can spend on the film. Starting with the idea and then deciding the budget, everything flows from that. How much I can spend on the script, on the director, the stars, the production—the post-production, which is different today—because so many pictures we do today use computer graphics.

LK: Roger, the film business is tough today for independents. Why do you decide to still produce films?

RC: I keep producing films because I love making motion pictures. I hope that they turn out to be good pictures and they are fun to make. Essentially, I love the game.

FIGURE 5.6 Producing legend Roger Corman seems perplexed by the positioning of LK's left hand.

REAL TALK ABOUT REAL ESTATE AND "REEL" MISTAKES

The other thing we Troma producers did—which now, I have to say, looking back, was rather genius—was we purchased some real estate! In the early 1970s, we rented a little janitor's closet in the offices of *McCall's* magazine. We then later moved to a "penthouse" in the Actor's Equity[17] building on West 46th Street. The landlord started to ream us, so we bought what would become the legendary Troma Building, a crappy slum in New York's then very dangerous Hell's Kitchen. We bought the building because (a) our landlord was

[17]This is the closest Troma has ever come to a union!

a shit and (b) we would be not only able to control our films but also our *space*. In tough times, we would not have to pay rent.

There was a liquor store on the first floor.[18] After that, it was the "Nearly New" Thrift Shop.[19] And then it was an animal hospital for about 10 years, where many Chinese restaurants came to get their dogs.[20] All of these businesses paid rent to us! After some time a McDonald's moved in next door. And—although their presence did produce a never-before-seen rat infestation in our building—I cannot be too upset at Mickey D's, for my hatred does account for some of the impetus and inspiration I felt to produce *Poultrygeist: Night of the Chicken Dead*, a shot by shot exact remake of the hilarious slapstick gore satire classic, *Schindler's List*.

Anyhow, we didn't take a mortgage out for the building. We paid for the building up front.[21] And the rent from the store on the first floor paid for our real estate taxes and more.

In good times, such as when the Troma film library proved especially lucrative with the video boom, we even paid ourselves rent. The lesson in all this? Go and Produce Your Own Damn Real Estate!

AVI LERNER REMINDS US THAT PRODUCING IS NOT JUST AN ART: IT'S A BUSINESS

LK: Why did you produce—why didn't you direct?

AL: The producer side of me is what I believe I'm better at. I would never be able to be a good director. One of the talents or things the director needs is a lot of patience and passion. Those two things—patience and passion—you have to have them in a way that sometimes are not logical. You see a director that is fighting and wants to do these shots in darkness...I would never be able to justify those kinds of shots that cost so much money in order to create something to my own satisfaction. You also need to have the patience to

---

[18]This liquor store is why we bought the building.

[19]I did all of my Christmas, errrr, Chanukah, errr Kwanza shopping there. Hail Satan!

[20]FOOTNOTE GUY: Hey, guys! Don't listen to Lloyd. He's lying about the Chinese restaurant thing. He's just trying to get a rise out of you. Not very healthy, Lloyd. Marianne Williamson would not be happy with your regression. As a side note, Lloyd, you don't have to work so hard to get a rise out of me! Just massage my semicolon.

[21]It was a crappy building in a dangerous neighborhood and life was cheap in 1979.

make a movie. Every day of a major movie you can shoot maybe one, one and a half minutes. Who has the time to sit there all day and do it again and again until you're happy or he's happy?

LK: Another reason why producing a movie for only $500K can be more fun—it goes a little faster.

AL: I don't see anything wrong with producing a movie for $500K. The only thing I can tell you, because it's so easy to do and so many people are making them, it's harder to then sell low-budget films. We always have to find something that's more difficult to make. The more difficult it is to make, the less competition there is from other productions.

LK: What about the young person who wants to produce?

AL: I'm not the producer. I'll never call myself a producer. I would call myself a person that puts the picture together and looks at the business. You have to, above all, be a business man. For example, if you manufacture bottles, you need to know what is the cost of the bottle and know that this bottle will cost 50 cents to manufacture and that you can eventually sell it for one dollar.

FIGURE 5.7 Avi Lerner uses his special time machine to meet John Travolta's grandfather, circa 1938.

FIGURE 5.8 Avi Lerner (right) with his two identical triplet brothers.

SIMPLE MATH IS MY FAVORITE KIND . . . CALL IT TRO – MATH

Now, if only we'd purchased a Troma Building in North Carolina in 1974, we'd be rolling in the money now—we would have made 50 times our investment instead of 20 times our investment. We eventually got bought out of our Troma Building in Hell's Kitchen (and I used some of my profits plus Pat's retirement fund to finance the majority of *Poultrygeist*). Regarding our new Troma Building[22] in Long Island City?[23] Ha! For what we paid for that, you could buy a skyscraper in West Virginia!

BRIAN YUZNA TELLS YOU HOW MONEY HAS CHANGED[24] OVER THE YEARS

WHO IS BRIAN YUZNA?

Brian Yuzna is a director and a producer, most notably of such hits as Beyond Re-Animator, Night of the Living Dead III, Honey, I Shrunk the Kids, *and* Bride of Re-Animator.

Financing has changed a lot over the years. It's all about any way you can get the money. You either have to have money yourself or family money or look to investors for money. It's all kind of personal. If you're in the industry already, there are other ways to do it. There is money from the people who are selling movies. These days, it has gotten very tricky to finance pictures. Normally, you would have to find a company to finance the movie. You would have to sell or pre-sell the movie. To me, there are three equal important parts of producing. One is financing, one is the production/making the movie and the other is exploiting the movie. If you don't know how you're going to exploit the movie, then you can't finance it.

---

[22]Our new Troma Building is definitely cleaner and less disgusting than 733 9th Avenue, but oh-so-much-farther away from the subway!

[23]By coincidence, the Long Island City Troma Building was formerly a Chinese food distributor. I was a Chinese Studies major at Yale. Louis Su is one of my peeps—what a co-inky dink!

[24]FOOTNOTE GUY: Yet another good pun, Lloyd!

A LITTLE MORE EXPLOITATION FOR THE ROAD

So you see, we Tromites were able to obtain money to produce our films through executive producing and financing other people's films and amassing a very valuable library collection of negatives of movies. This was also achieved by investing in a piece of real estate property that we were able to call our own and work out of, all the while having it increase significantly in value. Avi Lerner and Brian Yuzna don't even think about making a movie unless they know it is completely commercially viable—that it is a "product" they can sell and that it is destined to make a profit. You do have to take those exciting artistic dreams and balance them with hard-core financial realities. In the end, if you master this equation for yourself, you will stay happy and you will keep working. You may get violently stoned along the way here and there, but you will produce movies and have a career.

JIST SO THIS CHIPTER DON'T SEAM *TWO* POIFECT...

Most of my movies concentrate on the underdog. New Jersey is the underdog to arrogant Manhattan—not the underbitch, however. I love Jersey and have set our films in Tromaville, New Jersey, a fictitious town I made up—but many people today believe that Tromaville, New Jersey, is real! Not many folks know this, but at one point in time, Troma bought a building in Jersey City, New Jersey.[25] We were shooting *The Toxic Avenger* at the time in Jersey City, noticed that Jersey had great views of New York City, and thought it would be a good idea.[26] Our Jersey home had a big yard. We also used the basement as a kind of back lot in which to shoot a large part of *Class of Nuke 'Em High*. That's where the incredibly goofy monster scenes were shot. It was awesome. But, Jersey City was rough and not yet gentrified, and the building eventually got . . . torched. So we were forced to sell it. Now it's probably worth a fortune.

Did I mention that everything I touch is fucked?

---

[25]INDEX GYNO: Did you finally find a story you haven't yet told in one of your other books? Well, hooray, bee-atches! It's time to get down and celebrate.

[26]To my schnozzola, the permeating stench of garbage that reigns over the Garden State thanks to the abundant, plentiful chemical plants is the lovely "Aroma du Troma."

Intermission

Andy Deemer's Production Diaries

During the course of this book thus far, I have consulted with many experts on producing movies. I am going to continue describing, as best I can, how I have managed to get celluloid (or sell-u-Lloyd) up on that big silver screen. But I do not believe I am opening the window onto my producing world wide enough. I do not believe that I have given you enough "truth 24 frames per second."[1]

Therefore, I am calling on *Poultrygeist* Production Manager, Line Producer and Producer Andy Deemer to give you a taste of what it is like—the ambiance, if you will, on a Lloyd Kaufman production. Here are a few excerpts from Andy's diary. The last time I heard from Andy he was in Thailand and had sent me the box art for the Thai bootlegged edition of *Poultrygeist*.[2]

---

[1]This was the aesthetic slogan of filmmaker Jean Luc Goddard, but he said it in French. The French translation is "Lloyd Kaufman est le meilleur realisateur du monde."

[2]Which was a lot better than Troma's American version.

FIGURE INT 1.1 *The Thai bootleg edition is pictured here. The rumor is that a copy of this DVD cued up to a close-up shot of Lloyd (Lady Boy) Kaufman dancing and singing in fishnet stockings was found at the Bangkok scene of David Carradine's alleged death by autoerotic asphyxiation. This may not be true.*

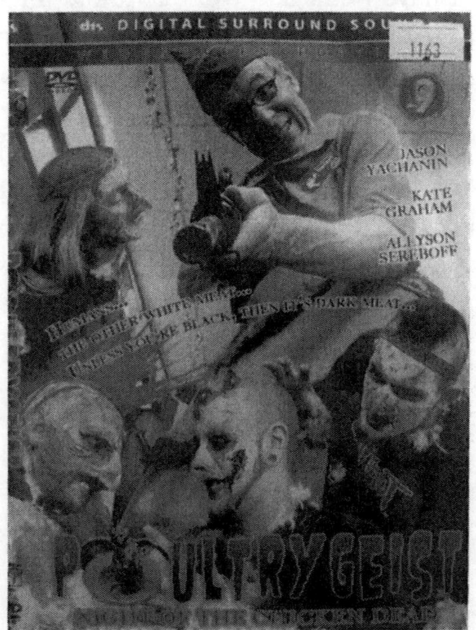

FIGURE INT 1.2 *LK is glad the good bootleggers of Thailand and China respected* Poultrygeist *enough to invest in creating their own DVD box cover art and menus that are better than Troma's! The Chinese bootleg edition is printed here.*

FIGURE INT 1.3 *Cover art for American Egg-dition of* Poultrygeist!

THURSDAY, JUNE 02, 2005

Traci

The incompetent, and possibly retarded PA, Traci, showed up late again today, despite repeat warnings. This is the girl who spent 20 minutes trying to work out why the Xerox was spitting out blank copies. (She'd left the original sitting next to the Xerox.) And countless other idiocies. Anyhow, it turns out she can't hack the hours, and so she quickly became the first PA to quit the film. I can't deny my relief.

posted at 1:12 p.m.

TUESDAY, JUNE 07, 2005

Another Producer?

Some serious character sent in his serious resume today, applying to be a producer or production manager on *Poultrygeist*. He showed a real familiarity with Lloyd's writings and work:

- "I can bring grown-up production management and producing judgment to Troma's project—and most importantly do things your way."

- "I know that Troma is the big time in independent film. If you hire me, I will stop at nothing to help you bring your project in safely, on time and under budget."
- "I cannot afford to work at no pay; however, I can commit to the entire summer and long hours if the pay rate is $1,600 per week, plus a reference letter at the end of the project. I'd be willing to work in any filmmaking capacity you need me."

Lloyd kept his reply short and to the point:

Sorry . . . this is fart . . . er . . . art; we do not have $1,600/week. Please try Michael Bay.

Nice.
posted at 8:17 p.m.

WEDNESDAY, JUNE 08, 2005

Cheap Bastards

Normally, when a film production comes to town, people get excited. Cash for the community, stars at local bars, a chance for the cute girl next door to be discovered at the candy store. Not the same for us.

In anticipation for my relocation to Buffalo tomorrow, I sent out an email to dozens of potential PAs, urging them to check their parents' basements for used beds, futons, couches, desks, tables, fax, photocopiers, old computers, printers—anything we could use—and asking that they pilfer office supplies for us. This really is a low-budget production.

A half-dozen responses came back immediately. "I can definitely cover you guys with a bunch of random pens, pencils, stuff like that," "a working computer with monitor and printer if you don't mind it being along the lines of a Pentium I," "I have a futon you guys can use. I am not sure I have all the parts anymore . . . In fact, I've been looking for an excuse to get rid of it for awhile!"

Ahhh, the high life.
posted at 9:59 AM

MONDAY, JUNE 13, 2005

Shooting schedule

For the last few months, Lloyd has been regularly freaking out about how behind schedule we are—we still haven't cast all the leads, we're behind on rehearsals, none of the vocals for the musical numbers have been recorded, we have nothing in the way of costumes or art, and the bulk of the FX[3] exist only on the written page. (He frequently screams in exasperation, "This film is about only two things: effects and beautiful young people! And we have neither!!! I am going to blow my fucking brains out!")

He's right. And we need as much time as we can to get these problems solved.

While freaking out today, he suddenly decided to cut a week of pre-production and start filming on July 26th.

I think back to the email that Trent Haaga sent me in warning. "No matter how much you plan everything out, Lloyd is still going to come up with some absurd last-minute request or change of plan to shoot himself in the foot and sabotage the film, thereby creating the drama that he believes causes the art."

posted at 5:54 p.m.

SATURDAY, JUNE 18, 2005

Weird PA E-mail

-----------------------Original Message------------------------

Hi Andy! This is Gary, I'm supposed 2 b a PA on *Poultrygeist*. I tried calling you but you r no longer available there. I have been delayed in getting 2 New York—I just got evicted from my apartment, my uncle just died and my grandpa just died this morning. I still want 2 come but it sucks that I couldn't get there on the 15th cause I wanted to get there b4 the other PAs so I could have a heads up. Anyway, My grandpa's funeral should be in the next couple days and I want to leave after that 4 *Poultrygeist*. Can you please e-mail me back or call me. I need to know what 2 bring . . . is there going to be a shower . . . should I bring extra clothes . . . do we really work 20 hour days and only get a cheese sandwich to eat. Please get back 2 me ASAP!

-------------------------End Message---------------------------

---

I really don't want to hire this guy.

posted at 2:52 p.m.

---

[3]FX: special effects.

SATURDAY, JUNE 25, 2005

Safety

Lloyd insists, on all Troma productions, that his laudable mantra be posted around the set:

SAFETY TO HUMANS
SAFETY TO PEOPLE'S PROPERTY
MAKE A GOOD MOVIE

He just realized that the posters throughout the New York and Buffalo offices read "Safety to *People*" instead of "to *Humans*." He's furious. I've already received multiple calls from Gabe and Kiel. I just assigned a PA to walk around the house and church hall and the McDonald's, fixing each of these signs with glue and cut-outs of the word "Humans."

After cutting out 30 copies of the word "Humans," the PA left her scissors sitting open in the middle of my office floor.

The irony is clear.

posted at 2:39 p.m.

Starstruck in Starbucks Asks Lloyd

Dear Lloyd,

Do you have any way of getting a name in your film? Horror names aren't too expensive.

Love,

Starstruck in Starbucks

Dear Starstruck,

You say you want a famous name in your film?

Just write a famous person's name on a piece of posterboard and have someone hold it up in a scene. That's what we did with Dee Snider in *Poultrygeist*, and presto! Dee is in *Poultrygeist*. Personally, I think it's some of his best work.

Other than that, just ask. You'd be surprised how many "names" are willing to support independent art by appearing for very little or no money.

I act in low-budget films all over the world every year, often just for the cost of airfare. And Popov.

XOXO,
Uncle Lloyd

Chapter | six

Pre-Sell Your Flick in a Game of Five-Card Stud *or* Go for a Straight *Flush**

*As in card games, bodily fluid removal *and* pre-selling your movie.

"We could make *Gone with the Wind*[1] and HBO wouldn't buy it."

—**Lloyd Kaufman**

ASSOCIATE PRODUCER: The producer's lackey or "bitch." The producer usually delegates a certain financial, creative or administrative responsibility to these individuals. In your case, this may be your mom, drunk rich uncle or the guy that collects the shopping carts outside of the Stop and Shop. This title (or the title of Line Producer) can be given to DGA production managers or the crack addict bum messing up my garbage at this very minute.

Synonyms: Creative Colleague, Step and Fetch It Dude.

[1]*Gone with the Wind* is also the phenomenon that happens to me when I eat fish tacos.*

*EDITOR'S NOTE: I love *Gone with the Wind*!

Example: "I need someone to figure out what time and which actors are called to set tomorrow to shoot the shit we need to shoot."
"Uh, I think maybe the Associate Producer can do that?"

It's January 20th, 2009[2] and I woke up awfully early today in nipply, brisk Park City, Utah, the adopted American hometown for the Tromadance Film Festival—http://www.tromadance.com—no entry fees, no snootiness and you can see all the movies for free! Plus, free metal pole lickings in winter!—Tromadance is where Troma fans and aspiring filmmakers have communed every third week of January for the past 10 years. Park City also hosts an obscure gathering of the rich and famous and their vassals, called Dance of the Sun,[3] at the same time. My beautiful wife Pat is here in her capacity as the New York State Film Commissioner. I rolled out of bed to discover Pat blaring the broadcast of Barack O's presidential inauguration.

Once I realized I wasn't watching *Dr. Strangelove*[4] and thanked my lucky stars that my darling Pat was giving me a break from Meredith Viagra and Matt Louchebag[5] lamenting the troubles of sustaining a makeover while teaching children to wrap themselves in saran wrap at night while eating a twinkie and playing *Guitar Hero* backward to lose weight, I became transfixed. Even I knew that I was witnessing a moment that will be remembered and talked about forever—the inauguration of President Barack Hussein Obama, the first part-black president since Warren G. Harding.

---

[2]INDEX GYNO: Lloydie, honey, it's becoming pretty darn apparent you didn't write these chapters in chronological order.*

*FOOTNOTE GUY: That's okay, Lloyd. Nobody's perfect! Not even you, Index Gyno.

[3]INDEX GYNO: That's the Sundance Film Festival, Lloyd. Both the Tromadance and Sundance Film Festivals are held at the same time as Slamdance (also a film festival), or, as I refer to it, Salacious Luscious Ass Mo-Fo's Dance.

[4]Vice Prexy William Cheney in the wheelchair in a black trench coat and fedora was a great touch of the sinister Lionel Barrymore in *It's a Wonderful Life*.

[5]Also known as Meredith Vieira and Matt Lauer, co-hosts of that morning monstrosity, *The Today Show*. Meredith is formerly of *The Shrew*, another vacuous morning talk show where women of various ages, races and political views sit around and talk about their differences with that woman from the crypt, also known as *The View* and Barbara Walters,* respectively.

*EDITOR'S NOTE: Readers, there is no such show and Barbara, if you're reading this, I'm a *huge* fan.

FIGURE 6.1 *When Lloyd attended President Barack O's inauguration, he was mortified to see U.S. Representative Barney Frank wearing the same ball gown.*

I didn't have to worry about anything concerning Tromadance just yet, as the festival wouldn't be having its opening night (mal)functions until later that evening. I had actually fallen asleep the night before dreaming about my upcoming board meeting with the Independent Film & Television Alliance (IFTA)[6] in Los Angeles the following week. Somehow, in my dream, a naked, aberrantly hard-bodied Anne Hathaway[7] has suddenly, magically replaced Pierre David[8] at the table during an IFTA board meeting. That's producing your own damn happy dream.

WHAT IS THE IFTA AND WHY YOU, MR./MS. PRODUCER, OUGHT TO GIVE A SHIT!

IFTA is a non-profit trade association of independent producers and distributors of motion picture and television programming worldwide. It was originally formed in 1980 by a group of independents

[6]PATTIE'S NOTE: Lloyd, sorry to interrupt—am I doing this footnote thing the right way? I think people should know that you are the chairperson of IFTA. It's a really invaluable organization and you should talk about it some more.*

*LLOYD'S NOTE TO PATTIE: Y-y-y-yes, dear, just don't hit me!

[7]One of Henry VIII's most intellectual wives.

[8]Pierre David is a hard-bodied, extremely successful, independent (largely TV) producer of such masterpieces as *She's No Angel*, *'Til Lies Do Us Part* and *A Nanny's Secret*.

whose main goal was to expand the independent film business by creating a world-class trade show, the American Film Market (AFM).[9]

JUST HOW DOES THE IFTA DEFINE AN "INDEPENDENT FILM"?

IFTA defines "independent" as a film that is financed outside the major media conglomerates, even though it may be distributed by one of those devil-worshipping international media conglomerates like General Electric-Universal-NBC. Under this definition, all three *Lord of the Rings* movies—$250 million dollar masterpieces (that's $250 million *each*)—as well as the Turner Movie Classic favorite *Tales from the Crapper* ($450 million budget[10])—are both considered "independent."

IFTA members have produced and distributed more than half of the films that have won the "Best Picture" Academy Award, including: *Gandhi, Amadeus, Platoon, The Last Emperor, Driving Miss Daisy,* ~~*The Toxic Avenger*~~, *Dances with Wolves, The Silence of the Lambs, Braveheart, The English Patient, Shakespeare in Love, Chicago, The Lord of the Rings: Return of the King, Million Dollar Baby, Crash, The Departed, No Country for Old Men* ~~*and Troma's Tales from the Crapper.*~~[11]

During 2009, IFTA members have continued to produce, distribute, and finance some of the world's most innovative and prominent films, including *Appaloosa, Atonement, The Band's Visit, Burn After Reading, The Great Debaters, Juno, Mad Money, Never Back Down, Nick and Nora's Infinite Playlist, Rambo, Righteous Kill, Smart People, There Will be Blood,* Tyler Perry's *The Family That Preys* ~~*and Poultrygeist, Night of the Chicken Dead.*~~[12]

---

[9]According to my Wicca Woman *Wikipedia*, founded in 1981, The American Film Market (AFM) is an annual event which attracts over 8,000 industry attendees to Santa Monica, California for eight days in early November. Participants from over 70 countries converge to buy and sell distribution rights for completed films or to gain financing for projects in various stages of production. Troma has taken a booth there from the beginning.

[10]EDITOR'S NOTE: In Zaire dollars.

[11]EDITOR'S NOTE: Nice try, Bernie Madoff.

[12]FOOTNOTE GUY: Lloyd, this is my favorite part of the whole book so far! It is so beautifully written!*

*EDITOR'S NOTE: Are these excerpts from IFTA's website, Lloyd? Even though it's more entertaining than your writing, you know that you can't fulfill a 323-page book contract simply by blatantly continuing to cut and paste "literature" from the Internet.

FIGURE 6.2 Rare picture of LK actually looking like he might have a shred of dignity. He is pictured here functioning as the chairman of IFTA at an American Film Market Press Conference.

WHY THE HECK I RAN FOR IFTA CHAIRPERSON

In 2007, I was elected to the role of chairperson of IFTA for a two-year term. I ran my campaign on the following platform:

1. To fight media industry consolidation,[13] primarily by using part of the treasury of our trade association to lobby Congress, the Federal Communications Commission, opinion makers and others in Washington, D.C.

The rules protecting the public against monopoly in the media have been done away with. The worst fallout from this is that it is now almost impossible for independent content to get on U.S. TV.

2. To fight for "net neutrality" on the Internet, the only democratic medium[14] we have left in this world. This means preserving the open, democratic, diverse and level playing field on the Web.

If you post or upload something interesting on the Internet, it will be discovered by the public, as opposed to humungous ad campaigns in the traditional media, which drive the public directly to an intended target, be it a movie or a piece of cheese. The MPAA has come out *against* net neutrality.

---

[13]Barack Obama later stole this idea from me when he ran for president.

[14]As Obama pointed out, Nancy Reagan had other mediums made available to her, but she is not democratic.

FIGURE 6.3 *On a recent trip to Washington D.C. to lobby for independent media, IFTA Chairman LK met with Congresswoman Diane Watson, Democratic whip for southern California. LK loves all kinds of whips!*

Yes, now the Internet is still free and open to everyone, everywhere. Whether it's Disney uploading the *High School Musical* multibillion dollar trailer or the beautiful subtle montage of *2 Girls, 1 Cup*, both have an equal chance of attracting a large public.[15] It's a true "free" market. Troma's website can get 500,000 hits a month; *The Huffington Post* site gets only 22 views per month.[16]

And why the heck did we have to form this Independent Film and Television Alliance in the first place? Well, to explain that, we have to go all the way back to the Glamour Age of Hollywood, to the *United States v. Paramount Pictures, Inc.* case, which the Supreme Court heard in the winter of 1948.

WHAT'S SO FRIGGIN' IMPORTANT ABOUT *UNITED STATES V. PARAMOUNT PICTURES, INC.* (1948)?

(and I really am going somewhere with all of this)

---

[15]You might guess which one I'm more attracted to.

[16]EDITOR'S NOTE: Lloyd, you are an unconscionable liar!*

*LLOYD'S NOTE: I am a victim.

You fledgling producers should know that, again confirmed by my little friend Wikipedia,[17] *United States v. Paramount Pictures, Inc.* was a landmark case that decided the fate of humungous movie studios owning theatres and holding exclusivity rights under which theatres would show their films. It changed the way Hollywood films were produced, distributed and exhibited. The studios were prohibited from owning or controlling the movie theatres and had to disgorge them or sell them off.

The Supreme Court held in this case that the existing distribution scheme was in violation of antitrust laws of the United States, which prohibit exclusive dealing arrangements. It was perceived as the beginning of the death of the old Hollywood studio system and set a precedent for vertical integration[18] cases. This opened the door for independent producers to get their movies into cinemas without having to go through the big oligopolistic[19] studios.

Well, that landmark case was pretty lucky for Little Lloydie. When I came onto the filmmaking scene in the late 1960s, there was hope for a fledgling producer. If a filmmaker made a movie the public wanted to see, he could actually get it into a cinema. No cinema wanted to book *Squeeze Play* (1976). We convinced an AMC theatre in Norfolk, Virginia, to give *Squeeze Play* a sneak preview. It ran with a Peter Falk/Charles Grodin feature, *The In-Laws*, and caused such a stir (in loins and laughter), that all of a sudden movie theatres across the country clamored for *Squeeze Play* and we eventually had to

---

[17]Not to be confused with my other little friend, whom I keep separate from the pack or Wicca* itself, which I briefly practiced post-Yale, pre-Pattie, while mistakenly falling under the spell of the 1970s Goth babe who worked in editorial at *McCall's* magazine, from whom we subleased our first janitor closet (office).

*Years later, Troma and I took a major ration of shit from Wicca-ites when we printed a catalogue of our new releases with a Wicca theme. They thought we were goofing on them! HA! IMAGINE THAT! Me goofing on someone—impossible! Producing Lesson #647: Be careful whom you insult.

[18]Companies united by a common owner. Can sometimes and often result in micromanaging, a singular, closed vision, or, put more clearly, "be my fuckin' bitch, BITCH!" syndrome.

[19]FOOTNOTE GUY: Uh, I'm supposed to define that here, but I'm having trouble spelling it, let alone pronouncing it!*

*INDEX GYNO: It refers to big controlling meanies who act only in their own self-interest.

make 400 35mm prints. Back then, it was the ol' "If you build it (and it's good), they will come" attitude.[20]

Dear Reader, I have to admit I was a little scared shitless when I signed on to do this book. I mean, I've been around a long time and somehow managed to make this crazy movie-producing world really work and I'm doing my danged best to share with you all I know, but the industry has since changed a whole heck of a lot. Flash forward from *Squeeze Play* to 30-plus years later, and we have maybe only twelve[21] 35mm prints of *Poultrygeist*, my best-reviewed movie to date. Only about 200 U.S. cinemas have played my fowl flick. And why is it nearly impossible for the little indie guy these days?

Well, that all has to do with a little blacklisting former president named Ronald Reagan.[22] The Consent Decree of 1948 was abolished on Reagan's watch and the media conglomerates were free to own and control the cinemas once again. But there's more bad news! Prior to Reagan and President Ford, there was President Nixon. And prior to Nixon, there was President Johnson.[23] And in the 1970s under Nixon, the Federal Communications Commission (FCC) created what became known as the Financial Interest and Syndication Rules (Fin-Syn).

WHAT ARE THE FINANCIAL INTEREST AND SYNDICATION RULES?

The FCC imposed this set of rules, which required the networks to license at least 35% of their content from independent sources. They also limited the content that broadcasters can own.[24]

---

[20]The same philosophy I had when erecting the leaning tower of plastic straws for the gentleman who works the weekend graveyard shift at the 7-Eleven on 42nd Street between 8th and 9th Avenues. Also a direct quote from *Field of Dreams*, the 1980s (yawn) classic starring Kevin Costner, the star of *Sizzle Beach, USA. Sizzle Beach, USA*, Kevin's very first movie, was produced and distributed by Troma and later remade as Costner's epic *Waterworld*. http://www.troma.com: BUY TROMA!!!

[21]INDEX GYNO: A dirty dozen.*

*FOOTNOTE GUY: A dozen makes for another egg joke!

[22]Reagan "named names" during the House Committee on Un-American Activitities hearing during the "Red Scare" period of U.S. history. He was an actor and SAG member before he became our 40th president. Just as we know in the casting department at Troma, a union actor is definitely not always the best person for the job. So it is true with regard to being President.

[23] President Johnson has nothing to do with this subject. I just like saying Johnson. Lyndon Johnson, My Johnson, Hairless Young Asian Boy Johnson.

[24]Laws put in place to protect you from the mega-conglomerates becoming your pimp.

Unfortunately, Reagan relaxed these rules[25] and so many companies ended up sleeping with the fishes. Soon President Clinton slept with a whale[26] and these rules were completely abolished (in 1993). Anyhow, back to the present day in Park City, Utah, and Obama's inauguration celebration.

Pattie was already chirping away in excitement over the new consciousness and confidence sweeping across America as she padded to the shower, and I scratched my balls. All of a sudden, it occurred to me! This was the historical dawn of a new era. In his wonderful inauguration speech, President Obama was encouraging all of us to be a part of our governmental process. I decided right then and there that I should sit down and write a letter to the president!

Eagerly, I scrounged around the drawer of the bedside table for some paper and a pen:

---

[25]He started there and kept right on relaxing through that whole giving weapons to the very friendly, open, welcoming, non-threatening, non-hostile country of Iran (Iran-Contra Affair) episode and continuing on to forgetting the whole dang thing when he died (of Alzheimer's).

[26]The whale being a blue dress-clad Monica Lewinsky.

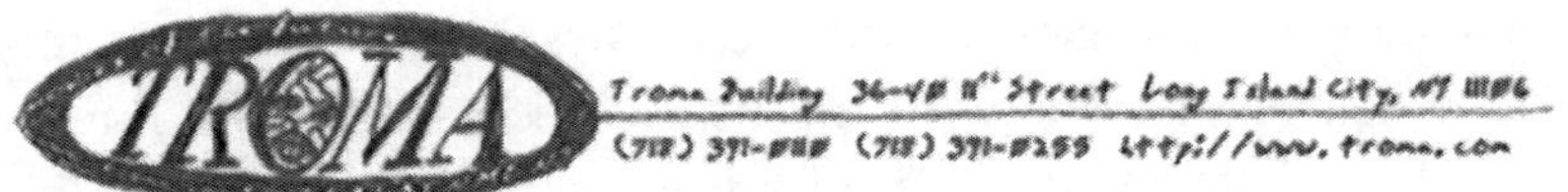

Dear President Obama:

Congratulations on becoming the next President of the United States! You've got a really big job ahead of you. (And you better do a good job, because I wouldn't want to disappoint Michelle if I were you. She looks like she could whip your ass if she wanted to --- or you wanted her to, for that matter.)

I heard your speech after Chief Justice Roberts messed up your oath (had he ever participated in the grueling process of producing a Troma movie, he would have had so much rehearsal he'd have been ready when the cameras were rolling) and you said something at the end that really, really moved me:

> "Our challenges may be new. The instruments with which we meet them may be new. But those values upon which our success depends --- hard work and honesty, courage and fair play, tolerance and curiosity, loyalty and patriotism --- these things are old. These things are true. They have been the quiet force of progress throughout our history. What is demanded then is a return to these truths. What is required of us now is a new era of responsibility --- a recognition, on the part of every American, that we have duties to ourselves, our nation, and the world, duties that we do not grudgingly accept but rather seize gladly, firm in the knowledge that there is nothing so satisfying to the spirit, so defining of our character, than giving our all to a difficult task.[1]"

Well, President Obama, my instrument is not new (in

[1] Obama brilliantly describes the antonym of 99% of the shitheads who are responsible for producing the movies in our cinemas and on our televisions. Also, reproducing this excerpt of his speech is getting me closer to the 323 pages my contract with Focal Press calls for.

Troma Building 36-40 11th Street Long Island City, NY 11106
(718) 391-0110 (718) 391-0255 http://www.troma.com

fact, it has almost 20 years on yours), but it is old and it is hard...er...true. You see, I sometimes come down to Washington DC representing the IFTA to lobby members of Congress and the FCC. Now, I know you're not particularly fond of Washingtonians getting into bed with lobbyists (and well, truth be known, my Pattie always asks that I do everything on the up and up --- she says it's the only way I'll respect myself in the morning and boy, if I didn't listen to her..., well, let's just say she could take Michelle --- she may be tiny, but she's surprisingly feisty)...anyhow, to return to the matter at hand, it is imperative that we independents make our cause heard, for the future of art in this country and the freedom to choose art and be exposed to art is at stake (and a man has to respect the right to be exposed, do we not agree, Mr. President?)

Anyhoo, I have this really awesome movie, my absolute best yet, in fact. It's called *Poultrygeist: Night of the Chicken Dead.* Everyone who has seen it has loved it. It got a pretty decent review in the 2 inches it was allotted in *The New York Times*, it kicked the ass of *Indiana Jones IV* according to *Entertainment Weekly* and it beat *Speed Racer* opening weekend at the box office. But here are some hardcore facts:

Even though it was the top grossing screen in the country the weekend it opened and made the most money of all of the other movies showing at Village East, it was kicked out after 2 weeks to make room for an aging Harrison Ford. Even after the theatre didn't want to get rid of us, they had to, for they face bullying by the movie studios if they don't do their bidding.

At this point, with the current laws and state of affairs as they are, this movie will not play on television. Anywhere. 15, 20, 25, 30 years ago, yes. Today, no. No large chain of DVD and video rental stores (meaning, specifically, Blockbuster, WalMart, Movie Gallery) will ever have *Poultrygeist* or a Troma film on their shelves.

I mean, look, I don't even have to list all of the atrocities. There's just too much butt fucking going on

at the top (and butt fucking is fine, it's great, but we need to balance it out and explore other ports of entry), that the little guys at the bottom are getting crushed without even being given a chance. Look, the fans, the audience, your public, your people, they speak for themselves and want to have their voices heard. So let them be heard, right? I think everyone has a right to be exposed to explosive shit (literally) on the screen, don't you?

So, if you can sort of silently (or very, very loudly) use your bully pulpit send your message to Congress to give everyone a chance to share, to be fair, that would be great. You can start rumbling about calling the Time Warners of the nation to congressional hearings about media consolidation. Then, maybe those Time Warners will start to shit their pants, worry about regulation (knowing no Metamucil's going to work this time) and volunteer to devote a substantial percentage of their television air time to truly independent content.

I mean, the stock of all the media conglomerates are approaching zero and that doesn't have them screaming, so we've got to resort to some drastic tactics here. Isn't it important that today's youth, this generation, continue their excitement in electing you? Let them realize that there are choices and plenty of diversity (like you!) out there — that not every movie is a regurgitated version of a Reese Witherspoon wannabe standing up for baby food ideals, not every TV show has androids starving themselves, complaining about their terrible, tortured lives and not every talk show sounds like Kathie Lee Gifford with a wrench lodged in her mouth to twist her face into perfection for an Oil of Olay spot.

Anyhow, Mr. President Obama, what it comes down to is that we are all just like you. I may be a white Jew who graduated from Yale, but I was raised a poor black dirt farmer in Mississippi.

We all want a chance. And it's time that we show America, the world, that every voice should be heard.

Yours truly,

Lloyd Kaufman

P. S. I've enclosed an autographed DVD copy of Troma's Poultrygeist for Sasha and Malia.

P. P. S. Please congratulate Aretha Franklin on the great hat she wore at your inauguration. Where can I buy one for Pat?

P. P. P. S. What's with the lame poetry reading?

So by now you're reading my letter to President Obama, thinking it's nearly impossible to get a movie produced and how dare I include a mention of butt fucking in a letter to the president of the United States. And you are thinking that once your movie is produced, it may also be impossible to get anyone to actually even see it.[27] And you're right. So we're back to unbridled passion as our fuel. Is there even no way to guarantee you will make your money back as an independent producer in this Obamanable age?

COMEDY CENTRAL PROVES MY POINT

Even after Trey Parker and Matt Stone's *South Park* became the hit it is, Comedy Central refused to play *Cannibal the Musical* on television. As their distributors, we at Troma received this rejection letter:

Dear Mr. Kaufman:

Thank you for submitting and ***re****-submitting* Cannibal the Musical, *but it is simply not up to our standards for broadcasting.*

Regards,
Comedy Central

No explanation whatsoever—just economically blacklisted, like all of the Troma films nowadays. I forwarded the above-mentioned letter to Trey's attention.

That rejection letter hangs on the wall of his office. Trey Parker's office is at Comedy Central.

It's eating shit like that Comedy Central letter makes me think about blowing my fucking brains out.

Well, Trey and Matt became famous through *South Park* and their fame increased the subsequent DVD demand for Troma's *Cannibal the Musical*. But without fame and fortune, what is the formula for immediately recouping your money that you had to lay out to produce your movie in the first place?

---

[27]Focal Press is offering full refunds to anyone who feels they are depressed, uninspired or angry about the contents of this book thus far, wanting to shout only "Fuck Your Own Damn Movie!" to the world.*

*EDITOR'S NOTE: Focal Press cannot and will not do any such thing, Lloyd. But there must be something to keep our young producers going, no?

BRIAN YUZNA GIVES YOU A LESSON ON EVOLUTION FROM THE VIDEO BOOM TO THE MODERN AGE

The money making wild west of the 1980s was driven by video. Mom-and-pop stores needed videos to fill up their shelves to meet the demand of their renters. These films were often independent, so it meant that anyone who made a video could sell it for rental and there was no competition from the major studio films. The majors were not using their own labels but were using *Vestron*[28] to release their videos. Because all of the international buyers were hungry for home video product, they would pay for the movies before they were made. Producers would pre-sell[29] five movies at a time and get advances against all five. Thus, movies were financed by pre-sale.

When you order something on a shopping channel and they say "six weeks for delivery," it's usually because they are waiting to see how many buyers they will have. Then they make the product and send it to you. That was how the movies were made. You'd pre-sell your film to a buyer from Japan. He, in turn, would pre-sell your movie to enough cinemas, video stores and TV channels in his territory, guaranteeing that he could make a profit within the territory. Home video drove everything, as there was a huge worldwide home video demand. However, in the United States, Blockbuster eventually took over the home video market from the mom-and-pop stores and it became like a monopoly. When the majors started putting out the videos themselves, independent video stores started to fold.

Put bluntly, Blockbuster became a division of Viacom-Paramount and economically blacklisted independent movies like Troma's.

So, you can see that with the aforementioned movie distribution state of affairs described by Mr. Yuzna, it is imperative that we penetrate the Blockbuster hymen by demanding that they and the rest of the world offer a true variety of independent films from which consumers can choose.

I happened upon the whole pre-selling thing when I was at the Cannes Film Festival years ago. Floundering in my guilt over eating too much of the heavy sauce with my fluke[30] the night before, I became a participant in one of the luckiest fish stories of my life (minus any actual sort of strategy) when I sort of miraculously

---

[28]The first successful video company.

[29]FOOTNOTE GUY: I just read ahead, and Lloyd—Kathy Morgan actually—explains this pretty soon. I mean, Paul sort of went into it earlier, but Kathy really explains it.

[30]FLUKE: A fish. Also my life.

pre-sold the rights to *The Toxic Avenger II*[31] to *mein* German distributor. He had "caught wind" of a toxic rumor that Troma had promised a rival German company *Toxic II.* Refusing to be left in the schnitzel, mein German offered us a hefty sum up front to make the sequel for his company. I later turned that money for one movie into two movies accidentally by shooting excessive, marathonic hours of footage. Michael Herz called me an idiot, but when *Toxic III* brought in big moolah, he called me a genius[32]. . . and he actually smiled.

WHAT *IS* PRE-SELLING?

Lloyd Asks Paul Hertzberg

LK: What is the budget for your upcoming project, *Icarus*?

PH: That's actually closer to the 5 million range.

LK: And the screenplay is something you liked?

PH: Yeah, it took a while. We tweaked it and got it to the point where I liked it, and then we took it to the Cannes Film Festival in May. At Cannes, we announced it and made pre-sales.

LK: So how do you do that? In other words, you have the script and. . .?

PH: We offer the script to people who might want it—including synopsis, artwork and pre-sale flyers with Dolph's picture on it.

LK: This is Dolph Lundgren, right?

PH: Yeah, Dolph Lundgren[33]. We probably sold 70 percent of the budget to major territories before we started shooting at the end of February in Vancouver.

LK: Can you explain what pre-selling is?

PH: It's a combination of finding the right buyers from the territories of the world who would want a Dolph Lundgren action film. You show them the script or the synopsis and let them know that the film will be successful as either a theatrical release, DVD and/or on television. An action film with Dolph Lundgren in the lead is a known commodity that will be good in theatrical as well as ancillary markets.[34]

---

[31]See *Direct Your Own Damn Movie* for more details. Also, pause for a moment to reflect on my sheer genius for then using that money from the pre-sale to make not one, but **two** *Toxic Avenger* movies. A total twofer! Also an accident. But a very happy one indeed!

[32]That was a while back. Unfortunately, he is back to calling me an idiot.

[33]Dolph Lundgren is a Swedish actor best known for his role as Russian boxer Ivan Frago in *Rocky IV*.

[34]ANCILLARY MARKETS: Circle K, 7-Eleven, Quik Chek, WaWa.*

*INDEX GYNO: He means to say that ancillary markets are secondary sales targets for a program that has already completed its first run on its initial delivery medium; that is, after theatrical distribution comes home video, TV, pay-per-view, Internet rights and so on.

LK: So how does selling to a specific territory go? Are there any independent distributors?

PH: It varies. In this particular case, we wanted to expand the type of buyer we attract, so we took some ads out in the trades[35] during Cannes, announcing the film. We had contacted a number of companies in different countries with whom we had never done business. So, we actually made some additional sales.

LK: Why can't everybody do what you do—that is, get money before the film is even shot?

PH: The reason we are able to do it is because we've been doing it for so long. We have credibility. Buyers know when we announce a movie that we are actually going to make it. There's a comfort level with the distributors—it's not about flyers or pieces of paper. We are real.

LK: Are there strong enough independent distributors?

PH: That can pre-sell?

LK: No, that you can sell to. Like say in Spain or France.

PH: Yeah, sure in Spain we just did an output deal[36] with TV6.

LK: Are they independent?

PH: No, they're a new TV channel. Actually, it's called Cuatro. They pre-bought a number of our movies. Orem, in Spain, bought a lot of our movies, Eagle, in Italy, has also pre-bought a number of our movies. We sell a lot of movies to TF1 in France.

LK: Are these independent distributors?

PH: Yes, they're independent and some are networks. We just sold *Icarus* to DNC in the UK and they're an independent distributor who pre-buy. Eagle is independent. We are with New Select in Japan and they're independent.

LK: So, in spite of the industry consolidation and the problems Troma faces, you're able to get around the conglomerates?

PH: We've been fortunate overseas, but in the United States it's been more difficult. Overseas, we have a steady list of buyers to whom we've been able to pre-sell so we can produce our films.

LK: Is there a particular genre that you prefer to produce?

---

[35]TRADES: Winds that blow hot and hard.*

*INDEX GYNO: Those aren't trades, baby.**

FOOTNOTE GUY: I know this one, I know this one! Examples of trade magazines are *Variety* or *The Hollywood Reporter*.*

***LLOYD'S NOTE TO FOOTNOTE GUY: In other words, FG, the self-promoting horn-tooting high school newspapers of Tinseltown.

[36]An *output deal* is a series of films you agree to license to one particular distributor. Also what I have with my friend at the 7-Eleven.

PH: Yes, in terms of genres, over the years we've tried dramas and we've tried comedies and all we could prove is that you can lose money with those on a regular basis, so we decided to focus on genre action films and genre disaster films. If there is a way to destroy the world, we will try to come up with it.

LK: There seems to be an explosion of horror. Everyone at Cannes seems to be pitching me a horror film. Should a young producer produce horror?

PH: We have not done a lot with horror, but only because there is so much of it out there and people produce horror really inexpensively. You even have some micro-budget horror films being done for $10K to $20K and they are selling for $100K and those producers are very happy. Let's say you are spending from $500K to $2 million dollars on a film and you only make $100K—you will not be very happy with sales. With producing horror, the competition is tougher and the field is already saturated. We avoid horror for the most part unless it's something special and we can stand above the masses and not get lumped in with the ultra low-budget horror movies. Troma has a kind of brand and cult following. That's different.

LK: That's easy for you to say. Our international sales today are ass. Is there an actor that you wanted and then finally got?

PH: In the past, that has happened on occasion, but our films are usually genre-driven, rather than cast-driven. We do a lot of work with the SciFi Channel. We have been able to pre-sell in the U.S. to the SciFi Channel on a disaster film, for example. The key elements are the CGI[37] and story. As long as we have good television or DVD-driven names, we're fine, because we are making the movie for a price, plus the profit.

LK: What would be a typical SciFi channel project and how does it get organized?

PH: Well, we've been working with the SciFi channel for five years now. We go to New York, or talk over the phone—we'll pitch concepts and they listen; they like them or dislike them. They're very hands-on. The pitch evolves from two paragraphs, to two pages, to a seven-act outline and eventually a script.

LK: What would be a typical movie that you've done with the SciFi Channel?

PH: We just finished wrapping up *Ice Tornadoes*. Try to picture tornadoes on steroids. We gave it a SciFi element, but with something people can still recognize. The new one we're starting to shoot in a month is called *Stonehenge Apocalypse*. I think people get the idea that something bad is going to happen around Stonehenge.

---

[37]CGI (computer-generated images) are used to create special effects on-screen.

LK: How do you produce these? Does SciFi put up all the money or do you have to put up the money yourself?

PH: They'll license it for the United States. Then, we put up a foreign guarantee and combine that with Canadian government and bank money. That's how we cobble together a financing structure.

LK: What are the approximate budgets for SciFi movies?

PH: They're primarily in the $2–$3 million dollar range and sometimes we go a little bit higher if it's more of an "event picture."

LK: Do they pay you up front, or do you have to deliver it first?

PH: They pay us when we deliver it.

LK: So you have to come up with the $2 million?

PH: Or more. We are able to take on higher budgets, because we get a piece of the budget from the Canadian government. If, for example, the budget is $3.5 million and I can get a million of that from the Canadian government, my net budget responsibility is only $2.5 million. If you get a bunch of that from the SciFi Channel and from foreign pre-sales, then you can have a good-looking movie with a decent budget. Sometimes, you can find yourself in profit right away—before the camera is even turned on!

LK: Can you talk a bit about movies with multiple producers? Do all of these producers get paid?

PH: Well I can't speak for them, because we don't do that. If there are a dozen producers, I hope they all get paid. Canadian regulations limit the number of producers. There can be three, four, or five tops.

LK: Do they get fees?

PH: I hope so.

LK: Is it like a percentage of the budget?

PH: Yes.

LK: Is there a limit?

PH: I think it's about 10 percent of the budget.

LK: So the producers can whack off 10 percent of the budget?

PH: Typically.

LK: For a young person today, how would you advise him or her to break into producing?

PH: Right now, there's no right way or wrong way. You can go to film school or you can attend a specialized program, like the American Film Institute (AFI) offers. If you find something that you're really passionate about, just get out there, put it together, and don't take "no" for an answer. The thing that's great now, is that with the new high-def (HD) cameras, it's less expensive to actually make a movie then it used to be. You can do it on video and you don't need film. The post-production work is cheaper and you can come up with the money from credit cards, family, and friends. If the story is good enough and if the acting is good enough, it can give you a springboard for your career.

LK: So, you're saying come up with a celluloid calling card and produce your own damn movie?

PH: Yes, or find some good material and control that material and the rights to it, because a good place to start your movie is with a great screenplay.

Meeting with Paul and hearing about all these foreign countries has me thinking about traveling abroad to Panama to seek financing for an Amazonian[38] San Blas Island adventure as my next Troma film. I can see it now—hard-bodied Cuna Indian lesbians in the jungle—there'd be monsters, gore galore, and 10 imported naked Brazilian Panamanian models. Maybe we can throw in Eric Estrada or Jan Michael Vincent. I would pre-sell the entire package of a Panamanian hot jungle love story on the strength of my own heaving, hefty, Caucasian-American package.[39] What a turn on. Oh, baby, I'm so juiced up I could work for Tropicana. Sorry, I get a little carried away, but I'll tear myself away from this waterfall of creativity to share with you some valuable insight from Kathy Morgan.

MORE ON THAT PRE-SELLING THING FROM A SALES AGENT (WHO, IN MY OPINION, IS ALSO A PRODUCER)

An Interview with Kathy Morgan About Her Game of Five-Card Stud*
(Actor, Director, Producer, Script, Domestic Distribution)

**For once, I am not referring to myself.*

WHO IS KATHY MORGAN?

Kathy Morgan is a very successful, smart and savvy sales agent. She will tell you just what that means.[40] Her company, Kathy Morgan International (KMI),

[38]INDEX GYNO: Lloyd, the Amazon is not in Panama.

[39]EDITOR'S NOTE: Lloyd, can you get back on point, please?*

*LLOYD'S RESPONSE TO EDITOR: Oh, I can get back on point, all right.

[40]FOOTNOTE GUY: And maybe define "savvy" for me?

specializes in the worldwide sales, distribution, marketing and financing of top-quality theatrical motion pictures. Kathy has repped such films as The Last Emperor, The Terminator, *and* Platoon. *She has also served as chairperson of the IFTA. As current IFTA chairperson, when I must make a decision, I think, "What would Kathy do?"*

LK: Why did you decide to get into producing, as opposed to writing or directing?

KM: Well, I use the term "producing" loosely, because I'm really a sales agent. A sales agent in my business pre-sells the rights to films, thereby enabling a film to be produced. Often we are given Executive Producer titles, because we are involved with the financing, but we are not in the trenches working on the film itself.

LK: Can you talk about *Crocodile Dundee in L.A.*, or one of your executive producing gigs? Most young producers don't know anything about pre-selling. Can you start from the beginning?

KM: The actual physical producer of the film comes to us with the script, talent and director and then asks us our advice regarding the "numbers," which is the value of the picture in the international market place. There's an old saying in the movie industry—I think William Goldman said it in a book[41]—"nobody knows anything." I think it's true now more than ever, because the marketplace is changing so fast. We're supposed to be the experts, and after 30 years, we at KMI have a good enough idea that banks will loan against our projections and investors will invest based on the same projections. We give estimates of what the value of the picture would be in the international market and then we go out into the marketplace, meet with buyers from all over the world and pitch them the movie. We attend film markets and festivals all over the world and we meet with some buyers in between.

LK: What are some the events you go to?

KM: We go to Cannes in May and Berlin in February and in between there are festivals, but we only go to those festivals when we have a film playing in that festival. We also attend Toronto, Venice, San Sebastián, Tokyo, and, of course, the American Film Market in Los Angeles is a great place to make sales. Each important festival supposedly has a market, but the main sales happen in Los Angeles, Berlin and Cannes.

LK: What happens? Can you tell us about *Crocodile Dundee in L.A.*?

---

[41]EDITOR'S NOTE: Please tell our readers the name of this book.*

*LLOYD'S NOTE TO EDITOR: The name of this book is *Direct Your Own Damn Movie.***

**EDITOR'S RESPONSE: Aaaaaggggghhh!

KM: That doesn't make a good case study because that was quite a few years ago. What we're finding is that the film business is changing today, like all businesses. Some of the models we applied long ago don't work anymore. We financed *Crocodile Dundee in L.A.* through international sales. *Dundee* was a strong franchise and we traveled around the world convincing distributors to license the film in their territories for a set amount of time. The normal term is between 7 and 15 years. They license the rights in the contract and our deals are "all-rights deals"[42]—meaning theatrical, video, and all forms of television, and so on. We then take these agreements to the banks. They discount the contracts and loan the money in a nonrecourse loan to the producers.

LK: What does it mean to discount the contract and why is it called "discounting"? Is it like Wal-Mart, where I can get a polyester sweatsuit at a big discount?

KM: Discounting agreements is the term used in all forms of business, not just the film business. It's the term used to describe loans against expected revenue, or, in our case, loans against distribution contracts.

Discounting a contract means a bank will loan the money based on just that contract. The banks know enough about the distributors and the reputation of KMI to have confidence that we will collect this money. This is a non-recourse loan, meaning that if something happens and the distributors don't honor their agreements, the banks' only recourse is to go after the distributors, not the producers or sales agents. Once we document these contracts and all the paperwork—

LK: Let's say you get 100,000 euros from France, does that mean the bank will only give you 90,000 euros?

KM: No, if the contract is for a good paying territory, the bank will discount 100 percent. In other words, they will lend you all the money, less their fees. Now, for countries that are less stable or don't have a good track record, their agreements may not be fully discounted. It depends on the bank or the territory.

LK: How about a recent film?

KM: It's interesting, you were talking about case studies, and the film business is very unique in that every single product you make is a "one-off." You can look at all of the money made in the film business, but each product has to stand on its own. The business is changing quickly, especially the value of any one project. Based on 30 years of experience and based on recent business trends, I can share a few of thoughts with you. Recently, we had a picture which was successful at the American Film Market, despite difficult business conditions.

LK: How did that movie begin and where is it going?

---

[42]An *all-rights deal* refers to when a buyer acquires every possible license for a particular title in a particular territory, as opposed to Troma, which pioneered the *all-wrong deal.*

KM: It's called *The Danish Girl*. It's something that is still in process and hasn't started shooting, but we already licensed most of the territories in the world.

LK: How did that happen? In Tromaville, we would not say "girls." We would say *The Danish Gyno* or *Danish Pastry*.

KM: The producer came to us with a script and an excellent cast including Nicole Kidman and Charlize Theron. Big stars are even more important for the international marketplace than the domestic. Sometimes the studios and the independents can have success pre-selling a movie that isn't a star vehicle. Recently, there was a movie called *Twilight*. An independent company called Summit sold it and it was based on a best-selling book, but we did not need big stars. *The Danish Girl* was also based on a best-selling book, but very different because it needed big stars in order to be sold internationally.

I will give an analogy. When pre-selling the movie, we're selling air. Pre-selling a movie is about risk management. We are securing distribution prior to producing the movie. So how do we get to do that? It's like playing a hand of poker. We travel around the world and meet people, mainly men, in hotel rooms, but everyone keeps their clothes on and we deal a deck of cards, so to speak. It's a game of five-card draw. We first put down the actor card and then the director card, the producer card, the script card and finally, the domestic distribution deal—but not necessarily in that order. The buyers bet on the cards and sometimes it's well into the millions. One time, I actually had 100 million dollars in pre-sales from international buyers alone.

LK: Woo-hoo!

KM: It was called *The Alchemist*. Again, it wasn't made yet and this is the difficult thing about pre-sales: sometimes we are successful in raising the money and for various reasons it still doesn't get made. *The Alchemist* is still in play. We are in as Executive Producers and Harvey Weinstein's[43] company is producing it. I think they are still working on the script. Anyway, back to my analogy. You have your five cards and the buyers will bet on how valuable your cards are. Will the movie that's produced a year or two from now with those cards be worth their bet? Those cards are really about helping the buyers market the movie. If the actor card is an ace, like Kidman and Theron, buyers are prepared to bet more.

When we make the pre-sale, that's not all we get. When we deliver the movie (and delivery is a defined legal term with a list of deliverables[44]), the

[43]Previously mentioned Harvey Weinstein really *is* one of the most loving creatures in the entertainment world. I am sure he will buy many copies of this book and give me a job. He is a giant teddy bear and must be a loving, devoted follower of Marianne Williamson.

[44]*Deliverables* refers to a list of what the producer is required to furnish, such as a letter granting the distributor lab access to your negative (to reproduce your film) and a video master for television broadcast, and so on and so forth.

minimum guarantee is then due and payable. The buyers will then market and release the film. We negotiate a deal called the back-end,[45] so if the picture does well in a given territory, the distributor will pay overages, or split profits with the producers. A producer doesn't have to sell for a flat fee and never see anything more. Some do, though. Also, at the end of some negotiated term, the rights will revert back to the producers, and the producer will still have an asset. It's still not the end of the story. In fact, as a sales agent, once we do our deal and get the money from the banks, our job is just beginning. We then need to collect the license fees by delivering the picture. We also need to check with every distributor around the world, asking, "What's your release date? What is your marketing plan? What are the holdbacks?" It is extremely important to coordinate foreign distribution with a big U.S. release.

LK: What's a holdback?

KM: A holdback means that a certain distributor is not allowed to release the picture in his or her territory until we, the producers, authorize it. Most of the time, we don't want the film to go out internationally before it is released in the United States. Statistically, 50 percent of revenues come from the United States. You do not want some distributor in Turkey releasing your film over there, having it flop and having that news leak, tarnishing the U.S. release. Another huge problem is piracy, especially in Asia. We wouldn't want a title to be pirated there, especially before its U.S. release. The same with video. You have to coordinate your windows—your theatrical, video windows, TV, and pay TV windows. You don't want one territory jumping the release gun and causing damage to a neighbor's territory.

LK: Wow! That sounds hard. How did your other film, *In the Land of Women*, differ?

KM: Warner Independent, which unfortunately is no longer in existence, developed that movie and financed it. At the time, their business model was to split rights—meaning that they released it domestically and then they had sales agents like my company selling it internationally. The riskiest way to make a movie is to go out there and make it without any distribution lined up in advance.[46] It would have to be a very low-budget movie to do it that way. You need to know how you're going to reach your audience before you make any investment. The major studios are different because they have a distribution pipeline they have to fill. With *In the Land of Women*, Warner Brothers made a decision that they would funnel it through their U.S. pipeline, but they didn't want to take a risk on it internationally. They wanted to spread the risk with

---

[45]EDITOR'S NOTE: I know what you are going to say about back-ends, Lloyd, and *don't*!

[46]Case in point: visit http://www.poultrygeistmovie.com!

these specialty films, so they went out to the independent distributors through sales agents like me and licensed the film around the world.

LK: Did *In the Land of Women* have stars?

KM: Yes, Meg Ryan, Kristen Stewart (who's now a big star in *Twilight*), and Adam Brody. It was a nice film.

LK: Does your method apply to movies that aren't "A" movies, or films without stars?

KM: It's very difficult, unless one of your other cards is an ace. There are certain "auteur" directors in Europe who are able to raise money year after year just because of who they are—Woody Allen, for example. Almost every spring, he has new movie. There are people in Europe who will go see anything Woody Allen makes. European distributors will finance him. They will finance a movie without any stars or any script, just based on the director card alone.

Now, can a beginning filmmaker do that? No. A newcomer has to have more than one good card. There are certain underlying materials like a book that is a bestseller—that can be an ace. It's built-in marketing. How do you get butts in the seats or eyes on the screen? Marketing has become a huge cost, because there are so many leisure activities that compete with movies. So sometimes, on the poster, you put a star's image or sometimes it's a book or sometimes it's a brand. But the buyers need to be convinced that a large audience will come to see the movie they are being offered.

LK: What do you suggest young producers do to break in?

KM: Well, I would say to find another career. But if you are passionate about it, be persistent. It's important to see older movies and understand film history. Get the best information and find a mentor. But still, you must persevere. A lot of people think it's really glamorous, but it's not. You must be prepared. It's hard work, but I love it. I travel all over the world, meeting friends and doing business with people who have the same passion I do, which is the love of film. I thoroughly enjoy it.

FIGURE 6.4 Kathy Morgan is a great leader, great success, a Goddess.

BUT WHY WOULD I NEED A SALES AGENT? I KNOW HOW TO HUSTLE!

BY JEAN PREWITT

WHO IS JEAN PREWITT?

Jean Prewitt is the CEO of the IFTA!

The dawn of the 21st century was supposed to bring a world without middlemen, where everyone (including film producers) could reach their loyal fans and customers directly, and where only the truly lazy had to pay someone to "handle their sales." So you, the reader and hopeful producer, are likely to argue when we say, "You need a sales agent." But trust us, you do! Here's why.

You are probably trying to make a living by producing movies (or at least to pay off your debts), which means that you have to generate revenue. The right sales agent knows how to do that. As Kathy Morgan explained, their job is to know whether an individual film will appeal to buyers just on the basis of who wrote or directed or starred in it, or its budget, or its subject matter and what type of license fee they will offer. They may tell you that the license fees could be improved if you enter the film in a film festival and get attention first (or advise you that going to a festival and getting panned could kill this particular dream). The sales agent has to take himself to film markets and meet with the buyers there and negotiate deal after deal after deal to make sure your film can be seen in as many countries and on as many different screens (big, little, over the air, at home, online) as possible to make you (and the sales agent) the money you need to do this again.

Now you are probably saying to yourself, "But I can do that! I proved I could hustle when I got the money to make this film in the first place and talked all these talented people into working for scale to do it. So, tell me again, *why* am I giving this sales agent a percentage of my own distribution revenue? *And* helping finance his trip to Santa Monica[47] and the south of France[48]?"

Because the sales agent knows the right buyers for your film and you don't. A "buyer" isn't the person who finally sits in a cinema and watches/laughs/cries over your film. A "buyer" is a hard-nosed businessperson who licenses your film exclusively for his home territory (or two) and down-sells it

[47]As mentioned earlier, the American Film Market (AFM) takes place in Santa Monica.

[48]The Cannes Film Festival unspools in the south of France.

to the theater chains, television programmers and video dealers. And he has to be convinced by your sales agent that this film can make him money in his territory in front of consumers who may not speak the same language and may not get your jokes or pathos—more money than the film the guy next door is selling. More money than something he could find at home, made in his own language with stars that his countrymen know. You can't even begin to know what choices he is making on a day-to-day basis to arrive at the price he is willing to pay. That's the third thing the sales agent knows that you don't (keep count here: which particular buyers want the type of film you've made; what will make that buyer like your film the most; what's the best price you can demand from him and still get the deal). And all of those things matter.

Finally, the sales agent will get a better price than a direct-selling producer pretty much every time. This isn't class discrimination. Getting the sale done on paper is only the first stage of fulfilling the producer's side of the bargain. After the deal is done, the film has to be finished (if it wasn't at the time of the deal) and then delivered. "Delivery" is a technical term that goes far beyond handing over the reels or a DVD. In the standard form contracts prepared and recommended by IFTA (more later), the delivery schedule runs to 50 or more items (including such things as music cue sheets and laboratory access letters) and will differ from territory to territory. Failure to meet the details of that schedule on time will negate the buyer's obligation to pay but also destroy his ability to meet the requirements of the sublicenses into which he has entered.

Experienced buyers know that a professional sales agent understands the importance of the "details" of delivery. They have no reason to believe that the producer—now on to his next creative venture—is able to meet these obligations to multiple buyers around the world. The price they are willing to pay the individual producer for the film will be reduced to reflect the risk of incomplete delivery or sloppy response on other items where time is of the essence.

You are now convinced that you actually do need a sales agent. So, how do you find one that's any good? That's where IFTA comes in! IFTA's 11 founding members created the American Film Market, held every November in Santa Monica, which now attracts 8,000 industry professionals from 70 countries.

IFTA now has 140 production/sales companies from 22 countries as members. These are not the only sales agents in the world, but they are the companies that routinely participate in the international marketplace. Every one of the IFTA members has a different business persona—some are adept at handling lower- to mid-budget range television movies; some have specialty divisions that produce or sell only high-concept horror (or low-concept, for that matter), or "women's films," or musical documentaries; others have a regular string of art-house films that grace the film festivals; and still others are known for their Academy Award–winning films over the years. And then there's Troma.

As a producer, you need to do your research and find the companies that feature (on their website, company literature, and on their stands at the AFM) films like yours. Really like yours, not just those you'd like to be associated with—remember that you are looking for the company that knows how to sell *your* film, not something else. See if you can meet with them. See if you like them and believe they will care about selling your film. Talk to other producers. Look at IFTA's Model Sales Agency agreement to see what you will be getting into. Pay attention to the details now and after the deal is done. Go ahead and find another project and do the creative thing you do best.

A final note about IFTA: IFTA members produce and distribute (sell) films and television programs that are financed, for the most part, independently of the six major Hollywood studios and they control the licensing rights for those films and programs in the major territories throughout the world. These companies take the financial risk to make programs that could not or would not be made in the major studios and would not be seen around the world without a strong infrastructure of independent buyers who choose to share the financial risk of releasing the films. We define "independent" to mean this very entrepreneurial sector of the entertainment industry.

IFTA delivers business services to support their business model, including creating the standard form contracts used throughout the independent distribution process; overseeing a professional arbitration panel that hears disputes arising from distribution agreements; providing research on business practices and realities in different territories around the world; monitoring and reporting on tax incentives that help producers reduce or recover production costs; lobbying governments to drop marketplace barriers that harm independent films and to protect the producers' right of payment for his works; providing umbrella stands for members to use at television markets; and producing the American Film Market in a manner that continues to attract thousands of film buyers and sellers each year. Stability in the marketplace and enthusiasm for independent film are the insurance we try to provide that your film and the next one will have a chance.

FIGURE 6.5 President and CEO of IFTA Jean Prewitt and Chairman LK are disappointed with stupid questions that they had to field from a *Variety* reporter.

MAN, THAT WAS GOOD SHIT! REALLY FUCKING GOOD![49] I learned a whole lot from Kathy and Jean. Anyhow, I think it's time we let all this pre-selling-movies knowledge simmer and move on to our next chapter all about how and why a producer needs to think about location. Don't you?[50]

[49]Oh, sorry, I was referring to those hard-bodied Cuna Indian lesbians in my fantasy, but it applies even more to what Jean Prewitt and Kathy Morgan have to teach and offer us.

[50]FOOTNOTE GUY AND INDEX GYNO: Yes! Please! Right here, Right here! This is the place! Uhhhh! Yes!! YES!! YESSSS!!!!!!!*

*LLOYD'S NOTE TO FOOTNOTE GUY AND INDEX GYNO: Hey, quiet down here! I'm trying to write a book!

Anxious in Anchorage Asks Lloyd

Dear Lloyd,

What is the best way to deal with the inevitable problems that will arise on a day-to-day basis?

Anxious in Anchorage

Dear Anxious,

1. Prozac.
2. Bloody Marys.
3. Yoga.
4. Staple removers.
5. Stain removers.
6. Couples counseling.
7. Zoloft.
8. Brass knuckles.
9. Meditation.
10. Masturbation.

Honorable mentions: pay people, provide edible food, practice Tai Chi.

XOXO,
Lloyd

Chapter | seven

Fuck Me Jesus on a Pogo Stick! Where Am I Going to Produce My Own Damn Movie? or The Secrets of the Location Vocation

LOCATION MANAGER: The guy or gyno in this role finds himself/herself saddled[1] with the responsibility of coordinating all logistics surrounding the securing of locations to be used on the movie and then making sure all legalities and expectations are managed successfully. This person serves as the face

[1]INDEX GYNO: Giddy-up, FG!*

*FOOTNOTE GUY: Yeeeee-haw! It's fun moving from the margins to the rear. By the way, speaking of "saddle up," animals are horribly difficult to work with. Try not to produce movies with animals. Lloyd doesn't even eat animals.

of the production to the local community in which you shoot and must address any issues that arise as a result of your movie's impact on the local community.

On location with Troma sets, there is often a double-edged feeling of sheer excitement (as evidenced by the hundreds of town residents who hanker to be actor persons[2]). And then there is the camp on the opposite end of the spectrum—the town residents who wish Troma would dump itself into a vat of toxic goo.

Synonyms: Coco the Loco LM, Scrounge and Scurry Shit, Head of Air Force One Photography Shoots at Ground Zero

Example: "How the hell am I supposed to find an estate with an Olympic-sized swimming pool for the naked water ballet scene?"

"Tell the Location Manager to get on it!"

The Location Manager is not to be confused with another very, very important manager:

UNIT PRODUCTION MANAGER: This guy or gyno watches over all of the below-the-line costs associated with your film and makes sure it gets delivered on time. Below-the-line[3] costs are anything associated with the actual production (i.e., everything you need while shooting and editing your movie—a crew, catering, facility and equipment rentals). Above-the-line costs refer to, well, those super-expensive highly overpaid Hollywood celebrities (or, in general, actors as well as musicians, directors, producers, story rights, etc.) you cast in your film.

My films have no above-the-line expenses. On *Poultrygeist*, the producer, director and script cost nothing, because they were all me. Because there were no expensive above-the-line stars, all $500K of the budget could go up on the screen. That's why *Poultrygeist* looks like it cost 10 times more.

Synonyms: **U**seful **P**erson **M**egastar, Panic Button Point Person.

Example: "How much does it fucking cost to rent the crane for two days?"

"The Unit Production Manager should know. She's over there, below-the-line for lunch, looking for her clipboard."

It's important to keep in mind the difference between Location Manager and Unit Production Manager as we dive into this chapter.

---

[2]We do not want extras to feel like lower-class degraded citizens on a Troma set, so we call *all* actors actor persons. That way, there is a kind of democracy on a Troma set and everyone can feel degraded together!

[3]INDEX GYNO: Sort of like how your humor is pretty much always below the line, right, Uncle Lloyd?

FIGURE 7.1 *On the set of* Poultrygeist, *LK is capturing a motherclucker in brilliant 35mm. Note that two 35mm cameras are burning film at the same time. That's a hell of a luxury for a low-budget film.*

Since Barack Obama has been elected president, I no longer have to entertain the prospect of moving to Canada. Although hailing from Pamela Anderson's native country would not be entirely without its own set of benefits,[4] the cold winters would be tough on me. Location is, as we know, everything. If you're not happy where you're at, how can you be happy where you're going?[5] More important, if you're not shooting your film in the right place, how are you going to end up making a great piece of art people will want to see?

LOCATION LOCUTION: CHOOSING A LOCATION AND GETTING IT IN WRITING AND LOTS MORE

We've already spoken about making the most use out of your fellow film collaborators' untapped locations—Louis Su's furrier factory, that abandoned warehouse Chuckie the Line Producer's father is trying to unload, you name it—don't be afraid to ask for it if it suits your movie's story.

---

[4]Anderson's Canadian benefits being the size of two giant melons. And, as described by Paul Hertzberg earlier, Canadian films get oodles of money from the federal and provincial Canadian governments!

[5]EDITOR'S NOTE: I saw a special about this on *The Tyra Banks Show* last week.

As producer, once you've decided on the locations in which you are going to shoot, get your agreement in writing in the form of a contract that includes the following:

1. How much you are paying for said location;
2. The shooting dates agreed upon by the individual(s) granting you access to the location;
3. The phone numbers, cell phone numbers, and alternate numbers of the primary and secondary persons involved in opening up the location for entry.

You don't just want a John Hancock on a piece of paper. If all of your cast and crew, food and trucks show up at 11:30 p.m. to shoot and the guy whose store you have signed up says, "Fuck off—you can't come in unless you give me another $25K," what can you do? Nothing, nada, zilch, zero. You are indeed ruined. Your signed location contract is pretty useless here. You can't sue someone in the middle of the night, can you? Threatening to blow your fucking brains out doesn't work either—I've tried it.

Sooooo, you need to make Ms. Owner of Location your very best friend. You want her involvement in your movie to be embedded in her soul. The location owner must have spiritual capital[6] in your production, making her feel like the active participant you are counting on. Also be sure to tell the other neighboring businesses, or, if you are shooting in a residential area, neighboring households, when and what you will be shooting, so they are prepared for the equipment (trucks, lights, cables), freak show and increase in intensity of ambient noise that they are about to experience.[7] Get them all to come aboard spiritually. If they like you, they won't shake you down. When I was the executive in charge of locations on *Saturday Night Fever*, I acted like I was running for Congress in Bay Ridge, Brooklyn. There was no one in Bay Ridge with whom I did not make friends, regardless of whether we were renting their location!

---

[6]EDITOR'S NOTE: Oprah believes in a spiritual capital commitment in all relationships, Lloyd! That's why your contract says that if you ask for one more extension on this book, Focal Press gets to own your soul.

[7]Let it be known that the freak show and volume control problems brought about by movie productions are not at all specifically applicable to Troma sets.

If you are going to be shooting at night, you may want permission from surrounding neighbors to put lights in their windows or use their power supply, if need be. You also want to be sure to arrange for parking ahead of time. Parking is always an issue, particularly on a low-budget film.

Most important, you want to get a place within close proximity to your shooting location that can serve as both the Green Room[8] and the bathroom (be it next door, on the floor above, wherever—just somewhere close so you don't have to MapQuest it to find it) so that people can do everything they need to do off-camera without disturbing the sound man (because your movie's no good if no one can hear the dialogue).

Then, once you've done all of these things, get a backup location, and wash, rinse and repeat as necessary all of the above-mentioned steps, because you will inevitably need at least one of these backup locations, whether due to inclement weather or, in my case, the fact that everything I touch is indeed fucked.

HANGER: A CASE STUDY AND MELVINA GETS HER GROOVE ON

In my quest to further the cause of independent film, I often agree to act in low-budget movies as a form of support and encouragement for the indie filmmaker community. Devoted Troma fans are fairly likely to buy the DVD of an unknown filmmaker (and their sheer numbers alone[9] can ensure that a producer is well on his or her way to making back some of the initial investment in his or her first-time, low-budget effort). Also, other better-known actors may have more confidence in agreeing to work for very low pay in a movie by a first-time producer if they know that Lloyd Kaufman is lending his name, time and incredible talent to the project.

Recently, I was "hired"[10] for a cameo in an independent horror film, *Hanger*, directed by celebrated special effects wizard Ryan

---

[8]The Green Room is the waiting room for actors and sometimes other production personnel as they wait to be called to set. As Troma productions are often shot in shitty locations, this room is more often brown than green—a very natural, manmade, earthy, solid brown.

[9]I know of at least six in the United States alone!

[10]If there is no budget, I act for free, which was the case with *Hanger*.

FIGURE 7.2 *Lloyd Kaufman, pictured here with a butcher's knife, acts in a Czech film shot in Slovenia,* Snimanjefilmawomansdaymarekadobea12. *Due to Iron Maiden flashbacks, LK can't remember well, but he thinks the movie is called* Moishe The Cut-Up! *Lloyd plays an absentminded rabbi who gets his briss work and butcher work confused, which is often met with hilarious and somewhat disturbing results.*

Nicholson. *Hanger* was shooting in Vancouver[11] in a building that was a cross between a dilapidated motel and a halfway house. The exterior of the building came complete with its very own set of realistic actor persons[12]—for example, shady furtive glances cast between two guys huddled against the wall of a building directly across the street exchanging something sketchy, and a lovely woman dressed for summer in the middle of a Canadian winter nodding out from heroin as she took a full five minutes to cross a street with a traffic light swinging from red to green and back again.

I thought I was going to be doing my usual cameo playing a doctor or a drunken bum. The director sent me the sides[13] just prior to my boarding my Air Canada plane. I took my miniscule middle airplane seat wedged in between two towering slabs of beef flesh, one consuming a fragrant corned-beef and sauerkraut sandwich, the other munching nonstop on Combos and honey-roasted peanuts, followed by several small containers of vanilla pudding for dessert. I started reading the sides as a sweaty, blubbery arm pressed against

---

[11]Still more on what Canada has to offer soon.

[12]Only these people were very, very real and *not* actor persons.

[13]*Sides* are the specific pages of the script from which an actor will be reading in an audition or, in this case, a shoot.

my arm. Skin on skin, battling for the armrest. Delightful. I began to read. I realized that I was going to be playing the pimp. Finally, I thought! A dream come true. Maybe young Nissim on the graveyard shift at the Santa Monica 7-Eleven would finally respect me and see me as the powerful man I am. It looked like an exciting scene, too! Slamming doors, screaming people, a big hoopla showdown with a gorgeous transvestite whore character named "Melvina" who gets a homemade sex change operation, courtesy of the flame from a kitchen stove. Very Robert Bresson.

The wardrobe department (a very tired, hardworking-looking gyno) approached me. "Put in on," she said wearily.

I eyed the skirt, fishnet stockings, and spike heels that she handed me skeptically. "What?" she retorted to my silence. "You don't think it's what Melvina would wear?"

And then it dawned on me. I wasn't playing the pimp. I was playing Melvina the tranny whore. Goddamn this business and its fucking predictable typecasting!

Producing Lesson #277: Give out the sides or script as far in advance as possible, so your actors can come prepared. Then again, don't hire actors like Lloyd Kaufman who don't bother to ask what role they are playing.

Decked out in my come-hither red lipstick, my panties got worked into a twist[14] when we learned that the very elegant tenants of the motel were complaining about the attention the production was drawing to their seedy affairs. Apparently, they wanted to conduct their nocturnal business deals and "social" networking in complete privacy. In the middle of my scene, the filmmakers were forced to wrap. Luckily, they had filmed most of my important shots. But I had to abandon my film debut just as I was finding my more feminine, tranny, natural self. My fellow actress and friend Debbie Rochon said my legs look incredibly sexy in fishnets. The producers had failed to talk to all of the neighboring tenants ahead of the film date to win them over. So that night the neighbors did not give a used condom about whether my scene was completed. Also, there was no backup location option arranged ahead of time. I was due

[14]INDEX GYNO: Readers, he also tries this alone at home.

FIGURE 7.3 *Sarah Jessica Parker (left) makes it clear to LK that there will be no sex in his city.*

on a plane to Los Angeles early the next day. So, the producers had to coerce one of the interns into wearing my sweaty, smelly panties ensemble in order to film cutaway shots of my lower body and finish the scene at another time. The sad part of the shoot being cut short was that Lloyd/Melvina was really getting her groove on![15]

WHAT *STATE* ARE YOU IN?

These days, I work with nonunion actors and crew in upstate New York, which affords me the flexibility (in terms of time and money) and unfettered time I like and need to translate the vision in my head from the page to the screen—New York State satisfies this necessity. Although I've had my share of foreign adventures turn out well (i.e., Toxie romping in Japan) and not so well (i.e., *All My Tainted Passovers,*[16] otherwise known as *Big Gus, What's the Fuss?* in Israel), I have found what works well for Troma. But, as we all know, what works well for Troma does not always work for ~~everyone~~ anyone else.[17]

These days, New York State and other states across our great country offer filmmakers tax incentives to shoot in their state.

---

[15]You can see the "shutdown" of this location unfold before your very eyes in the "behind the scenes" footage I shot concerning *Hanger* for the *Direct Your Own Damn Movie* DVD box set. http://www.troma.com: BUY TROMA!!!

[16]EDITOR'S NOTE: Not a real movie.

[17]INDEX GYNO: Maybe that Marianna Williamson *is* doing you some good after all, Lloyd.

WHAT IS A TAX INCENTIVE?

A tax incentive is an inducement* offered in the form of an abatement** of taxes.

***WHAT IS AN INDUCEMENT?**

An inducement is an incentive that helps bring about a desired state.

****WHAT IS AN ABATEMENT?**

An abatement[18] is a lessening in size, a diminution, a decrease, a reduction.

Now that you've learned all this useless cocktail-party terminology, you should understand that the real incentive is that some states will reimburse you well over one-third of your budget to produce your movie within their borders! In fact, Michigan will pay you 42 percent of your budget above and below-the-line. I'm really in no position whatsoever to talk about tax incentives, as I do not partake in them or apply for them. In fact, I had to have a suffering Troma intern look all those definitions up. See, in order for a film to be the recipient of a state's tax incentives, that film often has to hire a fancy accountant (or at least someone who can add) to handle and file all appropriate paperwork. Troma doesn't have the budget for Mr. CPA Fancy Pants. My wife, however, knows all about those handy, dandy tax incentives that can be a producer's great friend.

THE UNSTOPPABLE, LEGENDARY PAT SWINNEY KAUFMAN

WHO IS LLOYD'S WIFE?

Contrary to popular belief, I actually do have a wife. Pat Swinney Kaufman (a.k.a. Pattie-Pie) is my beautiful, loving, intelligent, far-more-legitimate-than-I wife. For years, she was the Co-First Gyno of Troma Entertainment, Inc. Pat has served as the Film Commissioner for the State of New York since 1995. The Film Commissioner's Office is a wonderful resource that serves as

[18]Not to be confused with the master-abatement, during which certain things actually *in*crease in size.

the filmmaker's liaison with city and local governments, state agencies, a network of statewide contacts, local film offices and professional location scouts. It is because of Pattie-Pie's efforts that (a) independent film is thriving in New York and (b) people still talk to me. I thought it would be helpful for her to share her knowledge regarding tax credits and other incentives.

FROM PERMITS TO CREDITS: PAT SWINNEY (KAUFMAN) GIVES THE SKINNY ON INCENTIVES AND WHY THE FILM COMMISSIONER OF WHERE YOU ARE SHOOTING COULD BE YOUR BEST FRIEND

When a production is first brewing, the first phone call a producer should make is to the local film commission in areas that are under consideration for film locations. A good film commission is a one-stop shop—it is a place a filmmaker can go to understand the available resources and infrastructure as well as the terms and conditions in the places he wants to film in.

At the New York State Film Commission, we have three primary responsibilities. First, we market New York as a place to do business, whether it is to come and do one film project or to come and locate your entire company (related to the film industry) in New York. Second, we do facilitate the film productions that decide to come to New York State. We have well over 100,000 location files that consist of photos and images of different places—it's a dream library for producers. If a location manager, production manager, director or producer comes into our office, we will help them go through the files. If time or distance are a factor, you can speak by phone with someone in our office or look at samples on our website, http://www.nylovesfilm.com. Your film commissioner will be enormously creative and helpful[19] in helping a

---

[19]One of Pattie-Pie's colleagues* helped us find a recently closed fast-food restaurant in Buffalo, New York, for our use in *Poultrygeist,* which then resulted in the decision to shoot the entire movie on location there! Yay, Buffalo and thanks, Buffalo!

*Pat always recuses herself from my film activities to avoid conflict of interest. She has tried to recuse herself from me in my non-film activities at home, but has not been successful. On the other hand, according to *The New York Times* (5/08/09), Stephen J. Friedman, while he was the Chairman of the Federal Reserve Bank of New York, did *not* recuse himself from being a director of Goldman Sachs and "held a substantial stake in the firm as the Fed drew up plans to keep Wall Street banks afloat." Friedman also bought 37,300 additional Goldman shares which the *Times* noted has risen $1.7 million dollars in value (whilst the New York Fed approved a request by Goldman to become a bank holding company.) Thomas C. Baxter, general counsel of the New York Fed stated, "With respect to Steve's purchases of Goldman shares . . . it is my view that

producer or director realize that he or she can bundle different scenes from a script into one location, thereby saving a lot of money, as every time a set must move location, it is at a cost to the producer.

A filmmaker might say, "I need a barn and it has to look like Ohio and be near a stream." We have multiple options and possibilities that will fit that description. We also help producers obtain the necessary permissions and clearances needed to shoot their films by putting them in touch with the local authority from whom they need permission. That could be the Department of Transportation, the City Parks commish, the military, whomever. We serve as an advocate and mediator, interceding to get you what you need.

The third thing we do is work on legislative and regulatory issues related to producing a film. For instance, we worked with the Department of Labor to write the regulations for child actors and we worked on the legislation that ultimately created the incentives for producing in New York State.

Regarding different states—not to mention countries—you really have to call the film commission and go to their website, because every state is not the same. New York State gives 30 percent of the below-the-line budget, and if you shoot in New York City, you get an additional 5 percent on top of that. In New York, you have to apply for the incentives ahead of time (before you even start filming). You have to meet with us and turn in an initial application. It's best to have someone on your production team who has experience and familiarity with Moviemaker[20] or other similar film accounting software packages. In our program—and again, every program is different—we give the incentive only to (1) full-length narrative feature films, (2) episodic television

---

these purchases did not violate any Federal Reserve statute or policy." What a sleaze! Is it any wonder the American banking system is in the toilet?

Meanwhile, Pattie-Pie has been known to pay her own way to the Cannes Film Festival when New York State can't afford it and often takes producers to lunch on her own dime in order to woo them to produce in New York State. She protects the interests of the New York State taxpayers like a pit bull. Furthermore, New York State has had great success with attracting billions of dollars in productions. Maybe Pattie-Pie should be the chairperson of the New York Fed, but when she was coming along, women could only be teachers or nurses. They weren't "made for investment banking" in those days! Oh—this just in! Stephen J. Friedman has "abruptly resigned" from his Fed post.

[20]I am told that Moviemaker budgets are some computer application thing that helps producers do their budgets. By contrast, Troma has patented its own unconventional budgeting system—we use recycled paper, a calculator, and chalk, pencils, crayons, eyeliner, spray paint—any appropriate writing utensil readily available (see "IHOP method" outlined earlier in this book.)

(and the pilots[21] that could lead to episodic television), (3) TV movies, and (4) some commercials. So we don't do soap operas, short films, documentaries, talk shows, or sports shows.

New York State has no minimum or maximum budget requirements in order to consider your film for the incentives program. Basically, we require that whatever portion of your movie is going to be shot on a sound stage,[22] 75 percent of it must take place on a New York sound stage. That can be as little as one day for a movie that doesn't demand a large use of sound stages. Our website has a list of qualified stages and you must choose from one of those.

If you spend more than $3 million at sound stages, then automatically everything else you do below-the-line is eligible for us. If, however, you spend less than $3 million at the stage, then you must shoot 75 percent of location days in New York as well in order to be eligible to receive the tax incentives on your other below-the-line expenses.

For example, consider *The Sopranos*.[23] That show shot 75–80 percent of their locations in New Jersey, but because they did all of their sound-stage work in New York, they were able to get the incentive for their New York work, as they spent more than $3 million and thus were able to qualify. Sometimes small films with budgets under $1 million crunch the numbers and realize that one day on a sound stage is going to cost them so much more than shooting on location that they forget about the sound stage.

Low-budget films like to shoot on location because you don't have to build the location and the front door; it's a "practical location." You may have to dress it differently or build a set, but it's a lot easier. The producer has to sharpen a pencil and do the math—is it worth it to spend a bit more for that one day of shooting on the sound stage as required by the New York State incentives?

---

[21]PILOT: A trial episode made in the hope of selling an entire television series. Also the really cool dude, Chesley B. "Sully" Sullenberger III, who landed a US Airways jet in the Hudson River.* A pilot about this pilot would be a cool thing. "I am producing a pilot about a pilot" is a cool thing to say. Maybe Pontius Pilate could have a cameo, too.

[22]SOUND STAGE: A soundproof, hangar-like structure (building or room) used to build and then shoot sets and locations needed for your movie. (I had to Google it to find out what Pattie is talking about.)

[23]*The Sopranos* was a very popular television series on HBO about a New Jersey–based devout, religious, conservative, nonviolent Italian family with lovely high-pitched singing voices. All the male actors are castrata.

No state is ever going to give you the money before you start spending it. Some states will give it to you incrementally as you start spending it, but generally, most places won't give you the money until you've actually finished the production.

People reading Lloyd's book might wish they could get the money up front![24] But you have to check out the incentive rules. In some states—though not all—the credit is transferable or assignable. For instance, if you are making your movie in Louisiana or Connecticut and taking advantage of the incentives that those states offer to shoot your movie there, but are not a resident of that particular state, you can monetize your credit and sell it to someone (at a discounted rate that falls in the range of 20 percent) who is a Louisiana or Connecticut taxpayer, who will then get a big tax write-off. You would typically use lawyers and go through a bank or broker to handle this. The good thing about a transferable credit if you are an indie filmmaker is that if you are able to sell your credit ahead of time, you can get the incentive money in hand to shoot in advance, but you don't get it all, because you sell it at a discount.

Our credit in New York State is not transferable, but it is refundable. When the film is over, you get the full value of the refund, even if you don't owe taxes. We ask for production reports and good record-keeping, in case of a future audit. You do have to be vigilant about keeping all receipts and be able to, at the end of the day, show exactly what you purchased if you're audited. You have to be able to prove that you did what you said you did.

New York City is exceptional and outstanding in that it gives free permits for shooting—there is no other city that does this. Your film does have to possess insurance and there are certain qualifications that your insurance must meet (you are out of your mind if you make a movie without insurance[25]) and with that you get two uniformed policemen manning[26] your set at no cost to you. Anywhere else you go, you have to pay for those policemen. You also get free parking—those movie trucks and trailers get those parking spaces for free—they get coned off the night before because the permit the city gives allows the production to use the parking spaces it needs.

In New York State, the costs of permits vary. Some places do not charge a big fee, because they are very excited to have the film in town and some will

---

[24]INDEX GYNO. Most people reading Lloyd's book might also wish they could get the money they paid for Lloyd's book back up front.

[25]Even I, the cheapest dirty Jew in New York City, take out insurance! Producers, you must insure your movie! If you are not concerned, stay tuned and read about what happened to Debbie Rochon.

[26]If it is a female police person, this would be a police gyno gyno-ing your set.

charge more and are less excited over the commotion. Part of the reason you go to the film commission is so they can help you navigate the road to obtaining permits.

The biggest mistake a producer can make is to not call the film commission and then find herself in a crisis, calling our office to say "We're shooting tomorrow morning and we just read the permit contract and don't like it, we've been told we don't have the right kind of insurance, what are we supposed to do?!" Our office is pretty good at pulling off miracles, but you should be calling the film commission and setting up a relationship, not waiting for the crisis to strike.

And that's sort of it, in a nutshell! Gosh, I hope this is helpful. Lloyd, can you please take out the trash now? Also, check the roof and pick up some cheese and milk on your way home.

FIGURE 7.4 Lloyd's lovely wife Pat Swinney Kaufman, fresh after her daily 6 mile run in Central Park and 2 hour cardio session at New York Sports Club.

Though I think it would be great if everyone in the world met my beautiful wife, New York State and New York City are not the only viable shooting location options you have. I am not sure and as crazy as it sounds, I have heard that many movies are produced in Los Angeles. What I do know is that permits in Los Angeles, in contrast to New York, are very expensive.

I recently acted in a no-budget modern day version of *A Midsummer Night's Dream* in Los Angeles. The young director Jake Metiva told me that the weekly permit to film in L.A. was so expensive that he had to shoot most of his film in one week. That sucks major bard ass! Shooting was continually held up by church chimes ringing every 15 minutes. The good church people refused to turn off the fucking church bells. In a scene shot with a puppet goat outside of a hospital, the cast and crew were told to leave by cops, due to "health concerns" in relationship to the goat.[27]

In places like Buffalo, the good citizens are not used to having films in their backyards, so even unwashed, smelly, and untouchable Troma crews are welcomed as glamorous movie people. I got a lot of free booze and more from the Buffalonians when I made *Poultrygeist*. In L.A., however, Angelenos are sick of being inconvenienced by movies on their streets and in their parks. So they'd honk their car horns right when I was uttering some profound Shakespearean iambic pentameter—or pedestrians would scream or whistle just for the fun of screwing up a sound take. Even worse, one night Jake and his cast were victims of a drive-by shooting—lucky for them the pain subsided and the red liquid pouring out of their clothing turned out to be paint from paint-ball guns and not real bullets. What fools these Angelenos be![28]

The important thing to do is—as Pattie-Pie says—no matter how big or how small your film is, to call the film commission where you want to shoot and see how they can help you.

Other countries around the world are offering enormous incentive programs as well. In 1997, Canada announced it was creating film incentives to try to bring film shoots there. They had nothing in place, but they wanted to attract Hollywood productions. By 1998, they were up and running. They were very successful in the beginning and then continued to get even more successful, first with TV movies. TV movies were too expensive to make in New York or Hollywood and had slim profit margins of what they could spend. TV movies used to be shot in South Carolina, but when Canada came along and launched the incentive program, the first places that really felt the blow were Utah, South Carolina and Georgia because all of a sudden, TV movies went north. Feature films followed and this trend

[27]The cops were correct. Puppet goat fever has now run rampant on *Sesame Street*. Kermit is very ill and the contagion has spread to Grover.

[28]INDEX GYNO: What up with the attempt to pretend you are some sort of Shakespeare scholar, Lloyd?

forced other states to hop on the incentives bandwagon. A film is a great economic boon to a community! It's a "clean" business[29] that brings great revenue and jobs along with caché to the locale where it's shot.[30]

PAUL HERTZBERG GIVES US A REASON TO STOP MAKING FUN OF CANADIANS[31]

LK: You get an actor and a script and you go overseas and negotiate a deal. Do they give you money or do you go to a bank? How does it work?

PH: It's a combination. We tend to shoot in Canada a lot. We shoot out of Vancouver, so we do bank financing. Primarily, the National Bank of Canada will extend credit to us as a company and sometimes they are backed by the EDC, the development commission out of Canada which guarantees our "paper."

LK: What do you mean by "paper"?

PH: If I sign a contract that I will pay a foreign guarantee of $700K, then they know we will be paying the $700K over a period of time and that if we don't, the Canadian government will pay.

LK: What does the Canadian government have to get from you in order to give you that loan? Is it based on a foreign deal?

PH: It's based on our corporate financials, our trust factor, and our history of doing movies with them. Moreover, they know we will finish the movie and deliver the movie and that they will collect on the film.

LK: So you get money from the Canadian banks or the government and they don't bank the contracts?

PH: No, they're banking us and we're trusting the contracts are good, and so far, we haven't been burned that much. We also get money from the Canadian government through subsidies and tax credits.

LK: If you film in Canada, do you have to deal with unions at all?

PH: Yes, to some extent. We deal with the Canadian actors in UBCP, certain below-the-line guilds and we work with a Canadian partner as well—in this case, Insight Pictures, who has been able to give us some reasonable rates.

---

[29]Well, Troma can be a little dirty. . .all those chicken parts and toxic green slime.

[30]EDITOR'S NOTE: I take my summer weekends in Mystic, Connecticut. *Mystic Pizza* is my favorite movie!*

*LLOYD'S RESPONSE: Let's put some *Fried Green Tomatoes* on that film and eat it.

[31]As hard as this is to admit, he does present a valid argument.

LK: Have you ever filmed in countries outside North America, such as Bulgaria, for example, and if you have, did you have to pay the Screen Actors Guild?

PH: We shot in Romania, but we haven't shot there in four years. Right now, we're shooting everything in Canada. In the past, it depended on the picture. For some, we did use the local rule, paying an actor or two out of SAG, and sometimes we didn't.

LK: So you shoot in Canada because the bank is there and the government gives you money?

PH: We get anywhere between 25–30 percent of subsidy money to shoot there, which helps to defray the budget, and happy days are here again because the U.S. dollar has gotten stronger. Therefore our buying power in Canada goes even further.

Think about movies like *No Country for Old Men*,[32] which had huge incentives to shoot in Texas, a location that really made the movie sing! Those Texas locations with dry, dust-blown, rolling brown hills and desolate, hot earth look fantastic and give the film production value it never could have gotten on the streets of Toronto or in Central Park, New York City. This is an example where the location really worked. Of course, in my capacity as chairperson of the IFTA, I was at a forum hosted by Congresswoman Diane Watson at which Jack Gerbus, Director of the Maryland Film Office, argued that incentives do sometimes have the ability to pervert[33] a movie by pushing a producer into making a movie that is not necessarily appropriate for its location. For example, filming *Brokeback Mountain*[34] on the streets of Detroit might not have worked, no matter how generous the Michigan rebates and incentives might have been. A film production creates jobs and brings business to many people—from restaurants to hotels to town residents. You do

[32] *No Country for Old Men* is a 2007 Oscar-winning movie written and directed by brothers Joel and Ethan Coen. It stars Javier Bardem as a vacuum cleaner–wielding serial killer with a very sexy haircut, not unlike the haircut of YouTube blogger Shawn C. Phillips (a.k.a. "coolduder").

[33] In this context, the emphasis in "per*vert*" is on the second syllable. When placed on the first syllable, it simply refers to me directly.

[34] Detroit could be an appropriate location for the *Brokeback Mountain* sequel with Heath Ledger playing a zombie.

want to make sure that you are balancing the art with the commerce and not letting the commerce dick the artist in you around.

BUNNY - HOPPING MY WAY TO A MOVIE OF THE FUTURE

Although I made many location mistakes in filming *Toxie II* in Japan,[35] I've pretty much stuck to domestic moviemaking location mistakes. For example, Michael Herz became impressed with India Allen, an actress and Playboy 1988 Playmate of the Year who had produced Troma's *The Rowdy Girls*, starring Shannon Tweed and Julie Strain. Michael felt the film showed a lot of promise.[36] Somehow Ms. Allen convinced us to shoot a scene from 2001's *Citizen Toxie* at the Playboy Mansion in Los Angeles. Michael went along with this, even though *Citizen Toxie*'s principal photography had long since been over. Also, the rough cut of *Citizen Toxie* was nearly three hours, so we definitely did not need another scene! Finally, how in toxic tarnation do we insert a scene of the exterior of this obscenely ostentatious mansion, with its zoo and lavish grounds into a Toxic Avenger movie taking place in Tromaville, New Jersey, the Toxic Waste Capital of the World?

The location fee alone was $25 thousand smackers. For $25 thou, we got one day on the grounds, inside the outside of the Playboy Mansion. We were not allowed inside the mansion. God knows how much that would have cost! The one "smart" thing we did that was ahead of our time and is chronicled in the documentary on the making of *Citizen Toxie*, *Apocalypse Soon*, was to have one of the very first Internet broadcasts/feed of a behind-the-scenes live stream of film shooting in real time. By "real-time behind-the-scenes," I mean an equipment-filled truck the size of Rhode Island, which cost another $25K. We had on-camera pundits placed at strategic locations on the Playboy Mansion grounds, giving us blow-by-blows[37] of the action in front of them (something CNN later ripped off in their 2008 presidential campaign coverage). Unfortunately,

---

[35]For example, the yen was so much stronger than the dollar, so everything in Tokyo cost about 40 percent more than it would have in good old Chinatown, New York City. *Not such a smart strategy for a low-budget production, eh?

*INDEX GYNO: You do know that Chinatown refers to China and not Japan, right Lloyd?!

[36]Yeah, promise in losing every cent invested!

[37]A very purposeful double entendre, meant figuratively and literally.

we did this in the year 2000, a time when no one was yet watching things on their computer. Gonzo porno webcams and streaming on the Internet were yet to be born.

Midway through the day, Hugh Heffner himself emerged from the mansion to lord it over the loping, aging, plastic surgery–pruned Playboy bunnies who were grazing on the grounds like retired race-horses saved from the glue factory. He staggered in the direction of our crew. Heff seemed to enjoy holding court in front of the camera. We offered him a line in the movie playing the president of the United States and he was touched. We wasted about an hour of precious winter daylight to film Heff as the sun started to dip below the horizon. In fact, it took so long to get a shot of him that we lost all light and didn't even get to shoot Locust, the brilliant live band we had lined up to film at the end of the day. A month later the "Page 6" gossip column of the *New York Post* published an item about Hugh and *Citizen Toxie*. His lawyers went nuts, sending us a letter threatening to sue us into the next century if we used any of the Heff footage from that day.

And what about all this footage of the mansion and surroundings? Thanks to the genius of our brilliant, long-suffering editor Gabe Friedman,[38] we converted the Playboy Mansion footage into a brilliant satire of the opening newsreel footage in *Citizen Kane*. It's probably one of the best and most sublime scenes in *Citizen Toxie*. Go see *Citizen Toxie* and let me know if you don't think the *Citizen Kane* scene is sheer genius. My e-mail is michaelbay@gmail.com.

Producing Lesson #192: If you are required to shoot in a location that has nothing to do with your movie, find a way to justify it and use it to tell *your* story. And whatever you do, don't use Hugh Heffner—unless you're using him in a book about producing your own damn movie.

---

[38]One of my most intelligent moves as a producer was to hire a brilliant editor and give him some freedom. Gabe Friedman edited *Terror Firmer, Citizen Toxie, Tales from the Crapper, All the Love You Cannes*, and many more. He did so much more than just editing. He raised the level of each Troma movie much higher than it would have been. He also wrote and is an uncredited producer on *Poultrygeist*. I believe that in giving Gabe a lot of creative latitude, it made him think he was having a fulfilling experience. He stayed with Troma for 10 years, even though he could have gotten a higher salary elsewhere—that's some rare good producing from Uncle Lloyd.

Gabe has moved to Los Angeles, far away from Troma in NYC. He has a great job at G-4, (a TV channel aimed at gamers), where much of his time is spent editing the movies he edited for Troma, which are now being broadcast on G-4. Quel irony! He can run, but he can't hide from Troma. HA HA HA HA HA HA HA HA HA! He's traveled 3,000 miles to get away from Troma and ends up editing Troma movies. HA HA HA HA HA HA HA!

MY CATERING STANDARDS

People continually tell me that actors like to eat. Not only do they like to eat, but also they need to eat. So I am told. I am even informed that crew members partake in this activity as well.[39] Though I continue to have my doubts, craft services on my productions does always look a little like Goldilocks and the Three Bears following an encounter, so there must be something to all of this.

I have found that the adage of one's eyes being bigger than one's stomach is far too often very true. Especially when it's 6:00 a.m. in the morning and people are convinced they will need a vat of coffee to jump start their day. Cups on a movie set are like gyno's purses. The larger they are, the more people will go out of their way to fill them to the brim.

Producing Lesson #49: Do feed your actors, as they tend to like that and it wards off a myriad of complaints and bad attitudes. But purchase cups that fall somewhere in between the size of a Dixie cup and the cup you drank your bug juice out of at summer camp for your actors and crew members to use to drink their precious coffee. If you don't, more of the coffee will end up in the trash than providing the much-needed energy of your cast and crew. Worse, those cups will end up littering your set and you'll be stuck with random white Styrofoam floating in the background of your shot.[40] If they want more, they can go back for more. You want every available cent to end up on the screen, not in the toilet.[41]

HOW DO YOU EVEN PAY PEOPLE TO BEGIN WITH? SETTING UP AN LLC

You are probably wondering how, if you, as the producer, are the guy or gyno responsible for writing the checks and actually paying the cast and crew, how are you supposed to keep track of all of the money you're spending? One of the best options available to you is to set up an LLC.

---

[39]Me, I survive on the animal lust of my raw sex drive. This is enough to keep me going for months at a time, like a camel.

[40]This doesn't happen with only low-budget movies. Check out the *Direct Your Own Damn Movie!* DVD box set to see how a bright white Styrofoam coffee cup fucked up a scene in the ginormous budget movie, *Gamer!*

[41]Literally. Caffeine is a diuretic, you know.

An LLC is a Limited Liability Company[42] wherein the company participants or members are investors, but not partners or shareholders. The most important aspect of the LLC is the fact that you, as the producer, and your investors are not *personally* liable for any debts incurred as a result of the film production. Your (ass)ets are completely separate from the LLC, so they cannot be seized.[43] To put it more lightly, if someone dies on the set, you are protected personally unless you murdered them, as your liability is limited only to the extent of your investment. Additionally, members are only required to pay taxes on their *profits* (as opposed to owning General Electric[44] stock, where they are subjected to both corporation and individual taxes). Once you set up the LLC, you can open your account and get checks and a check ledger from your bank. You're ready to start signing those checks and you can keep track of every cent related to the film production, rather than mixing your production expenses with your regular utility, cell phone, Internet and porno charges. This LLC record-keeping will come in handy when trying to get that incentive money Pat discussed earlier.

What is most important to know is that the full amount of each member's investment can be immediately deducted from his or her income tax, thanks to Section 181 of the U.S. tax code, which former President George W. Bush[45] championed to encourage American entrepreneurial endeavors. Avi Lerner's company used Section 181

---

[42]INDEX GYNO: Major yawn factor, Lloydie.*

*FOOTNOTE GUY: That's OK, IG; these long, boring, completely useful passages for producers are giving us a chance to produce . . . some hot LLC-ing monkey love of our own!**

**INDEX GYNO: (Sigh!) Oh, FG. Why, why, why didn't you tell me that Little FG's throbbing backslash was like one of those sponges you put in a jar of water and it just grows and grows and GROWS?

[43]It always gives me great relief to know that my full collection of days-of-the-week panties and good friend the Flowbee will always be protected.

[44]It is hard to find a worse investment than one of my movies, but General Electric may indeed be one. GE stock has cratered from around 60 to 6 and it has been shown to be a house of shit. The obscenity is that widows and orphans have been conned into owning GE—whereas only rich people who can afford to lose all their money are allowed to invest in my so-called risky movies, which, for 40 years, have rarely lost money.

[45]George W. Bush is regarded as the greatest economist since Adam West. Bush has also been one of the greatest friends of independent film since President John Adams.

to build a studio in Louisiana and is now able take advantage of the generous rebates provided there 24/7.

WHATEVER YOU DO, GET INSURANCE!

Just as it is a cold, hard fact that all gynos are lesbians, so it is a cold, hard fact that moviemaking is dangerous. If you are shooting a movie, no matter how little money you have, you must insure your production. If you learn nothing else from me with regard to producing your own damn move, please learn this: insurance protects human beings and your personal assets. For *Poultrygeist*, whose budget was $500K, insurance cost us a lot of golden eggs. But it protected us and those who worked for and with us against all sorts of calamities, such as injury, the loss of human life, and damage to property.[46] You can even get what is called *negative insurance*, under which if the lab screws up in processing your film or Kodak gives you defective stock, the insurance company will give you money to reshoot the damaged footage.

HOW DEBBIE ROCHON DID NOT GET A HAND *OR* CAN YOU DIGIT?

BY DEBBIE ROCHON

WHO IS DEBBIE ROCHON?

Debbie Rochon is a queen (and by that I mean sheer royalty) of independent cinema. She has starred in hundreds of films, including Vampire's Kiss, Nowhere Man, *and* Ladies and Gentlemen, the Fabulous Stains. *She's appeared in Troma's* Tromeo & Juliet, Citizen Toxie, Terror Firmer, *and our television series* Troma's Edge TV. *Debbie has won prestigious awards for her acting and co-hosts a weekly show with* Dee Snider *on Fangoria Radio, which can be found on Sirius Channel 102.*

SAFETY FIRST

Troma's classic rule, as punctuated in the 1999 release *Terror Firmer*, is: "Safety to Humans." Lloyd didn't just pull this saying out of his ass. He may enjoy pulling many things out of his ass, but this saying wasn't one of them. It

---

[46] A 35mm lens can cost $75K.

should not only be a rule to live by on film sets, but also in life in general. You think accidents don't happen on sets? Here's a list of what I have actually witnessed on movie sets, not including my own disfiguring hand accident.

1. Actor person fell down a set of stairs while shooting a chase scene and broke his foot. Had to complete movie with cast on. It was a pain for him and pain for the director who had to shoot around the foot cast and was unable to shoot that character running any more. Luckily, they had insurance. Foot was shattered in 15 places.[47] Very expensive to fix actor person's foot.
2. Gyno actor had hair catch fire. This gyno was a professional fire eater, but because not everyone on the set was completely focused on the action taking place before the camera and being awake and alert when the fire eater accidentally caught her hair ablaze (due to the intense hair spray that the make-up department had used), the fire extinguisher was "lost" for a few seconds longer than it should have been! The extinguisher should have been right there. It wasn't, because somebody spaced out for a moment. That "space" cost the fire-eating gyno one-fourth of her hair! Luckily, they had insurance. She sued for lost wages for a year. That would have been very expensive coming out of pocket.
3. Crew person tripped on electrical wiring and broke his elbow while trying to break his fall. Hospital bills, worker's compensation. Luckily, the production was covered. Crew person would have sued the producers' butts off otherwise. He had just won a settlement from another production company a year before.

NEVERS

1. Never hire klutzes. You can hire them for paperwork jobs back at the office, but never for on-set work.
2. Never hire space cadets. They are jettisoned into space by unknown forces and cannot be relied upon to be "present."
3. Never hire people with an axe to grind. While you need to have insurance to protect the cast, crew and yourself, you don't want your second-in-command to be looking for a reason to sue you and put your ass and bank account in a sling, thereby royally fucking the production.
4. Never hire people who talk trash about every employer they have had prior to you. People that do this are pathetic, weak and blame the world and everyone in it for all of their problems—especially authority

[47]This is no good, unless you are producing *My Left Foot*.

figures, employers and anyone they have to take direction from. Your name will get added to that impressive roster, so just nip that problem in the bud and never hire them in the first place. Keep your eyes and ears open for red flags when assembling your team.

5. Never hire your girlfriend or boyfriend. You shouldn't shit where you eat and people will hate you for it. Look at how people enjoyed the failure of the film *Gigli.* All because a happy "A-list" Hollywood couple who happened to be having sex in real life (and enjoying a good 69 session here and there), added insult to injury by starring in a movie together and getting engaged. This infuriated the movie-going public. Given that most people have only a left hand to rely upon, who wanted to imagine Ben Affleck and Jennifer Lopez penetrating each other!? The public also hated this film because it sucked.

There are a multitude of reasons people want to become film producers. But very few are really good or realistic reasons. Most aspiring movie producers think a good reason to go into this part of the filmmaking field is because they will attain one or more of the following:

A. Become powerful.
B. Become rich.
C. Get mucho cooch or crotch (depending on preference).
D. Be known as the ultimate do-gooder, helping your friend's art by saying you'll produce their film.

Although all of these reasons to become a big-shot producer are possible in the world of filmmaking, they are not good reasons to become a producer. If you're reading this book, then let's face it: you're most likely looking to put together something cool, low-budget and original. You're not looking to be Ron Howard's next Brian Grazer.

MORE RULES TO LIVE BY

Important qualities for an indie film producer:

1. Don't take "no" for an answer. Where there is determination and blind stubbornness, there is a way.
2. Be hardworking and willing to be on-call 24/7 during this process. I mean on-call to troubleshoot for the film you're producing, not on-call for the "Men for Men" section on Craigslist.
3. Know what you're talking about when speaking to potential investors, actors or anybody you need for the film. Read, research and ask questions. Never answer a question with a guess. I once asked a producer

if I was being provided with wardrobe or had to bring my own, and he said they would take care of it. Turned out there was no wardrobe department and I had to wear what I walked off the plane in—jeans and a T-shirt. It would have been OK, but playing the ruling queen of the entire universe in this wardrobe was less than believable.

4. Have paperwork for everything! Never base deals on a handshake or the spoken word! Get it in writing. Document everything. If you had a conversation with the person who owns a potential location for your movie, make a note of it. If someone refers you onto someone else, get their names. If you were constipated for three days straight, make note! You can never have too much information, but you can definitely have too little.
5. A small but important document called the RELEASE should become your middle name. RELEASE should be your preferred sexual position! RELEASE will keep you safe on a cold winter night. Just remember you want to RELEASE, not sustain problems.
6. Get some genre people involved! Although I don't recommend approaching big genre people before you get your financing in order, I do think it's a valuable asset, depending on the names you go after. It's a waste of everyone's time to ask someone to sign onto your film before you have the financing in place, or at least part of it. I have been on mass email lists for films that have been looking for financing for years. After the first reply email I may send supporting all efforts as an actor, I don't have much to say until they're ready to talk schedule.

   I think you burn out your actors if you get them involved too early. Let's face it: if it takes two years to put the film together, it takes two years. When you first asked the actor person to become involved, they were probably very happy and excited. Over the years it has taken you to gather the $5K or $50K together to produce your movie, the actors may have lost the emotional steam to be excited about the project. Wait until you are realistically within about six months of shooting (or less) before approaching the genre stars.

   Also, you would be surprised how few people use a spellchecker when sending out a note of inquiry. Or how few people know how to put a sentence together in a way that makes them sound professional, or even just above the age of five. As producer, you are the representative of this film. You are creating the impression on which people will base their saying "yes" or "no" to your project.
7. **GET INSURANCE**. Under no circumstance and no matter how small your budget is, you do not want to skimp on purchasing insurance for your shoot.

WHAT IS THE SOUND OF ONE HAND CLAPPING?

A film set has many people milling around, many pieces of equipment propped up on tripods, and electric cables and outlets everywhere. The environment is hazardous and the probability of something dangerous happening if you're not careful is very real. Please don't be a backsliding irresponsible producer and think you can just sidestep this issue by writing releases for your cast and crew to sign that absolve you of all responsibility for their well-being while making your movie.

Insurance is cheap.

It should be your number-one priority.

I worked on a set where the filmmakers did not get location insurance. I didn't know they hadn't. I would not have been there had I known. As I prepared to shoot a scene, they switched out a prop knife for a real machete. I did not know it was sharp and "real"—I assumed it was made safe by the weapons department. The scene called for me to stab someone with all my might. A moment after the director called action, I whaled down on the fake body with the knife as hard as I could, trying to give the best performance possible, when my hand slid right from the handle onto the blade. In a split second, my four fingers on my right hand were severed completely, except for the bone. All the tendons and nerves were cut and destroyed.

I have since had two operations and have gained about 70 percent use of my right hand back, but it will never be completely corrected. The cost of this, because the filmmakers didn't have insurance and did not try to help with the medical bills,

FIGURE 7.5 A young Johnny Depp faints at the beauty of actress Debbie Rochon.

landed me in bankruptcy court. It cost me my entire life savings, my apartment, and everything I owned, *plus* a couple hundred thousand dollars in debt.

Trust me. Get set insurance. You want to be able to sleep at night and not have to live with having permanently disfigured an actor or crew person, plus the long legal battles, costs and time you'll spend in court, just because you wanted to save a small chunk of cash by not getting insurance.

FIGURE 7.6 Debbie Rochon (left) and a young Jane Fonda (right) canoodling on the set of *Hanger*, over producing *Hanoi Jane Goes to Yemen.*

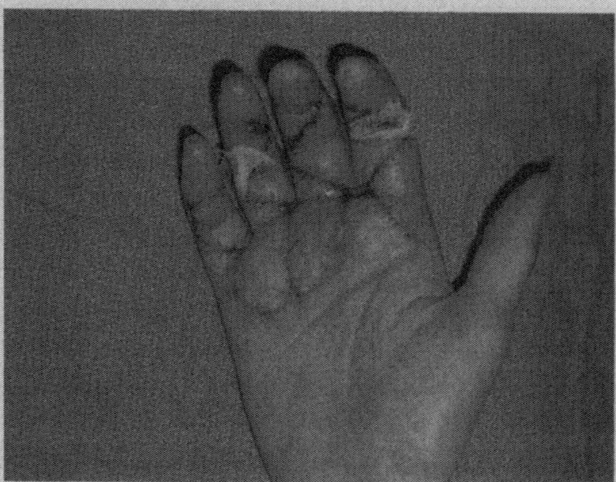

FIGURE 7.7 There are no special effects here! This is Debbie Rochon's hand after being sewn back together. Some retarded producers didn't read my "3 Rules of Safety" and used an actual machete on set instead of a prop weapon.

Jesus, Debbie! That story is horrifying. Those producers should have their balls meet a machete. Toxie and Marianne Williamson have taught me that you truly just never, never know and safety to humans is more important than any movie, even *Step Up Part II: The Streets.* That's why safety plus insurance is paramount . . . oh, shit! I just wrote the name of one of those evil giant movie studios!

BRIAN YUZNA ALSO DEFECTS NORTH

LK: How do you get a movie like *Hard Wire* done, with Sony, in such a difficult economic climate as today?

BY: Well, we had produced another film for Sony that did very well for them called *Line Watch.* It was a film set in New Mexico about current politics and border patrol and what happens on the border in Mexico. That film did well—so well, in fact, that Sony called us up and said, "Look, this was a great experience. You made a great movie for a good price, so bring us another project." So we made *Hard Wire.* We did *Hard Wire* because we thought it would be a good project for Cuba Gooding, Jr. and because it had a science fiction element. He hasn't done many science fiction movies and we also thought it would add to the marketplace, because there aren't many smaller budget science fiction movies being made today.

LK: What do you mean when you say "smaller budget"?

BY: Traditionally, if you look at the science fiction movies produced by the studios, they don't make any for less than $50 or $60 million dollars, plus the $40 million spent on marketing around the world and North America. For us, we thought we would make a reasonably priced science fiction movie for about $5 million dollars in 24–36 shooting days, shoot in HD on a camera that allowed experimentation with shots, and have another world-class actor besides Cuba Gooding, Jr.—in this case, Val Kilmer. And then we shot in Vancouver to take advantage of the great tax incentives in a studio with soundstages and sets already used on other movies.

LK: Do they pay you money in Vancouver or is it a tax credit?

BY: It's a tax credit, but in order to access the best tax deals—whether it's a credit or deduction—you have to use a Canadian local producer or Canadian writers and directors. We were able to have the Canadian government subsidize at least 35 percent of the film.

LK: For tax purposes, don't the films have to be profitable?

BY: No. In the current economy, U.S. states and cities as well as foreign countries offer incentives to film productions in their respective locations. The idea is that if you bring a whole crew and actors there, they'll spend money on the hotels, restaurants and more. It's a ratio of 4 to 1, so every dollar spent or Canadian dollar or Euro spent has a ratio[48] of four times that amount to the local economy.

LK: When you make the movie, do they just give you back cash?

BY: In this case, Canada gives you three levels of credit—the national level, state level and city level. You're given a percentage that you know you're going to get and after you're finished, you're given an audit. The audit is done to make sure that what you say was spent was spent and then the government writes you a check for the full amount of your credit. Many people like myself don't want to wait the 18 months for the film to finish and the audit process to be completed and approved. There's a risk that the producer didn't spend money on what he said he spent it on or that something catastrophic happened on the film, so what we do instead is we take the credit and go to a local bank and say, "Look, we have these credits, here's our budget, we have a bond from the completion bond company, we have local tax credits and you're a Canadian company and you deal with the government. Why don't you discount the credits for us and give us 80 or 90 percent?" So that's the scenario that happened to the film. We were able to cash in our hands fast.

TRENT HAAGA GETS THROWN IN THE TRENT-CHES ON LOCATION

LK: What's the worst producing mistake you've seen?

TH: There were times where, for instance, we went and secured a location in the desert and it was a blank, uninteresting location. It was more of a transitional shot to get to another shot. We thought they had everything squared away. It was supposed to be a state-owned spot, so we did it really cheap. Lo and behold, we arrived and our trailers were there and we found out that it was co-owned by a private owner and the private guy shows up and he was like, "The state never got a hold of me about that and you're going to have to pay me X amount." By that time, it was like extortion. We had all of our cast and crew out there. We were at the point of no return! So we ended up paying a lot more for the location than we had originally planned for it. On top of that

---

[48]This is called a "multiplier." I believe New York City's former Mayor Edward ("How'm I doin'?") Koch (three terms) said that movies in New York had a "10" multiplier—that is, one dollar spent by a movie in a community had the power of ten dollars as it flowed through the local economy.

came a lot of rules about when we had to get out of there. Owners of locations will do that all the time and you have to try and get the tightest location contracts you can, because in pre-production they'll tell you that you can do anything and then when you get there to shoot, they stick you for every penny you've got. Another example is MacArthur Park, which is kind of a sketchy area. We were filming and a group of screaming homeless people came by with pots and pans, waiting for the producer to walk by and give them $20 a piece to leave the set alone. It was a public park and they could do that. In L.A., even drunken bums know how to disrupt a set to get some booze money.

BRIAN YUZNA RAN FROM THE INDIES TO THE ANDES IN HIS UNDIES—OR AT LEAST FROM INDONESIA TO SPAIN

LK: What was it like to produce movies in the United States versus Spain or Indonesia?

BY: Well, it's different from both a practical and financial point of view. I made *Re-Animator* with private money. I tried not to get money from people who aren't in the movie business, because they have unrealistic expectations of what they will get out of it.

One of the typical ideas in movie making is that if you make ten movies, at least one would be successful. One of those could click. For an upside in the movie business, that's what people play for. The other thing is, if you can own the pictures, it's like a library—real estate that you create. That's why Troma owns a ton of movies in its library. I once knew a distributor who said, "A movie is like a sack of flour—when you're all done, there's still a little bit more in the bottom of the sack." A movie is like that. After you have sold the movie, exploited it, sold the video, done everything, who knows? There is always a new technology or new country or territory to sell to.

When I was in L.A. and not using private financing, I'd go to companies that would buy the movies. I would go to Trimark, which is now Lions Gate, and pitch them something, find a script or just talk to them about making a movie. Sometimes they would say, "We want a sequel to *Silent Night, Deadly Night*," or "Hey, let's make *The Dentist*," or "*Return of the Living Dead 3*."

Most of these companies wouldn't make movies in-house, but we would create a corporation to make the movie. They were cash-flowing the production and we made sure the accounting and dailies were fine. Distribution companies don't do that, so that's what producers do.

It is getting harder here to work from a level that I work at, which is low-budget. I make small movies, because I haven't been able to be financially successful with big-budget movies. In the 1990s, I decided that if you can make a label for yourself, you can keep the same crews and you don't have to advertise their cost. If you make three movies a year, because you have a line of production, you can benefit from economies of scale. Also, movies as a label have more value. For example, I'm a big fan of the Hammer films—I go into a video store and I see *The Lizard Woman* and I have to rent it. It's part of a package. Troma is one of the few genuine labels. In L.A., I tried to take this idea to many people. One was *The Seven Deadly Sins of Horror*. I'd get actors and directors from horror together. Each would do one movie based on one deadly sin. Miramax picked it up and we started developing the idea. I had Toby Hooper, Stuart Gordon, George Romero and Dario Argento. As it turned out, they never greenlit one of the projects. One of them was eventually made and that turned out to be *Idle Hands* with Seth Green. It came out about ten years ago and was supposed to represent the deadly sin of sloth.

LK: Do you think that idea influenced the cable TV concept of *Masters of Horror*?

BY: I think so. The idea of doing it for cable was better than my idea. Good ideas are abundant, so as a producer, I hesitate to verbalize an idea, because when I come up with one, it can be taken already. Normally, they say you have to have an actor, director or a script, because these elements are sellable. I think most people who go into the movie business want to make movies and don't see it as a business, but as an art. Production is the most fun part of it all because you are spending the money fast. If you have solid financing, it doesn't mean you have a good movie, but it's a solid start.

In L.A., that can mean if you don't have a relationship to a big studio, you might not be able to make a movie. I looked outside of the United States. When I was in Spain, they said, "Do you want to make a movie?" and I said, "No, I want to make a label." We called it the Fantastic Factory and I developed a production system there for the development, productions and sales of movies. In Europe, you always use government subsidies, so you want to take money from the government. By the time we were getting to the end of my duration with the Fantastic Factory, we had co-productions with England. England has a subsidy scheme wherein you can get 35 percent of the movie budget from the government—and if you produced this project in the UK, you'd get another 18 percent. The European system is like Canada and all based on subsidies. That's what I did for eight years.

LK: Do they have unions in Spain?

BY: They don't have unions like we have here, but the government does many things that the union does—they take care of the workers. They give you very few hours to film. In Spain, they have ten-hour days and three-hour lunches. They drink alcohol on the set all day long. It's a little less in your face, but it's also less commercial, so when I was there I tried to make it more commercial, like a Hollywood movie, or what I call an "international" movie. It's not like I said, "We need to make this like an American film." I was just trying to make it more commercial. For instance, when you're in the car business, you make a car like a Toyota, because they are the standard for the world. You wouldn't make a Ford, because a Ford model is an imitation of a Toyota. You also wouldn't make a BMW, because it's too high-end. It comes down to standards. I'm not saying "Make a Japanese car," I'm saying, "Make a Toyota." When I tried to tell that to the Spaniards or other Europeans, I explained that I'm not trying to be Japan-nationalistic, I was trying to create a standard, and this had nothing to do with the content or other things. That's one of the challenges of going overseas.

LK: Tell me about Indonesia.

BY: One of the reasons I left Europe was because the euro became so expensive. The authorities on the financing side also started getting sticky about the content. In Indonesia, you don't have any subsidies and you just go and you shoot there, because it's very cheap. We recently made a deal with Komodo films to produce 3D films in Indonesia. We approached the Singaporean government and asked them if they wanted to be our partner, as governments can be interesting partners. So we have our theatrical exhibitor and the government behind us. It's all about the finances.

The great thing about being a producer is that you're still involved with the movie after it comes out—making the extra materials for the DVD release or trying to distribute it for a new market. When you produce a movie, you're really involved with it for totality. Today, we believe the director is the auteur of the movie, but it's actually a group of people—three to six people—creating it. In some cases, the directors actually change, like in *Gone with the Wind.* But that movie was the producer's, Selznick's, and that's the way a lot of movies are. Sometimes a producer only puts up the money and isn't involved with the filmmaking and other times he is the movie.

I've been a producer, director and writer, but when I'm directing, I'm not trying to produce and when I'm producing, I'm not trying to direct. I tried to do that when I started and I was all over the place and got in everybody's way. When I was in Spain, I tried being the "creative" producer by deciding who the director was going to be, what the project was going to be, how it was going to develop, how we would make the script better. A director that has a good creative producer is really lucky. One who doesn't have a good producer can find himself floundering. I've worked on projects where I've found myself without good production support and it's amazing what a miserable experience it is and what a terrible movie is made.

Troma was involved in one of the very first joint American/Indonesian movie co-productions, an action flick called *Jakarta*. An Indonesian producer had seen *Troma's War*, loved it and approached us about doing something similar. While I manned the Troma office fires at home, I sent my more talented brother Charles (*Mother's Day, When Nature Calls*) over to Indonesia to produce and direct *Jakarta* on location. My sister Susan (producer of *I Am a Teenage TV Terrorist* and production designer on numerous mainstream movies) also went as Charles's production designer.

LONG BEFORE THERE WAS CHARLIE KAUFMAN, THERE WAS CHARLES KAUFMAN

WHO IS CHARLES KAUFMAN?

Hello. My name is Charles Kaufman. Lloyd and I have been brothers for all of my life and most of his.

CHARLES DOES NOT HAVE INDO-AMNESIA: THE DIRECTOR OF *MOTHER'S DAY* SUCKLES AT THE BREAST OF PRODUCING IN A FAR AWAY LAND

At the memorial gathering for R. L. Kaufman, our mother, Lloyd told the story of Jigger and Batsy, a pair of miniature Doberman pinchers we had as pets when Lloyd and I were very young. Batsy became very, very sick. His brother Jigger was perfectly healthy. One day, six-year-old Lloydie came home and both Jigger *and* Batsy were gone. He asked my dear mother where they were. "I put them *both* to sleep," she answered. She offed both of them. It was cleaner that way. That was the way my mother rolled. Lloyd claims from that day on he made sure that I was always well-fed and in the peak of health.

I wish Lloyd's concern for my survival had extended into adulthood. In my thirties, Lloyd landed me a job producing, directing and writing a feature film in Indonesia. I'd just finished making *Mother's Day* (horror) and *When Nature Calls* (comedy) and wanted to try an action film.

One New York afternoon, Lloyd introduced me to the Punjabi brothers: big-shot Indonesian distributors who had also admired *Troma's War*. We talked about producing an action film in Indonesia. "No problem!" said one of the brothers. I asked the basics: "Do you have camera equipment, lights, dollies, a dolly track?" "No problem!" said the oldest brother. I had two months before my next planned film assignment. "One month pre-production and one month shoot should do it. Right?" I asked. "No problem!" the second brother answered cheerily. "By the way," inquired the third brother, "What time does your watch say?" "3:30," I answered. "That's funny . . . because MY WATCH CAN'T SPEAK!" And with that, all of the brothers collapsed laughing.

Maybe that should have been a clue. After casting Chris Noth as the lead (his first feature role;[49] later of *Law and Order: Criminal Intent* and *Sex in the City* as Mr. Big), I packed for a two-month trip to Jakarta, Indonesia. I returned to my New York apartment over a year later. The Punjabi brothers *did* tell me the fabulous watch joke, but neglected to tell me the following few informational reasons why producing *Jakarta* on location took so long.

LANGUAGE: Indonesians speak a different language. By Indonesian law (previously unknown to me), the film crew had to be 97 percent Indonesian. I could hire two American crew members. Because Lloyd got me, his younger brother, involved in this nightmare project, I did the only moral and correct thing and forced my younger sister Susan (who had art-directed, designed, and propped numerous commercials and prestigious films, including Woody Allen's) to be production designer.

I would also like to take this opportunity to publicly apologize for forcing my dear friend costume designer extraordinaire Ellen Lutter (from almost all of Adam Sandler's films) to come halfway around the world. The rest of the crew was Indonesian. After the first day of shooting, when one of the scenes called for "25 soccer balls" and the crew instead brought me 25 goat balls, it became pretty clear that either the entire crew had to learn English, or I had to learn Indonesian. Guess who learned basic Bahasa Indonesian? I'm convinced that if I hadn't, I'd *still* be over there directing *Jakarta*.

WEATHER: It's hot in Jakarta. No, actually, it's fucking hot in Jakarta. Fact: Indonesia is located directly on the equator. Try standing outside and shooting day after day in 105-degree weather with 98 percent humidity in a pollution-choked Asian city that uses exposed canals to move its sewage along. And of course there are the requisite hot and cold running rats. It's my understanding that germs were originally invented in Jakarta. It was like living in a dog's mouth for over a year. I remember one shooting day, lying on a piss-stained city sidewalk, not being able to stand, nearly dead with the flu and throwing up again and again into the crap-filled gutter. Glamorous city.

RELIGION: Indonesia is the largest Muslim populated nation in the world. The Punjabis neglected to mention that a month after Susan, Ellen and I arrived, Ramadan would begin. That's the religious holiday during which Muslims are basically not allowed to eat, at least while the sun is up. Oh yeah,

---

[49] Actually, he appeared very briefly before that in big brother Lloyd's *Waitress!*

and this holiday lasts *for an entire month*! Try working with a crew that speaks a different language and that hasn't eaten for more than 12 hours.

EQUIPMENT: They didn't tell me that for all intents and purposes no one had ever made an action film in the entire history of Indonesia. In fact, they'd never *moved a camera* before. The camera had always been on a tripod. Into this setting, I had written a script and was expected to produce a film that had more than 25 moving car chases, explosions, and the like. Dolly track on which to put a dolly and move the camera? They had some. The Punjabis hadn't lied. The first day my sister and I arrived in Jakarta, they took us down to their studio basement and we saw a huge, completely rusted and solidified mass of dolly track. Years ago, there had been a flood and the dolly track had rusted into one giant metallic glob. We had to begin from scratch and make an all-new dolly track. No camera rigs at all—and we had numerous car chase scenes and explosions where cameras had to attach to all kinds of vehicles, buildings, etc. Camera rigs, cranes and everything had to be made from scratch. Come to think of it, even the scratch had to be made.

REALITY: Jakarta is the capital of Indonesia and located on the island of Java and, as such, the people have what is called an "island mentality." Things are the same on Java island now as they were three or three hundred years ago. So deeply rooted is this concept of time that even their language makes no distinction between past and present. If I made an appointment to meet someone at 2:00 p.m. on Thursday, I was lucky if he or she showed up by Monday the following week. Try working and coordinating a 74-man crew, car chases, explosions, a town that literally gets destroyed, and more in this atmosphere.

LOGIC: Other things I'd always assumed and taken for granted were turned upside down. One example: Indonesian street addresses. Not progressive. No. 6 Jalan Suharto Street could be next to No. 1215 Jalan Suharto, followed by No. 12. You get the idea. Frankly, I still don't know how my sister and Ellen managed to find any of the stores to buy any of the massive amounts of props and costumes.

LIFE: I'd scheduled a stunt for the first day of shooting. I'd never done action/car chase stunts before, so I was relying on our Indonesian stunt coordinator. The scene was a motorcyclist driving at full speed into the side of a taxi; the cyclist flies over the hood, landing dead on the ground. My experience had been that stunt coordinators were the experts and they would design and rig the stunts and decide how the action would be cut up for shooting. Like if a guy jumps off a roof, you'd have a shot of a guy jumping, followed by a shot of the stunt guy flying through the air, and finally a closeup of maybe the guy's body slamming onto the ground. Film tricks.

So, on the first day of shooting, I ask the stunt coordinator for the first shot and we set up for the motorcyclist to take off. The guy revs his motor, pops the clutch, gets up to about 60 MPH and slams into the side of the taxi and is catapulted on top of the cab, unconscious. Five crew guys run over, grab the stuntman, and load his body into a car to go to either a hospital or morgue, whichever is more appropriate. I'm stunned. The stunt coordinator comes over and apologizes to me that the guy didn't fly over the cab. "Next take, we'll make a little ramp so he really flies!" he says. I look over and he had another *new* stunt guy in the same costume on the motorcycle waiting for the action cue. Not exactly the "in the editing room film trickery" we use in

FIGURE 7.8 Charles Kaufman, circa 1988, on set of *Jakarta*, shows that he is a true fashionista, both with his car and clothes. Note: In back, local motorcycle stuntmen are waiting for their cue to die.

FIGURE 7.9 Charles Kaufman, pictured in sunglasses and moustache, is worshipped as a god by the good people of Jakarta. He and his followers prepare to bathe in the sacred Lake Fecal Matter on the set of *Jakarta*, circa 1988. Here pictured with Chris "Mr. Big" Noth (left).

America. More like the "wave theory" of stunt work: stuntman gets hurt; bring on another stuntman.

TASK SOLVING: See Diagram 1 in Figure 7.11 below.

Although producing a film in a third-world country was a total nightmare (and this may be why I now own a bakery in San Diego), living in Jakarta,

FIGURE 7.10 Shirtless and in sunglasses, Charles "the hunk" Kaufman cooling off and relaxing on the set of *Jakarta*, circa 1988.

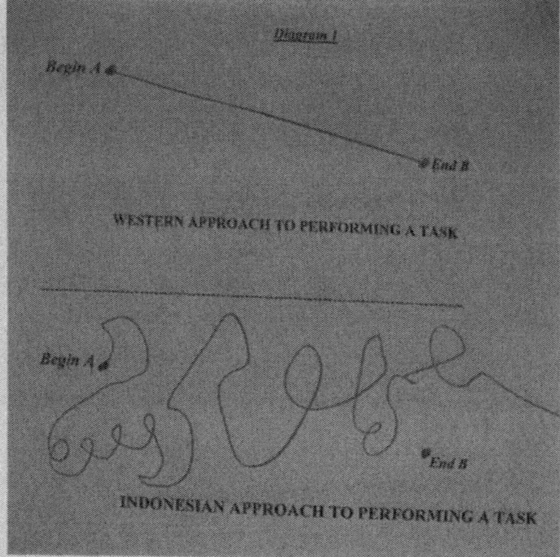

FIGURE 7.11 Diagram 1.[50]

[50]Lloyd asked me to include a diagram that would help him reach his page quota with his editor. Does this take up enough space in this chapter, Lloyd?

Indonesia, for over a year was one of the best experiences of my life. It shook things up and made me rethink everything I'd always assumed to be true and obvious. Indonesians are a wonderful, spiritual and amazing people. And ingenious—they could make a new car out of paper clips or paper clips out of your new car, if you were not careful. Producing *Jakarta* in Indonesia altered and enriched my view of the world, my life, and myself almost as much as seeing my first Troma movie.

Writing this book is still making me think that maybe I'm in the wrong line of work. You know, Charles has long ago given up filmmaking to run Bread & Cie. He has about 450 employees and a very nice life. He's out body surfing in the Pacific Ocean while I lug my Willy Loman suitcases of Troma memorabilia to Tromapalooza[51] events in Denver. Charles recently had a group of orthodox Jewish singles tour his bread factory. As they remarked on how fresh and delicious the bread they had sampled on their tour of the café was, he said, "Really? Would you like to know much the challah[52] cost?" (Say "challah cost" out loud.)

Now, Charles, a successful businessman and community leader, produces one-liners and the best bread in the world, while I'm still producing my own damn movies, sleeping on the floor, eating cheese sandwiches three times a day and defecating in a paper bag.

[51]Tromapalooza events are mini music festivals of live band entertainment run by rabid fans around the country in support of the Tromadance Film Festival (http://www.tromadance.com). Yeah, Troma fans, we love you!

[52]CHALLAH (pronounced "HOLLA"): Not to be confused with the word meaning "to yell loudly." Example: "When the owner of the location tried to shake me down, I hollahed bloody murder and tried to blow my fucking brains out."

Pumped Up in Peoria Asks Lloyd

Dear Lloyd,

I am currently raising money to make the most awesome movie ever. A few of my friends and I got together and made these leather jackets with the movie title on the back. I am sending you one of the jackets right now! I would love you forever if you would wear it and promote the movie.

Thanks! ☺

Pumped Up in Peoria

Dear Pumped Up,

I am constantly amazed how people seem to have money to make jackets and hats and novelty shoelaces, but not enough money to make a film that doesn't suck.

Why not skip the jackets and put that money on the screen where it belongs? In fact, all of that creative energy that you are spending on jacket design might be better channeled into *writing a script*! Worry about promoting the film when you actually have a film to promote.

That being said, I do need a new winter coat, so please send the leather jacket to the Troma Building in Long Island City.

XOXO,
Lloyd

P.S. I hope it's real leather. Pleather makes my arms chafe.

Chapter | eight

How to Do It Hollywood-Style *or* I am the Herpes of the Film Industry: I Won't Go Away

ASSISTANT PRODUCER: In effect, this term is interchangeable with that of "Associate Producer," yet falls several notches lower on the producer totem pole than the Associate Producer. This job is perhaps better understood by adding the tag line "and cleans the toilets" at the end.

Synonyms: Producer's Bitch

Example: "Joe is the Assistant Producer on this film."

"Oh, is that like the Associate Producer?"

"Yeah, except that he'll also be cleaning the toilets."

You may find this difficult to believe, but I didn't grow up with the intention of becoming a depressed old man who makes movies about chicken zombies and spends his weekends in the parking lot outside the Stop and Shop, selling books about chicken zombies out of his 1989 Subaru, all so that he can afford to make more movies about chicken zombies[1] and iconic deformed mutants of superhuman size and strength. In the words of Amy Winehouse, "No, no, no". At one time, many, many moons ago, I was just like you. I wanted success, and early in my filmmaking career, I fully expected to get it, effortlessly. Of course, this was back when I was still a dumbass.

Most people don't know it, but once upon a time I did have a big-shot Hollywood agent named Jim Maloney. He was a great guy, really optimistic and encouraging of my blossoming talent. He originally took me on thanks to two strong scripts I had written. The first was a Hitchcockian story about a little boy who pushes a hot young woman down the stairs. My other "original" script was the story of group of guys in a carpool[2] who keep getting victimized by people on the road. Neither ended up going anywhere, but I was young and optimistic.

Maloney was my big connection to the Hollywood producers. He'd ring me up and say "Lloydie, this one's gonna be big! *Real big!*" He'd go on to say that the studio would read my script, it was a slam dunk, they would be totally stoked to do the movie, bring me on board and pay me vast sums of money for my artistic masterpiece. He convinced me that my movie and I were a "sure bet."

So, on a nice 100-degree Los Angeles day, I'd get all spiffed up with my neatly pressed bar mitzvah suit,[3] bow tie, and saddle shoes and

---

[1]I'm thinking *Poultrygeist II: The Other Thigh*, starring the big-boned ghost of Heather O'Rourke. Any takers? Anybody?

[2]See?! I had the whole "environmentally friendly" thing down way before Al Gore came on the scene. And, unlike Al Gore, I don't waste millions of gallons of fuel flying around in a private jet. I mean, I could if I wanted to, but I have a conscience.

[3]In accordance with Jewish law, my bar mitzvah occurred when I turned 13 years old. Luckily, at the age of 23, I hadn't grown an inch and the suit still fit like a glove. A powder-blue, ugly, polyester-with-velvet-trim glove.

head out to Paramount Studios. I'd arrive at the check-in gate, pull my sunglasses off and give them my name. I'd spell my name backwards, forwards and in Chinese. But still, my name wouldn't be on any entry list, official or otherwise. There was no studio pass waiting for me. I'd have to turn around, irritating the drivers of the other cars lined up behind me. Then I'd have to find a pay phone to call Jim. And of course by now, my bar mitzvah suit would start to become soaked in sweat. Those pay phone booths were really hot inside!

Jim would apologize, make a quick call to the studio to clear up the studio incompetence, and I'd go back. They'd let me in and I'd be directed to park my car somewhere near Guam. I'd have the fun of hauling two 60-pound 35mm Goldberg cans[4] of one of my movies that spoke volumes of my talent, my promise, my gusto. And, of course, after the half-mile traipse in the blazing, hot sun to my meeting, my suit would be so completely dripping with sweat that it would shrink to a Pee-Wee Herman size. As I would sit on the studio exec's plush white Rodeo Drive couch, hoping my swamp ass wouldn't leave a stain, it became crystal clear: the "suits" were only honoring a courtesy call and they had not read my script, nor did they intend to. I'd leave them scratching their heads in confusion as to whether I was the filmmaker or the sweaty carpet salesman pushing plush wall-to-wall with automatic casting-couch stain remover. I tired of this studio bullshit pretty fast and decided to bypass it completely from then on by producing my own damn movies myself.

Fast forward to 2009. I was thinking about this experience of mine from last century when I came into the still new-smelling offices of the Troma Building in beautiful downtown Long Island City one recent blustery March afternoon. My personal assistant,

---

[4]Goldberg happens to be the grandfather of my present agent, Jerome Henry Rudes.* Old Abe Goldberg** and his brothers invented the hexagonal tin can used to transport film reels securely. Their invention became an industry standard.

*LLOYD'S AGENT'S RESPONSE: The Goldberg boys made the executive decision to sell off the business when I was a child. I am now forced to live out the prime years of my life not as the scion of an American success story, but rather as the miserable, grossly underpaid literary pimp for Lloyd Kaufman. And no, Lloyd, I will not take your free passes to the Manhole Club in lieu of my paltry commission for your next book.

**Old Abe Goldberg's young wife Beatrice had a great figure. So the name "Goldberg Cans" was a tribute to Beatrice's breasts.

FIGURE 8.1 *In 1979, LK was an associate producer on the 1979 film* The Final Countdown. *Pictured here: Martin Sheen's chest hair meets LK's facial hair.*

Matt, informed me that thousands of e-mails from fans[5] about this book were pouring in on MySpace and Facebook.[6] Always willing to listen to a devoted Troma fan, I decided to get my feel of the pulse of our base.

Hi, Lloyd!

I have always wondered how you balance both directing and producing on a film set. Frankly, I'm surprised that you can do either. HA HA! No, seriously, how do you do it?

Sincerely,

Wondering in Wichita

Dear Wondering,

You're hilarious! And thanks for the great question. The fact is, it is a difficult balance to find, but because I've been doing it that way for so long, I would have a hard time being just the director or just the producer. I hope this answers your question.

XOXO,

OctoMom's Sperm Donor

My response to Wondering in Wichita was truthful, but in hindsight, I probably could have been more specific about how I balance producing and directing responsibilities. Also, if I have learned

[5] A few of the most intelligent of those e-mails from MySpace, Facebook and Twitter are reproduced herein.

[6] MATT'S NOTE: I think my estimate was closer to around four e-mails.

FIGURE 8.2 *Misty Poteet, a.k.a. Super Tromette Anorexia, shares a proud moment with one of the thousands of fans showing off their Troma love.*

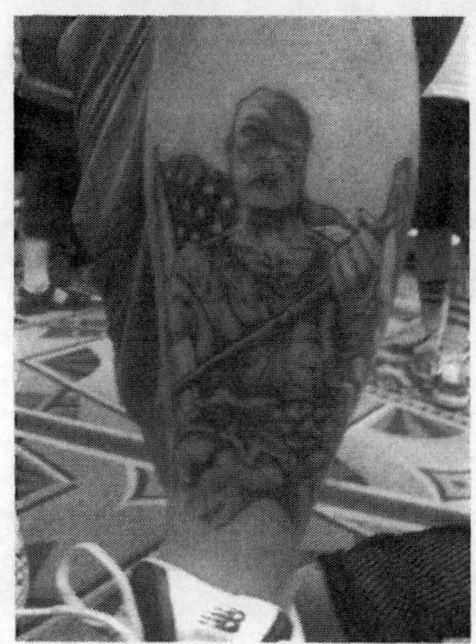

FIGURE 8.3 *Troma Love from a Troma fan via a Toxie tattoo.*

anything from Marianne Williamson, it is about the importance of "follow-through"[7] in my life's journey. I did promise that we would devote some time to that gazillion-dollar Hollywood model I vaguely remember mentioning somewhere in Chapter 1. I don't really know anything about that model, because I don't make those kinds of movies and I don't know how to, anyway. Someone who

[7]EDITOR'S NOTE: I am hoping you are going to "follow through" on your promise to deliver this book on time, Lloyd.

does and is incredibly talented, however, is James Gunn, a former Troma employee, who has made his own damn big-time movie, and will probably make more, because unlike me, he is a Hollywood insider and very talented. He knows all about balancing both producing and directing! Also, stay tuned after James: because I know nothing about the subject of this chapter, I'll be calling on a number of my friends who do.

FIGURE 8.4 *Troma fan Alan Carroll spreads the Troma love to Pres Jimmy Carter.*

PRODUCING, DIRECTING, AND LLOYD, OH MY

BY JAMES GUNN

WHO IS JAMES GUNN?

James Gunn is a writer, filmmaker, actor and cartoonist who began his career co-writing Troma's Tromeo & Juliet *and Lloyd's first book,* All I Need to Know About Filmmaking I Learned from The Toxic Avenger. *Fortunately, he was not permanently scarred from his Troma experience and went on to write* Scooby-Doo *and to direct* Slither *for a mega-conglomerate. Or maybe he was scarred. We'll never know. Come back, James!*

The Troma style of directing (and by "Troma style," I mean the "Lloyd Kaufman style") works for Troma, and wouldn't work almost anywhere else. The one thing I really learned from Lloyd—and I think this has been both to my benefit and my detriment—is that he is *truly* a director/producer. By that I mean, when he's directing, the production is on his mind, just as much as the directing, if not more. He was the first director I really had intimate contact with[8] and worked with on a constant basis. On *Tromeo & Juliet*, we spent twenty-four hours a day together, so Lloyd imprinted on me and I took that with me.

Sometimes I think I was too influenced by Lloyd's approach. Producers and studios love me, because I'm always thinking about going over budget, by avoiding such things as the day's shoot going into overtime. I'm always thinking about all these production concerns, and you have to as a director. That is a big part of the job. But sometimes, I think more with my producing brain than with my directing brain. At times, I can't sacrifice things for the sake of production, and that is a little like Lloyd. That's what people never talk about when they talk about the "Troma Way."

That's because they don't understand how much of a producer Lloyd is when he's directing. And that's the reason he's crazy. He doesn't get crazy because of the directing, but because of the producing. When he loses his temper, it's not because somebody's performance isn't good enough, it's because a second or third take costs more film, more time, more money.

Everything on a Troma movie is "cartoony." Lloyd loves *MAD Magazine* and he loves Looney Toons. It's over the top, it's extreme, and that's a hard style to pull off. On a Troma movie, you'll see that, due to the lack of money to hire experienced or union talent. Good actors are few and far between. Lloyd gets a memorable performance out of everyone. But you'll notice that everyone in the movie acts like Lloyd because Lloyd doesn't really know how to talk to actors like a director does. Lloyd *shows* actors how to act, so everybody on a Troma movie is usually doing a bad imitation of Lloyd. This results in a very strange aesthetic that focuses on a lot of actor persons making Lloyd faces all the time. I've noticed other directors imitating this method, oddly enough.

Sometimes, because I think like a producer, I've lost my temper and I have a ferocity on set that is equal to Lloyd's. I'm usually a pretty nice guy, but I can definitely get upset if things aren't getting done well. I'm not afraid to show that, and I think you have to as a director. There are those directors out there who are able to keep an even keel and never get upset, but they always have a good producer taking care of things. If you are the producer, then you need to do that bullshit. It's great to be a nice guy, it's great to like everybody, but every once in a

[8]There are many, many layers to the word "intimate" in this context. James Gunn masturbated on my desk one night. Unfortunately, I didn't get to watch. But now I can masturbate to the image of James Gunn masturbating on my desk. I know when he reads this he will masturbate to the image of me masturbating to the image of him masturbating on my desk. Now, *that* is creative producing and it can have a main *stream* . . . salty and creamy, but main.

while, I have to lose my temper a little bit to show people I'm serious about what I'm doing. On *Slither*, I think I lost my temper three times on set. Two of those times it was completely calculated. Another time, I was 100 percent furious.

For you wannabe producers out there, listen up to Lloyd's cautionary tale. Even though he's dealt in sophisticated subjects such as Shakespeare (*Tromeo & Juliet*), the dangers of chemical waste (*The Toxic Avenger*), and women's liberation (*Squeeze Play*), Troma doesn't get a lot of respect, because it revels in being lowbrow and vulgar. When you have farting and a shitload of gore and naked women and you mix that with really esoteric obscure themes, it's not always going to get the greatest critical attention or respect from the masses.

On the other hand, I think that Troma is misunderstood. Lloyd's movies are often lumped together in the same category as Ed Wood's movies or other bad flicks from the past. I think if anybody is like Lloyd, it would be Russ Meyer[9] or John Waters.[10] Both Waters and Meyer took elements of lowbrow and put them into their films, yet they had some integrity about it. They knew what they were doing. Russ Meyer's movies actually played in those seedy porn flick houses on 42nd Street in Manhattan. There were a lot of people who were going into the movie theatre to jerk off and watch a big-breasted movie. They had no idea about a quality film. *Mudhoney*, which screened on 42nd Street, is a fantastic film—one of my favorites—and a lot of heart went into it. Russ Meyer knew about the commercial aspects of his movies, as Lloyd does. Lloyd has integrity, but he is also a businessman and thinks about what it is that will work commercially with audiences. And the easiest way to get people's attention—John Waters even said this—doesn't matter what your first movie is, just make sure it has a lot of sex and violence. There are always people out there who will buy sex and violence. Lloyd adds in social and political satire and singing and dancing and Shakespeare. His productions are unique.

I think there's always been something offensive about Troma. When you watch a Troma movie, you get a little offended, you get a little freaked out, but it's also hilarious. Lloyd's making light of something that's ridiculous: the AIDS jokes in

---

[9]Russ Meyer was an independent film director ahead of his time with his use of satire in film in Hollywood late 1950s and early 1960s. His first feature was a nudist comedy titled *The Immortal Mr. Teas*. He then went on to make *Faster, Pussycat! Kill! Kill!*, *Vixen*, the popular mockumentary *Mondo Topless* and the cult favorite, *Beyond the Valley of the Dolls*.

[10]John Waters is an American director who rose to fame with such movies as *Hairspray*, *Cry-Baby* and *Cecil B. Demented*. As Lloyd is known for his bowtie and awesome good looks, John is known for his trademark pencil-thin moustache. He is smart, however, to base the majority of his films in his hometown of Baltimore, Maryland. Because his roots there go deep, Baltimore is a city in which he has the strength and investment of his community's spiritual commitment.

Troma's War, the wife-beating in *Tromeo & Juliet*. Normal everyday society says, "Don't make a joke about this," and then one guy, Lloyd Kaufman, who's willing to make jokes about that stuff and shove important themes right in people's faces years before these themes become fashionable. And that's why I love him.[11]

FIGURE 8.5 James Gunn and LK in this year's new hit buddy movie *Young Gunn and Chronic Kauf.*

FIGURE 8.6 Producer Kaufman has Joycian epiphany about upcoming project *The Toxic Twins: The Toxic Avenger 5.*

[11]Last sentence added by Lloyd Kaufman.

I love you, too, James! I'm not quite sure what in the world James means by my "losing my temper," as that *never* happens.[12] From the stack of messages in my Facebook inbox, I picked out another gem.

Dear Lloyd,

Your movies rock. You bravely dealt in unpopular, risky themes 20 years before Al Gore and Michael Moore. When I finish film school, can I come work for you for a little while and then, based on my impressive experience with you, get hired to work for another cool producer like Michael Bay[13] *or Brett Ratner*[14] *who also make really awesome movies, only bigger and more popular?*

Your fan,

Big Budget or Bust in Baton Rouge

My heart soared, but I didn't have the guts to tell Big Budget or Bust in Baton Rouge that there was a large chance that having Troma on his resume would indeed make everyone scream and clamor, and also probably put a pox on one's career. I considered my response to the message carefully, attempting to find a balance between tact and truthfulness.

Dear Big Budget or Bust,

No.

XOXO,

Lloyd

Many people have asked to work for me. Few have survived. There is always someone who wants to know what that's like.[15] Working for Troma can indeed prepare you for producing your own damn movies. It can also prepare you for ruining your life! Some might say you've got to be very smart and have thick skin to survive the Troma producing boot camp. Just ask Caroline Baron.

---

[12]MARIANNE WILLAMSON'S NOTE TO LLOYD: Stop the denial, Lloyd. Don't backtrack in the progress you've made.

[13]Michael Bay is an American film producer/director well known for his big-budget action films, such as *Transformers*, *Pearl Harbor* and *Armageddon*. His style was lampooned by Trey Parker and Matt Stone in *Team America*, and therefore it seems overkill to make fun of him these days.

[14]Brett Ratner is an American film and music video director best known for *The Family Man*, the *Rush Hour*, series and *X-Men: The Last Stand*. He is also an executive producer on the television show *Prison Break*. He is currently remaking my brother Charles Kaufman's *Mother's Day* and is very rich, so I will suck your dick if you don't tell him that I made fun of him.

[15]NOTE FROM MATT LAWRENCE AND SARA ANTILL: We've been there—save thyself!

WORKING AT TROMA ISN'T ALWAYS TOXIERRIFIC!

Who is Caroline Baron?

Caroline Baron is a talented producer of such Hollywood films as Capote, Monsoon Wedding, Flawless *and* The Santa Clause. *In 1999, she founded FilmAid, a nonprofit organization that brings educational, informative and entertaining films to displaced refugee populations. It's definitely fair to say that Caroline fell into the producing business by accident, way back in 1984 while working on the set of* The Toxic Avenger.

In 1983, I graduated with a degree in English from Brandeis University. Being that there were no possible career options in sight, I moved back home with my parents for two weeks. During that time my brother got a job volunteering on a movie called *The Toxic Avenger* as the Assistant Casting Director. And he said, "Caroline, you've got to come and work here because it's like summer camp!" And I said "Okay, sounds fun! I'll give it a try." And the next thing I knew I was the PA (Production Assistant), working for free, on *The Toxic Avenger.* I had zero experience. Then I was promoted to Costume Designer (still zero experience) and Lloyd told me to go out and buy a costume for the Toxic Avenger. I was warned that I could not spend more than $2. That was my budget. I was very upset because I had found the perfect hat at the Salvation Army, but it cost $3.50! I apologized profusely and Lloyd agreed to make up the difference and took the hat. Next thing I knew, everybody with any experience on that movie had quit and I was given a second promotion, this time to Production Manager, still with no experience beyond my stint as student body president in junior high school and my summers as a camp counselor.

Because I was incredibly loyal and had nothing else to do that summer and Lloyd was crazy-cool, I was extremely hard-working. We spent many days, hours and nights on the second floor of the Troma Building in Hell's Kitchen. Actually, it was the third floor. The second floor was the executive "suite" where Michael and Lloyd worked. It was fully air-conditioned and very comfortable. The third floor where we worked was kind of like, oh, I don't know, working in a flaming inferno. It was really, really hot.

At one point, Lloyd put me in charge of interviewing people for Production Assistant positions. We put ads in the local trade magazines looking for interns and all these film students came looking for jobs. I interviewed them one by one (again, without having any real PA experience myself). Suddenly, out of the kitchen came Michael Herz, demanding: "Did you just tell that guy I'm an asshole?"

"Oh, my God, no," I said. "I would never, ever say that!"

"Well, that's your fucking problem," retorted Michael. "I *am* an asshole and all of these people are going to quit unless you tell them the truth, that working here and producing movies is really, really hard! And tell them Lloyd is bonkers, too!"

That was a lesson I never forgot. Making films *is* really hard and you really don't want any quitters. . .and Lloyd really *is* bonkers.

THE TWO HEADS OF LLOYD KAUFMAN

As James told you, we don't produce movies at Troma like other folks do. I myself become a two-headed dragon and each of my heads—producer and director—talk to each other incessantly. But you know what? You've heard so much from both of my heads already, I want to let a high-powered producer like Avi Lerner clue you in on how they do it in LA-LA-LAND, but first let me take a look at the next MySpace posting that my assistant just tossed on my desk:

Uncle Lloyd!

I want to produce my own damn movie, but I want to make sure once I do that, people are gonna see it, because I don't want to end up like you. Any advice?

Your biggest Poultrygeist *fan,*
Cluckin' in Carmel

Dear Cluckin',

I share your fear. Often, I don't want to be me, either. Ironically, my advice on how to avoid becoming me is to read my books, starting with Produce Your Own Damn Movie! *You may just learn enough to avoid becoming me!*

XOXO,
Lloyd

Cluckin' in Carmel and I could both learn a lot about getting our movies in front of big audiences from the experiences of some of the following top producers I talked to especially for this book: Avi Lerner, Mark Neveldine, Brian Taylor, Jay and Mark Duplass, Larry Cohen and Brad Krevoy. These people have shot movies around the world and made tons of money doing it. You can learn something, too!

AVI LERNER: A *RAMBO*-STYLE REBEL IN HOLLYWOOD

LK: How did you produce a huge movie like *Rambo IV*?

AL: I was always a fan and wanted to work with Sly.[16] One day I heard that Miramax was selling the rights for *Rambo*, and that Sly was buying the rights.

LK: Carolco[17] was one of scores of big movie studios that have gone out of business over the last 40 years!

AL: Yeah, Carolco went out of business, like so many businesses nowadays. I called them and they agreed to sell it to us. I approached Sly with the idea that Sly would be the mentor and then the script would follow someone younger. We then decided to change it so that Stallone would be the main character.

LK: As a result of getting to know Stallone, you decided the make him the main character?

AL: After reading the script.

LK: Did you write the script?

AL: No, Sly wrote the script. We helped him with the idea of placing the story in Burma. Burma is one of the most unknown dictatorships in the world, but it's one of the worst.

LK: How did you get Sly to sign on?

AL: Like any other actor, we approached his agents and asked. That's the producer's job to do.

LK: Stallone said he wanted to write the script?

AL: Yeah, we had some other script, but he didn't like it, so we and he decided to write it from the beginning. We shot it in Northern Thailand, near the border of Burma.

LK: Were there any incentives to shooting in Thailand?

AL: No, there were no incentives for shooting in Thailand, but the location was correct—its proximity to Burma gave it the feel we needed.

LK: Do you have to raise money to make a movie with a huge star like Stallone?

---

[16]Sly is Sylvester Stallone's nickname, short for "Silly." I acted the part of the drunken bum in *Rocky*, but I always called Sylvester "Syl."

[17]Carolco Pictures was an independent movie production company that produced such blockbuster successes as *Terminator 2: Judgment Day*, the first three *Rambo* movies and, of course, one of the most moving epics of our times, the *Sophie's Choice* of its day, *Showgirls*. Of course, with *Showgirls*, Elizabeth Berkley's naked breasts are more profound than Meryl Streep's throwaway performance in *Sophie's Choice*.

AL: *Rambo* was not the most expensive movie we made. We made *16 Blocks* with Bruce Willis and *Righteous Kill* with Robert DeNiro and Al Pacino—both of those cost far more money.

LK: How did you raise the money for *Rambo*?

AL: Like any other independent company, we invested some of our own money (we had managed to save some after making 300 pictures) and then we secured the director and the cast and were able to pre-sell, country by country.

LK: So you didn't go to the mainstream media conglomerates first?

AL: No, we don't believe in the studio system. The studio system does not want to accept the independent company. Even if you do well, they'll find any reason not to buy the movie.

LK: Why is that?

AL: They find out that the independents can do a movie for half the price, or a quarter of the price. Studio execs are very lazy. Sometimes they don't even come to set. They don't know who's who on the crew—they don't even know how many gaffers or grips you need. Their money is shareholder money and they don't care about that or the budget, because it's not coming out of their pockets. Therefore, when we bring them a movie like *Rambo* and say we made it for $40 million, they would say it has to be $100 million. There's no justification when they explain why the movie costs so much money and independent movies cost half or even a quarter of the price.

LK: Can you talk about how you raise the money for $40 or $50 million budgets?

AL: Sure. We pre-sell the movie to different parts of the world.

LK: We talked about that with Paul, Kathy, and Brian earlier, but can you tell our readers how *you* pre-sell? There seem to be different ways to go about it.

AL: Basically, France pays for 10 percent of the film and England pays for 10 percent of the film and Spain will pay 8 percent and all the big territories, and so on. You go to 40-something territories to pre-sell it, making sure you cover 75–85 percent of the film from the market. Hopefully, the film does well and you have a company that will distribute it, such as Lion's Gate or Overture.

LK: Overture[18] distributes; isn't it part of Time Warner?

---

[18]Overture Films is a fully integrated studio that produces, acquires, markets, and distributes theatrical motion pictures. Its affiliated companies make Overture Films available domestically via Internet, home video and television. Paramount works exclusively with Overture on its international distribution.

AL: Yeah, Overture is "independent with stars." They bought *Righteous Kill* and *Mad Money*, so they're working for us.

LK: Why is it that so few companies survive? Overture is still here, but Rysher[19] and so many others are gone.

AL: If we were to look at the list of companies that were here 15 or 20 years ago or go to the Cannes Film Festival then, you would see Carolco, Hemdale[20] and Rysher.

LK: What's the mistake these companies are making?

AL: I think it's a combination of a few things that we have to take into consideration. It's very difficult to be an independent producer. You, Lloyd, are unique. Troma has survived for. . .how many years?

LK: 35.

AL: Whoa! With you as the president? The Cannes festival is a tough business because you have to create something with a certain amount of money and then you have to sell it. Some people make a movie and they don't care about the cost to make it. We look at the most important thing: how much we can sell the movie before we make it? And for the amount of money we can sell the movie, we will do the movie at the budget of 10 percent, 5 percent or less than what we will definitely sell the movie. We will never ever make a movie if the cost will be more then what we can sell it for. So that explains why my partner and myself and maybe you, Lloyd, have been in this business longer than anyone else—over 35 years[21]!

Producing movies is wonderful, it's creative—you are putting a vision up on the screen—but the basic thing and something fledgling producers must never forget is that you are running a business, and in order to run a business, you can never break the golden rule of making a film that will cost you more than what you can sell it for—this is the very basic model for success. Of course, we make mistakes, overestimating or underestimating, but at the end of the day, as long as you remember that it's a business, you will survive.

---

[19]Rysher Entertainment is the owner of TV and film programming content, primarily distributed around the world by CBS Television Entertainment and CBS Home Entertainment. Select rights are also distributed by Warner Brothers, Lions Gate, Sony Pictures, MGM, and others. Today, Rysher is owned by 2929 Entertainment, a division of Wagner/Cuban.

[20]Hemdale Film Corporation is yet another independent film production company and distributor that found itself an early grave amongst the other dead production companies. It produced *Platoon*, among other films.

[21]Actually, I never know if Troma movies will make any money up front, because usually nobody wants to pre-buy.*

*FOOTNOTE GUY: They also don't want to post-buy your movies, Lloyd. I'm still waiting for my check for footnotes in *Direct Your Own Damn Movie*, goddammit!

LK: Now, I don't think we've talked at all about contingency. Can you explain what this is? You were shooting *Rambo IV* in Thailand—did you have a contingency built into your budget?

AL: Oh, yes. Part of the budget or one paragraph of the budget is contingency. Contingency should make up approximately 5–10 percent of your budget in case something goes wrong.

LK: Were there any surprises when you produced *Rambo IV*?

AL: In every movie you make there are always surprises. Burma is a dictatorship and while we were filming near their border, they sent people to threaten us. We had to get security and they had to send a special car for Stallone's use that could take bullets—a car that cost an extra $100K. If you prepare yourself ahead of time by breaking down the script and the budget—if the line producers are crunching the numbers correctly and putting all the right numbers into the budget, then there shouldn't be any surprise. For instance, if you know that every day is going to be a 12-hour work day, budget an extra hour for security.

Even though Troma budgets are microscopic compared to Avi's, we, too, know the importance of building in a little contingency, because you never know when you might have to go back and reshoot something! And, although it sounds like some broken-down, drunken old manic depressive's hackneyed advice: better safe than sorry.[22] Take Buddy Giovinazzo, director of *Combat Shock*. He recently finished shooting his feature film *Life Is Hot in Cracktown*, an optimistic, upbeat story about how cocaine has infiltrated inner-city life. He had a 10 percent contingency built into the budget and used some of it in post-production to go back and shoot one day of exterior and establishing shots of a bodega at which one of the main characters works. With those few long shots of the store on the seedy street—full of drug addicts and prostitutes—placed strategically within the film, Buddy was able to create the illusion of compressed time and evoke a heaviness of the reality the characters lived in. While you're thinking about building in that little bit of "just in case" money,[23] let's get back to Mark Neveldine and Brian Taylor. They can tell you how to start creating on the cheap.

---

[22]INDEX GYNO: Lloyd, the 7-Eleven cashier told us that you used this same line on him when you flashed him your free Barack Obama condom last fall.

[23]I always keep some money available for filming during post-production. Elske McCain's wonderful Goldberg Cans never would have made it into *Poultrygeist* had I not put aside money to film during post-production.

MARK NEVELDINE AND BRIAN TAYLOR *CRANK* IT UP

Who are Mark Neveldine and Brian Taylor?

Mark Neveldine and Brian Taylor are producers, directors, screenwriters, and lovers[24] *who made cult favorites* Crank *and* Crank 2. *Their soon-to-be-released $80 million production* Gamer *features Lloyd Kaufman as a "genericon." Almost as important is that Gamer is the first big-budget mainstream production to use the revolutionary Red Camera.*[25] *Lloyd Kaufman also has a big three words of dialogue in* Crank 2: High Voltage.

LK: How did you get your first producing and directing job?

MN: *Crank* was our first directing job. This is how we got it. We had a script, we called it *Crank*, we wrote our own damn script. We sent it out to a bunch of agencies, and we had the classic bullshit where they wined and dined us.

BT: They sixty-nined us.

MN: They waxed our chest. And those agencies were really excited. We chose one and they sent it out to the studios. Lakeshore[26] got behind the script. They really got behind *Crank* and made it happen.

LK: Tell our readers the value of agents.

MN: You don't need an agent. Our first movie happened to be a studio film, so we did have an agent. Our feeling is go make your own damn movie.

LK: But did the agent get you the gig?

BT: The agents put you in contact with people, but at the end of the day you are still basically closing the deals yourself.

LK: Starting off their careers, do producers or directors need agents?

MN: Absolutely not. All they need is a camera and a computer. That is it. The only thing a young producer/director needs is a cheap $500 dollar camera and a $500 dollar PC or Mac—Macs are a little bit more expensive, so then get a PC. And go out, like Brian said—

BT: I'm really PC.

---

[24]EDITOR'S NOTE: The Fact Checking Department has come back to say that this is not true. Mark Neveldine and Brian Taylor are not lovers. If they were, that would be fine, as Focal Press is an equal opportunity supporter (and employer), but we do not feel it is appropriate to give our readers false information. Mark and Brian also wrote me an e-mail to thank us for our diligence and said they next time they come to NYC, maybe I can take a train down from Boston and go out to dinner with them in Chelsea.

[25]To see the Red Camera in action and Lloyd Kaufman as a "genericon," see the *Direct Your Own Damn Movie* DVD box set "behind-the-scenes" piece on *Gamer.*

[26]Lakeshore Entertainment Group is an American film production company founded in 1994 by Tom Rosenberg and Ted Tannenbaum (1933–2002). Lakeshore produced *Million Dollar Baby.*

In fact, the Duplass Brothers echo Neveldine and Taylor and expound their philosophy of just keeping on creating—no matter what, keep creating films.

THE DUPLASS BROTHERS' MOTTO: "MAKE MOVIES, NOT MEETINGS"

Who are the Duplass brothers?

Jay and Mark Duplass are brothers, actors, writers, directors, producers and lovers.[27] *They have gone from no-budget indie movies to "A"-quality studio pictures with stars. They first got noticed with their sleeper Sundance hit* The Puffy Chair *in 2005, which was produced for $15K and was edited entirely on their computer. Following the theatrical and DVD release of* Baghead, *they are now in post-production on about 17 different projects, one of which is a big-budget "studio" film currently called* The Untitled Duplass Brothers Project, *starring John C. Reilly, Jonah Hill, Catherine Keener and Marisa Tomei.*[28] *They are the best!*

MD: If I wanted to be producing movies, if I had no money, no nothing, what I would do is buy a used DVX100 camera for $1K or less and a laptop. I would then pirate some editing software and buy a boom mic and a boom pole or mike stand if I needed it. I would put them all on my credit card. Then I'd rent them out on Craigslist to pay them off, then shoot movies and also say, "Hey, I have equipment you can use for free. Look, I'm a studio, I'm Roger Corman or Troma 2009, come produce a movie with me! We'll pool some money for food and gas and shoot all this stuff.

JD: I would then go to a couple of film festivals a year, maybe in your town or your region, and meet the filmmakers who are making interesting stuff and meet the actors that you think are really talented. The thing that people are often really surprised by is how many established people will collaborate with you if you have something to offer. Lloyd, you're very open to helping young talented people, right?

People want to make art and all you have to do is put yourself out there—get in touch with the people you generally feel are doing good stuff and it will happen. The main thing Mark and I are talking about is action—never stop moving. Our big motto is "Make movies, not meetings."

---

[27]EDITOR'S NOTE: Goddammit, Lloyd. I am going to blow *my* fucking brains out. Stop it!

[28]One of Marisa Tomei's very first movie appearances was in *The Toxic Avenger*! I'm eternally grateful that she remembered this and mentioned it once in an interview, or I would have never known!

The Duplass Brothers are right. Making movies and not meetings is the way you young producers out there are going to get into the game! I hate sitting at meetings. Ask Michael Herz. He thinks I have ADD—no, he thinks I am retarded. I get up during meetings and walk to my desk and fidget and check my e-mail, get distracted by any and everything[29] and then start talking about a subject that has absolutely nothing to do with the meeting. But there is no question that networking and meetings are important. You've got to like it and be good at it and not be retarded.

So now hear what Brad Krevoy says about that and how he has become a great success as a producer. Like me, he has produced comedies—except that his comedies are mega-hits. Comedy may be the most difficult kind of film to produce. When you read Brad's wisdom about how he produces comedy, you'll know why. Read on!

KINGPIN BRAD KREVOY UNMASKS THE HOLLYWOOD MYSTERY

Powerful Agents Make Powerful Films Happen In a Powerful Way And The 411 About Producing Powerful Comedies

WHO IS BRAD KREVOY?

Brad Krevoy is a major American producer of more than 100 television and movie projects, including Dumb and Dumber *and* Kingpin. *He is the founder/chairman/CEO of the Motion Picture Corporation of America and directly responsible for jump-starting the careers of people like Vince Vaughn, Paul Rudd, Kirsten Dunst, Reese Witherspoon and the Farrelly Brothers.*

LK: Was *Kingpin* before *Dumb and Dumber*?

BK: *Kingpin* was the second film written and directed by the Farrelly brothers, who I believe are Troma fans. It was a screenplay that they always wanted to do. It represented their early days in Hollywood, when both of them were facing tough times. When *Dumb and Dumber* was produced, we didn't know whether it would be a hugely successful film, a moderately successful

[29]Sometimes people we are meeting with to talk business think this is some kind of clever strategy—but it's just me being a jerk.

film, or a big bomb. Jim Carrey got hot, so when *Dumb and Dumber* was released, it did a huge amount of business for its time. It did $130 million at the U.S. box office alone and if you add up DVD, pay TV and Free TV, it did at least that amount and more—and that's just North America. If you add in the international, then it probably grossed about half a billion in all media. So when *Dumb and Dumber* hit, we thought, "Okay, let's do another film together."

The Farrellys had another script called *Kingpin*, which was actually something they had written before *Dumb and Dumber*. At the time a lot of the agents and studio executives did not know what to make of *Dumb and Dumber*—were the Farrelly brothers one-hit wonders? Were they just plain lucky? We sent *Kingpin* to all the major studios and they all rejected it, even though the Farrelly brothers revenue on their last film was half a billion dollars. It was remarkable. I'll never forget what happened to make it happen. It seems every year, new investors come to Hollywood, and in this case a new company, Rysher Entertainment, came into formation just as we were starting to pitch and market *Kingpin* to the various studios. I believe they were funded by Tribune Broadcasting Group, who had given several hundred million dollars to Rysher to find projects. I'll never forget the moment when the movie was greenlit, because the head of the agency, Creative Artists Agency (CAA), one of the best agencies in the world, drove out to the valley to be with his clients, Peter and Bobby Farrelly and us, to pitch *Kingpin* to Rysher.

Richard Lovett had just become president of CAA at that time. I realized the power of the agency when Lovett said to the studio people in the room, "Look, maybe you don't see the opportunity here with *Kingpin*." (By the way, many people didn't see the opportunity with *Dumb and Dumber*.) "The Farrelly brothers are the real deal," said Lovett. We made the pitch and then the bosses said to us, "Please leave the room; we're going to talk it over internally." After a while, they invited us back in the room and said, "We're going to make the movie." Lovett made it happen. The power of the powerful agent!

LK: How did you meet the Farrelly brothers? How did you discover their talent?

BK: I had a good friend, Thomas Gottschalk, who is a big star in Germany. He hosts a talk show there—sort of Germany's David Letterman—and he asked me to help him find some work in America.

We had become good friends at the time Euro Disney was opening. I called up Michael Eisner and said, "You know, you're going to be opening up Euro Disney in Paris. You're going to want to have customers across the continent of Europe, especially from Germany, which is a great market for anybody." I said, "I'll tell you what, if you help my friend Thomas Gottschalk find some movie parts in the U.S., I will make sure that he helps you in Europe, promoting Euro Disney in Germany. Maybe if you have enough good clients,

Thomas might find a spot for them on Germany's #1 TV show." The next week Michael Eisner said, "Come in for a meeting," and we hammered out a deal for Thomas, where Thomas would promote Euro Disney in Germany and be given the opportunity to find work in Disney family movies.

LK: How did you get Michael Eisner's attention?

BK: I basically sent him a letter. Early in my career, I made it a point to attend as many industry events as possible. There's nothing stopping anyone from introducing himself to someone else, so I went up to him, introduced myself, and over the years we developed a friendship. He's a very decent guy. I had already known him for one year before I called him up to make the Gottschalk deal. Long story short, I made a deal for Thomas to be in some Disney films and Thomas and I started attending meetings with producers for Disney, who had films coming up. There was one film coming up and this is why *Dumb and Dumber* was made.

We all met for breakfast at Hugo's[30] on Santa Monica Boulevard in West Hollywood. At breakfast, it was myself, Thomas, my friend Charlie Wessler, and Adam Bernstein. We were talking about the film *It's Pat* (based on the he/she character made popular on *Saturday Night Live*) and Thomas went off to the bathroom. I said to my friend Charlie, "What else are you working on right now?" and he said, "You'll never believe this, but I have the funniest screenplay in my car. Why don't you help me get it going?" I said "Okay." We walked outside to his beat-up VW, he opened the trunk, handed it to me and said, "Look, here's *Dumb and Dumber* and it's the funniest screenplay you'll ever read in your life." I got it on a Friday morning in the summer. At that time, I was living as a bachelor on the beach. I had a nice girlfriend and I said to her, "Okay, tonight we're going to stay here and read this script, because my friend Charlie said it was the funniest script he's ever read in his life." When we finished it, I said, "This is going to be the next movie I do." The next day, I called up Charlie and said, "This is a fantastic script, tell me some more about it," and he said, "Well, the script has been around for seven years. It's fantastic, isn't it?" and I said, "Yeah, why hasn't it been made yet?" and he said, "Well, it has a back story."

I later found out that John Hughes,[31] a prominent writer/director in Hollywood at the time, actually helped with the story for *Dumb and Dumber*, but he never took credit and didn't want people to know he was involved.

LK: Why was that?

---

[30]Hugo's ain't IHOP!

[31]John Hughes wrote and directed *Sixteen Candles*, *The Breakfast Club* and *Ferris Bueller's Day Off*, all classy hit comedies with a youthful bent—not much explosive diarrhea in his films.

BK: I don't know the circumstances, but every couple of years I send a letter to John Hughes, saying "Thank you so much for being involved with the script, because it changed my life."

Charlie explained the situation. He said, "The guys who wrote it, Pete and Bob, want to direct it and nobody in Hollywood wanted to give them a chance as first-time directors." Many people don't understand the screenplay. I sure do. I am a student of comedy (at least I like to think of myself as one), I love the Zucker brothers—who could forget *Kentucky Fried Movie*, *Airplane* or any of those classics? I always remembered something the Zuckers said when they were asked about the key to their success. They said, "In the comedy genre, you have to write and direct your own material." So I've always been pro-writer/director in my career. Of the 100 films I was involved with, 75 percent were done with a writer/director. And I've given many writer/directors their first chance in Hollywood. You write and direct, don't you, Lloyd?

In my opinion, the comedy genre is the hardest to execute, because it's all about precision and timing, unlike an action film, where you can reshoot or manipulate via editing or a horror film where you've got a lot of blood, guts and gore. It's all about if the joke is funny or not, because you can't "get it" funny, you can't edit or cut. The writer must be able to be funny on the written page, then one can make the film equally funny on screen. If you do a horror or drama, it's up to the director to get the performance out of the actor. Also, as a producer, I have learned that in addition to the writers, great comedy rises on the shoulders of brilliant performers. If you're doing a comedy—and especially a traditional comedy—the best performers are those who have a big say in how the films are directed. So, if you're someone like Mike Myers, with Austin Powers, or Adam Sandler, or Jim Carrey especially, they always have a special relationship with the directors, where the directors allow the actors to shoot and execute the scene themselves, the way they see it as hilarious. That's how I produce, too.

Remember, it's the comic who performs in front of an audience on the stage. He knows what's good and bad and it's the brilliant writers who are absolutely necessary. So, long story short, I was happy with Peter and Bobby directing the film.

Another one of the reasons *Kingpin* was greenlit was that when we made our big pitch, the Farrelly brothers had this comedy shtick that I don't want to talk about here. They did it on the guys at Rysher and they laughed so hard that they were peeing in their pants. Peter and Bobby did the same thing to me when we had the meeting for *Dumb and Dumber*. I looked at my girlfriend (now my wife) and I said, "These guys are funny guys. They're definitely going to be able to direct this." I told them: "Come back in on Monday and we'll discuss the project." They came in on Monday and I said "Tell me everything.

What studios have seen this script, what actors have seen it and who do you want to be in it?"

Through a seven-hour meeting, I learned one key piece of information: There was someone out there who was not a big motion-picture actor but was a prominent TV actor, Jim Carrey, who loved the screenplay. Some of the studios had had discussions about his being the lead, but they said, "Jim Carrey, who's that? We need a comedy actor, not a TV actor." I said, "Okay, let's meet Jim Carrey and see why you Farrelly brothers want him for the lead." So we had the meeting and it was so obvious that this guy was a genius. He's the real deal, just as funny as Charlie Chaplin was in his heyday. Robin Williams has that same quality. At the time, Jim Carrey had just been given the lead in *Ace Ventura*, produced by Morgan Creek[32] and to be distributed by Warner Bros.

I knew that Morgan Creek sold their movies territory by territory outside the U.S. I picked up the phone and called all the people who had pre-bought *Ace Ventura* and asked what they thought. My friend from Sweden who works for the biggest distributor in Sweden said, "Brad, this stuff is really funny, this guy is going to be a huge star, sign him up, now!" At the time, New Line liked the screenplay, but they weren't ready to commit to Bobby and Peter as the directors. I said, "Okay, now I have the script, Peter and Bobby are directing. By the way, don't you have another Jim Carrey script in the can? Something called *The Mask*?" and they said, "Yes, we do," and I said, "How does it look?" and they said, "We're really bullish on the film." I said, "Why don't you double down? It's going to cost you $20 million to market it and you'll spend another $20 million making it. If *The Mask* opens huge, then you'll want to use Jim Carrey again and stay in his good graces, because he'll be a big star when *The Mask* comes out. You'll have further protection, because Ace Ventura comes out before *The Mask*, so you'll get a free look-see. How about it?" They said, "No, that doesn't work for us," and I asked "Why not? Think about it. I'll gladly take your call when *Ace Ventura* opens, if it opens as big as people think." And, of course, *Ace Ventura* opened huge and I got the call. When I went to see them, they said, "Okay, Peter and Bobby can direct and we'll hire Jim."

By that time, there was a salary dispute, where Jim was asking for $1 million and they were going to pay him in the neighborhood of $300K. We heard about the salary difference and said, "What's another few hundred thousand dollars, when you're making over $40 million?" They got tired of me whining and said, "We'll produce the Jim Carrey movie without you" and I said, "Best of luck with *The Mask*." I knew that if *The Mask* did well, then Jim would only

[32]Morgan Creek Productions is an American film studio co-founded by James G. Robinson and Joe Roth in 1988.

become more valuable, so we just waited. I got the call to sit down and talk but they still weren't willing to give Jim Carrey his fee. Then *The Mask* came out and did huge and every studio approached us and asked if they could do the movie. At that point, Jim Carrey's agents got smart and realized his $1 million salary was chicken feed. Now they were asking for $6 million for him. I offered part of my salary to cover the difference and ultimately the film went to New Line.

So we did *Kingpin* after the success of *Dumb and Dumber*. But now they didn't want to do the movie, because of Jim Carrey not being in it, which was ironical considering their previous position. *Kingpin* was not as successful as we'd thought it would be. It opened during the 1996 Atlanta Olympics and there was a bomb scare that weekend, so no one wanted to go out to see a movie—ours or any other. The film did okay theatrically and it had a good following overseas, but when it was released on video, it did fantastically and developed a huge cult following. Whenever you're on a college campus, someone will always recommend *Kingpin*.

LK: How did you develop *Dumb* and *Dumber*?

BK: We picked up the script and I optioned it with my own capital and we made deals with the Farrelly brothers and Charlie, who did *It's Pat* before Jim Carrey was successful, we were going to produce it as a low-budget movie.

I think of every movie as a diamond in the rough. You have to polish that diamond, then find a girl who wants that diamond and court her. Every movie and every buyer is different. We knew there would be many buyers for that diamond in the rough.

LK: How did you get international distribution?

BK: American comedies usually don't translate well abroad, especially in Asia. We made a deal for world rights with one studio, New Line. At that time, New Line was part of Turner, which had bought the MGM library. So the bankers gave us very good terms.

LK: What happens if you don't deliver the film to New Line or your star dies?

BK: A bond company backs you up, saying, "I'm going to guarantee that the movie is going to be made." They charge between 3 and 8 percent of the total budget of the film. If you do not pay a bank back or you hurt the bond company, you're out of the business, because that's big money. You could be working at McDonald's the next day if that happens.

LK: Has that ever happened?

BK: Sure, if the director or an actor goes crazy or if there's an earthquake, the bond company has to come in and complete the movie. Everyone has to work together.

LK: What's the biggest mistake that producers make?

BK: I think, as a producer, you're as good as your last film. It's all about execution and marketing. You'd better not have an ego as a producer. A producer on set is an oxymoron. Working behind the scenes is fine, but don't have an ego. Yet, some of the best producers do have really big egos.

LK: How do you become a producer?

BK: The people closest to pop culture are younger, so if you're trying to break in, guys like me are looking for an education on what's going on in your life. And with IMDB, things are much easier, because anyone can search and contact a producer to offer his/her services.

I guess Brad doesn't think IMDB is "ass." Apparently, it has other uses. Brad's interview also shows how much time and hard work go into developing a big-time movie. Calling Sweden, making deals for German TV stars in order to advance a film, attending Hollywood networking events in order to connect with Michael Eisner—this is full-time work. I hate that shit. I remember when Oliver Stone and I were just starting out, how he and his then-wife Najwa would be out every night at parties, discos, clubs and trendy restaurants. He would call this "work." I didn't get it. To me, this was just the kind of frivolous jet-setting waste of time I hated. I'd prefer to go to the Thalia Cinema in New York City and see John Ford's *The Searchers* or *Cheyenne Autumn*—boy, was I wrong. Oliver's "work" paid off. The next thing I knew, he was getting an Oscar for best screenplay for *Midnight Express.* Reading my dog-eared copies of *Cahiers de Cinéma*[33] huddled under my covers at night,[34] I thought Oliver was out of his mind to think of partying until 4:00 a.m. as critical work, but it turned out that he knew what it took to make it in this business—he was further grounded than I was in that reality, that truth.

Speaking of truth, not too long ago, I went to my talented and prolific director/actor friend Robby Benson's[35] class at Tisch School

---

[33]*Cahiers du Cinéma* is the French magazine published by the Cinémathèque Française that propounded the auteur theory of filmmaking (i.e., that the film is the director's event: he or she must be in complete control). This philosophy formed the basis for my entire career and led to my becoming a crazed dictator on my movie sets.

[34]We didn't have Internet porn in those days.

[35]Robby Benson is an actor who starred in *Ice Castles*, *Death Be Not Proud*, *Tribute* and many other films. He has written several screenplays and produced and directed *Modern Love*, starring Burt Reynolds, Carla DeVito and himself.

of the Arts at New York University (NYU) to speak to aspiring filmmakers. After I regaled Professor Benson's class with sophisticated, hi-tech behind-the-scenes how-to lessons in head crushings, car crashes and choreographing hard-bodied lesbians in unmentionable acts, Robby and I retired to his NYU office, where he paused a moment to reflect on my upcoming book. He reminded me that the most important thing we must do as producers is to tell the truth, no matter how brutal it is, and exercise good communication skills at all times.[36]

FIGURE 8.7 *Robby Benson in the film* One on One *(1977), which he also co – wrote at the age of 17.*

It's important to tell the people who are working for you whatever the particular truth of reality may be, as early in the game as possible. For example, says Robby Benson, the worst thing a producer can do is turn around at 11:49 p.m. and surprise a director by stating, "We're pulling the plug in five minutes," and then, when asked "Why?" respond with "Because we had to be out of here at 11:00!" Robby also talked about the importance of the screenplay: "It used to be that if you sent a script to the studio, they would want it to grab their attention in the first 15 pages. Then it was

---

[36] I, too, am good at telling the brutal truth, but it almost always results in a brutal punch to my face.

the first 10 pages. Now it's on the first page. And you have to have a story to back up the attention-grabbing moment. You need some sort of great obsession and a great psychological battle. In most movies, there's always an apparent defeat and then a renewal of hope and then you follow the journey of whether or not the characters are going to come out on top." Larry Cohen, Mark Neveldine and Brian Taylor share Robby's belief in the power of the written word in getting you the opportunity to work with large movie studios.

FIGURE 8.8 *Robby Benson (left) and Jack Lemmon (right) on the set of* Tribute, *circa 1980.*

FIGURE 8.9 *Robby Benson in the film* Lucky Lady *(1975), in which he starred alongside Gene Hackman, Liza Minnelli and Burt Reynolds!*

THE WAY IN: HIGH-VOLTAGE WISDOM FROM MARK NEVELDINE AND BRIAN TAYLOR WHILE LARRY COHEN SAYS "GOD TOLD ME TO WRITE A GREAT SCRIPT"

WHO IS LARRY COHEN?

Larry Cohen is a prominent Hollywood producer, director, and screenwriter of such movies as Q: The Winged Serpent, Bone, God Told Me To, Phone Booth *and the* It's Alive *trilogy.*

BT: Here's the really important thing: you need to have a script, you need to write. You need to have a complete script, so get out there and just write, find the story that you love and just write it. That's the most important thing.

LK: Do the studios interfere with you creatively?

MN: The more money you have, the more they want to get involved. But the fact is that they help you out—they give you money to make your movie. You sometimes have to battle them to make the movie you want to make. You have to be tough; you have to be thick-skinned with the studio.

LK: How about with *Crank 2: High Voltage*? You seemed to have been able to do whatever you want.

MN: We were smart with *Crank 2*, in that we did not ask for a big budget. We had a budget that was very similar to the first *Crank* and we did that specifically so that we could make our own damn movie. We even could risk putting Lloyd Kaufman in the film![37]

LK: So Larry, what advice would you give a young up-and-coming filmmaker who wants to produce his or her own film?

LC: If you want to produce your own film, don't let anyone talk you out of it. Just do it. Equipment is so light and so easy to acquire and you can produce a movie with a skeleton crew, so there's almost no excuse not to make your movie. If you're not making one with SAG performers, and there are plenty of talented crew and actors who are not in the guilds, you don't have to pay union wages. There is a high probability that your film will not get distributed, but you can always hope for the best and you'll have the experience of producing the picture.

---

[37] I play a power plant worker in *Crank 2: High Voltage*. My line of dialogue, "Better call 911," is destined to replace *Night of the Living Dead*'s "They're coming to get you, Barbara" as cult cinema's most memorable line.

If you make an unusually good movie, then it will get distributed and it will get seen. It's entirely up to the talented people—or the untalented people—who are going to make the film. The most important thing to do is to get a good script. Going out and shooting something that isn't any good to begin with will get you nowhere. You have to have a good story, you have to have good characters, and you have to have good actors to bring those characters to life. There's no sense in going through all the trouble to go out there and shoot something that you know from the beginning is not right and not good. So, get the script ready, because if it isn't on the page, it's not going to appear on the screen. Some magical element isn't going to turn a bad script into a good movie.

A movie is like a building. The architect has to lay out a blueprint, and that blueprint has to work. Otherwise, the movie will collapse. The basic plot and characters and development have to go somewhere. I also suggest that producers, if they can avoid it, not make movies so depressing and so debilitating that it becomes agonizing to watch them. Too many movies are downers with little or no real commercial potential. You don't have to make *Spiderman*, but you can certainly make some kind of a story that has some commercial appeal, if you want people to see it. You need to have to have a good concept and a good execution of that concept. Take your time and don't rush to go out and shoot just anything. Make sure you know where the film is going and how it will be edited together.

A lot of people start producing a picture, and then run out of money to shoot the ending. So sometimes the last part of the film is rushed or undercovered. Always shoot the ending toward the beginning of the shoot,[38] when you still have a lot of money left and everyone is still fresh and energetic. If you wait until they end, you may be desperate. People always remember a movie when they walk out of the theater by the last 10 or 15 minutes of it. You can have a great beginning and a great middle, but if the ending is lousy, they think of it as a lousy movie. If you have a mediocre middle, you should have a good beginning, because you have to hook people and make them watch the picture. If you have to compromise anywhere, do it somewhere around the middle, and try and make it as short as possible and get onto the final climax of the picture and make that look terrific. People will walk out of the screening room or the theater and respond to what they saw in the last fifteen minutes of the picture and say "That was terrific!" You should spend your effort making the ending even stronger than the beginning.

---

[38]Trey Parker did this on *Orgasmo*. He shot the last scene with my part on the first day. I don't do this. I shoot in sequence. But I am fucked.

LK: Have you ever come up against the studio? Have they wanted to cast somebody else?

BT: People complain about the studio, but they're giving you money to make the film. So if you don't want to deal with collaborating or working with them, don't make studio movies. It's really simple, it's like any other business. I really don't know why studios are demonized—there are a lot of really smart people that work at studios and there are a lot of really dumb people that work at studios. It's like any other line of work. You've got to try to work with the smart ones. We've been pretty lucky so far. If you don't want to deal with that, then be an independent and don't work with the studios. They're spending hundreds of millions of dollars to produce your damn movie. So they're going to have a say—why shouldn't they? It's their money. If you don't want them to have a say, then just do it the Lloyd Kaufman way. That's great, too![39]

Man, all the great advice and illuminating anecdotes from James, Caroline, Mark, Brian, Jay, Larry, Robby, Buddy, Avi and Brad are great! Their wealth of different experiences are all so valuable to producers, young and old![40]

Right now, dear reader, you may be saying to yourself, "Boy, did Lloyd blow it—these guys are all megasuccesses. Lloyd eats at IHOP and sleeps in Motel 6. He can't sit through meetings, he's getting old and he's economically black-listed. He'll never make it into the mainstream even if he wanted to. It's over for him!" Well, as I said back at the beginning of this chapter, when I began my career long ago, I did go to meetings with a great agent, Jim Maloney, but I always had a very empty, unsatisfied feeling. Around 1972, after numerous useless hours spent in waiting rooms, restaurants and trendy hotel bars frequented by studio executives, and repeated incidents of sweat-stained bar mitzvah suits and swamp ass, (as detailed earlier), I decided just to produce movies and not to waste time on anything else. Well, I did get married and have kids. But I never again wasted time trying to "pitch projects" to studio personnel. Now, after 40 years, they are finally coming to me!

---

[39]FOOTNOTE GUY: Hey! IG! Are you thinking what I'm thinking?!*

*INDEX GYNO: I think so, FG. Let's blow this book and go. . .produce. . .our own. . .damn but very tiny movie!

[40]Not to mention the wealth of their bank accounts.

The mountain comes to TroMa-ohammed. I do not remember the last time I had swamp ass on the soft couch of a Hollywood studio bigwig, but recently, the big-time guys are starting to visit the capital of swamp ass—the Troma Building in Long Island City, New York. Mainstream producers have been trekking to our dump to ask for remake rights to our films, and they have actually paid us some serious moolah for Charles Kaufman's *Mother's Day* and *The Toxic Avenger*! Not only that, but there are producers out there who want to remake *Class of Nuke 'Em High*, *Sargeant Kabukiman NYPD* and *Poultrygeist, Night of the Chicken Dead.* I know that there is a lesson here, but I do not know what it is—other than the Hollywood big shots are out of ideas.

Perhaps because Troma's visionary, now classic productions have been under-utilized due to economic blacklisting, the mainstream cartel can make some serious loot by remaking them. Or maybe it's just because I have great ideas and come up with great stories, but produce and direct crappy films, that the big-time producers are eager to turn my chicken shit into chicken salad! No, goddammit, I make *great* films—and that is exactly why the big boys finally want to play with us after 35 years of Troma![41] I am the herpes of the film industry; I won't go away!

But I think I am all Hollywood-ed out for now. I'm also wondering what's in store next in this crazy movie-producing world? What do we have to look forward to? Marianne Williamson tells us the answer lies within the question. All we have to do is ask it.

[41]INDEX GYNO: For many years, you've had to play with yourself, Lloyd, and you sure are good at it. I've looked up from down here to watch you during those moments of writer's block.

Frustrated in Frankfurt Asks Lloyd

Dear Lloyd,

What's the best way to get a crew together? Also, how do you handle problems with the crew? It's hard to pull rank without being an asshole, but sometimes it really seems necessary.

Sincerely,
Frustrated in Frankfurt

Dear Frustrated in Frankfurt,

I would like to begin by telling you how much I appreciate your city's invention of the hot dog. No one likes putting a small, moist, vegetarian sausage in a bun more than I do, and without the ingenuity of the people of Frankfurt, I wouldn't be able to say that without getting myself in trouble. So thanks.

Now, if you're interested in learning how not to be an asshole on your film set, my advice would be to read someone else's book. Because, as you would know if you had read my other books, watched any of my "behind-the-scenes" documentaries about films, or spoken to anyone who knows me, I am, in fact, a giant asshole. Some who have worked under my producership suggest I might even go so far as to be a giant hemorrhoid-filled anus.

However, I have found that—in addition to being an asshole—guilt trips are also very effective. Tell your crew that this movie is the last one you may ever make and if it doesn't get made on time and on budget, you'll blow your fucking brains out.[1] They

[1] See *Terror Firmer* for several effective variations of the phrase "I'll blow my fucking brains out." Sometimes I like to scream the words aggressively, whereas sometimes I like to throw in some quiet weeping. See what works for you!

may be willing to skip a cigarette break and get the movie made on time. Or, they may think you're an asshole and they'll actually want you to blow your brains out. It's a catch-22.

Good luck. Please review this book on Amazon!

XOXO,
Lloyd

Chapter | nine

Face the Music: Post-production and Distribution *or* Pump Up Your Production to a Higher Level

INTERNET: A global network of interconnected computers that enables users to share information among multiple channels. The Internet is a great tool for producers! Through web browsers, computers give us wonderful things like e-mail and social networking sites such as Facebook or MySpace. Even some-one as technologically agnostic as I am is on Twitter. Sites like Redtube.com and YouPorn.com . . . er, Craigslist.org and Mandy.com... can relieve a lot of the stress of finding a cast and crew who will work for little or no pay. The Internet is also a great way to market your production[2]!

Synonyms: World Wide Web, the Net, Porn Superhighway

Example: "Mom asked if the Internet is open on Sundays."

It's Monday, April 20th, Hitler's birthday (oof! gotta remember to bring flowers home), and I'm stuck on a subway train headed to the Troma Building in beautiful downtown Long Island City, stalled on the tracks and going nowhere for no apparent reason. In an effort to quell my rising impatience, I repeat my mantras[3] and take in my surroundings. I can't help but notice the huge book advertisement (complete with a photo of four pimped-out pastel-zoot-suit-wearing gentlemen) posted above the doors on that N train:

> Single Husbands *by Mary Honey Morrison*
> "Publishers Weekly[4] *says Morrison certainly knows her way around the bedroom."*
> *Warning! Adult fiction!*

WOW. Produce your own damn sex book, I thought. Someone had poured some hefty advertising bucks into *Single Husbands*. I started thinking that maybe Troma should have peppered the NYC subway cars with posters about single chicken zombies. But then the mothers of small children (not to mention single husbands) probably would've cried "Fowl."

I glanced at my watch. I was going to be late for my interview with *The New York Times*. It was ostensibly about the upcoming

---

[2]See the upcoming *Distribute Your Own Damn Movie!*, published by Focal Press and edited by Elinor Actipis.

[3]My favorite mantra is the one Marianne taught me: "Our deepest fear is not that we are inadequate. Our deepest fear is that we are powerful beyond measure." I've morphed this to better suit my beliefs: "I am as powerful as the Toxic Avenger."

[4]FOOTNOTE GUY: What is *Publisher's Weekly*?*

*INDEX GYNO: Who cares?**

**LLOYD'S RESPONSE: *Publisher's Weekly* sure didn't write about *Direct Your Own Damn Movie*. Maybe if I . . . er . . . Louis Su had written the novel *The Newcomers*, *Publisher's Weekly* would have written about it: "Louis Su sure knows his way around the bed."

premiere of *The Toxic Avenger Musical* off-Broadway and my book signing for *Direct Your Own Damn Movie!* at the Strand Bookstore in Union Square the following evening. My cell phone rang. Due to the glare of the sun, I couldn't see who was calling. So I took a chance and answered:

"Hello?"

"Guess what?" I heard the familiar voice of my better half.

"Pattie-Pie! What? Guess what? What am I guessing?"

"The opening night movie at this year's Cannes Film Festival."

"OK, you stumped me. What's the title?"

"It's *Up*."

"I know they announced it and you got the news first, so what's it called?"

"*Up*! The movie is called *Up*."

"Oh, okay. *Up*?"

I drew a total blank.

"It's a big-budget animated Disney movie! Pixar made it. Whoops. I'm sorry, I've got to go take this other call, Lloyd, see you later, just called to wish you a great *New York Times* interview!"

"Bye!" I could barely eke out a farewell.

What is this world and crazy movie business coming to I wondered? Cannes,[5] the premiere film festival in the world, the most international one of them all, and they'd chosen a Disney animated film for their prestigious opening slot! Had they become so corporate? Was the economy so bad that Cannes couldn't even afford to invite human actors to walk the red carpet? I mused about this state of affairs as I began jogging through the streets of Queens to make it to the Troma office in time for the start of the interview. I started panting in the humidity of the spring rain.

Suddenly, my ass buzzed.

---

[5]The Cannes Film Festival is where Billy Baxter* would introduce me to Robert Altman and other stars. Billy and I would get drunk, he'd get into a fistfight, and I'd get into a hooker and get V.D. The festival is where I met Rossellini, Goddard, Chabrol and John Wayne Bobbitt.

*Billy "Silver Dollar" Baxter, a larger-than-life character, directed the documentary *Diary of the Cannes Film Festival* starring Rex Reed. Billy was infamous for both his generosity and his outrageousness; he got his nickname from the American silver dollars he bestowed as tips during the festival. He arrived at Cannes with 2,000 of them, which he had to ship ahead of time. As Roger Ebert said, "Billy Baxter was the epicenter of the festival for many people. His gift was that he cut through the crap."

Ahhhh, I thought. That feels good. D'oh! I pulled out my vibrating BlackBerry from my back pocket and squinted at a text message from Evan as I kept jogging to get to the interview in time: "Office is PAST Crescent Street." Dammit. Apparently the whole Troma staff knows I can't always find my way to work in Long Island City.[6]

I looked up. Up! "Heh-heh," I said weakly, under my breath. No Disney pun intended. The sign read "Crescent Street." I was in luck. My watch said 11:38 a.m. and the interview was in seven minutes. I was just going to make it.

I hurried up the stairs double-time and Matt handed me the phone with the journalist on the other end. "Is this Lloyd Kaufman?"

"Yes!" I said, breathlessly. "This *is* Lloyd Kaufman.

"Well," the voice from the *Times* asked, "Tell me more about you and *The Toxic Avenger Musical*!"

The interview went on and on and was a great success, at least from my vantage point.[7] Just as I hung up the phone, I knocked over yesterday's cup of tea. While hurriedly cleaning my incredibly messy desk[8] and digging down through layers of paper to wipe up all of the liquid, I discovered a letter with another, older distinct brown tea ring adorning it, hidden under piles of pieces of unopened mail and junk postmarked several days earlier. It's a good thing I am a klutz and spilled the tea, or I never would have come across this letter!

The return address was marked "The White House." Holy shit! President Barack Obama was sending *me* a letter?! Had he gotten *my* letter, I wondered? Had he actually read it? I tore open the envelope, half in eager anticipation, half in disbelief:

---

[6] I grew up in Manhattan, which has an idiot-proof grid of street numbers so you can't get lost. Long Island City is the opposite!

[7] An impressive article about *The Toxic Avenger Musical* did run. It took up a half-page of the Sunday Arts & Leisure section. Nowhere did it mention Lloyd Kaufman or Troma!

[8] My desk is piled high with useless stuff—old papers, food, collectibles that fans send, Troma special effects props, books, scripts and more. It looks like a 14-year-old boy's bedroom.

THE WHITE HOUSE
WASHINGTON, D.C.

March 27, 2009

Lloyd Kaufman
Troma Entertainment
36-40 11th Street
Long Island City, NY 11106

Dear Mr. Kaufman,

Thank you for your letter and for making time in your busy day to write to me about your concerns facing young producers and young Americans. As president of the United States, it is my hope that we can begin to address the needs of the "little guy/gyno" in all industries, so that your voices are not stifled. My administration wants to provide a safe haven in this country from which to create and view art.

Following your visionary example, Lloyd (I think we're both cool enough to address each other on a first-name basis), I myself have done my best to make use of modern-day technology to communicate to the nation. I take pride in updating my Facebook status and choosing my brackets for March Madness online. But most of all, I am proud that the Executive Branch has gotten behind me in producing my own damn presidential addresses via YouTube.

I've given a lot of thought to your situation, Lloyd, and I think that other young[9] producers will make use of this wonderful platform as well, for there is still so much unexplored territory. You should encourage them. Independent artists look to you to lead the way. You are my favorite film director. You are so hot. You could turn me to that love that darest not speak its name.[10]

---

[9]HA HA HA! The Prez thinks I am young!

[10]EDITOR'S NOTE: Oy vey, Lloyd, times 10. You will burn in hell for this.

Thank you for the tickets to the premiere of *The Toxic Avenger Musical*. Michelle and I would love to attend the show (especially because of our interest in all things ecologically enlightening), but we will probably be wiped out completing our first 100 days in office in only 72 days. They also just told me that The Beast[11] would have trouble navigating Manhattan streets (not to mention all the comp tickets your producer would have to offer my Secret Service boys and gynos). I will, however, make sure that Air Force One and an F-14 buzzes around Manhattan, the Statue of Liberty, and Ground Zero to promote *The Toxic Avenger* Musical. Aretha Franklin dared me.

Thank you as well for the *Poultrygeist* DVD. It is an egg-cellent flick. We were hoping to share it with Sasha and Malia when they turn ~~18~~ 38, but we lent it to Hillary and she refuses to return it.

See you on Twitter. Please follow me.

Respectfully,

Barack H. Obama
President of the United States

P.S. As a fellow brother, I am happy to hear that you, Lloyd, who were raised as a poor black dirt farmer, have come so far with your life.

P.P.S. Although I am the coolest president ever, I think your use of the term "butt fucking" was inappropriate in a letter to the President. Next time, I suggest you use the more politically correct phrase "ass pirate."

Well, that was really nice of President Obama to take time to write me back! He was right. I need to encourage young producers to use all media, and especially the Internet.

Troma's had enormous success with promoting our movies online. And thanks to YouTube, I've been delivering my own damn chairman (of IFTA) address direct to people's computer screens,

[11]The Beast is President Obama's extremely secure, souped-up vehicle.

defining media consolidation and doing my damnedest to stop the homogenization and suppression of independent art by the vertically integrated media conglomerates!

Thanks to the Internet, short-form entertainment is staging a big comeback. So maybe you can produce your own damn short film, post it on YouTube, get a million views and attract the attention of mainstream producers who are scouring the Internet looking for talent. Years ago, Trey Parker and Matt Stone used an ingenious viral method of getting a production deal for the *South Park* TV series before the Internet became the Internet. When Trey and Matt were trying to get a producing deal for *South Park,* they told me they sent about 800 copies of their home-made pilot for *South Park* to those they considered powerful people in the Hollywood media industry. They did this anonymously. Soon, there was a big buzz about this mysterious, hilarious, primitive-looking, cut-out-style cartoon called "Spirit of Christmas." The result was that Trey and Matt got to produce their own damn animated Comedy Central smash hit series.

We can view movies these days on screens no larger than 2 inches wide by 2 inches tall. Maybe you can tell stories in three-minute episodes, then edit and upload them to the Net. Once something goes viral, it has the potential to receive hundreds, thousands, even millions of views. Your independent production can live on through the Web and you may develop a following or, like me, a loyal collection of fans.[12] At Troma, we have created many shorts and put them on the Internet to entertain as well as to call attention to our many feature-length movies.

The music video is another short form that can help you work your way up to producing feature films. The music video is really a kind of mini-movie in itself—a showcase for your talent. The first music video I directed was for the Luna Chicks. One of the Luna Chicks acted in *Terror Firmer* and her record company thought that if my name was on the music video as director, their song "Say What You Mean" would get on MTV. In 1999, MTV was still a big deal. Nowadays, no one even really cares about MTV, a television station on which very little, if any, actual music is played. But now bands produce those videos and put them up on YouTube. If you direct one, anyone and everyone can go and view your work.

[12]Not just fans, but air conditioners, too.

And, most important, except for nudity, there is virtually no censorship, as there is on TV. I've produced/directed[13] videos for Not the Government, Entombed, Korable, Purple Pam, Dingelberry Dynasty, Faggot, Municipal Waste, New Found Glory and others. Some made it to TV, and they're all on YouTube. All I have been asking is that bands allow me to shoot their clips on some form of celluloid,[14] which I know doesn't sound very high-tech. So I'm old-fashioned. I like the texture of film! Nobody's perfect![15]

FIGURE 9.2 *Night Flight Comics in Salt Lake City, winner of the Will Eisner (the equivalent of an Oscar in comic-book land), is a 10-year sponsor of the TromaDance Film Festival. The fourth Jonas brother is pictured far left.*

JOE LYNCH LIKES MAKIN' MUSIC (VIDEOS)

WHO IS JOE LYNCH?

BY JOE LYNCH

Joe Lynch is a producer/director who got his start at Troma as a grip[16] and background actor on Terror Firmer *and worked his way up to 2nd unit director (an arduous task involving the careful choreography of hundreds of unpaid background actor persons on any Troma set) and Troma staff writer. An avid horror*

---

[13]I usually do not get paid. I do it because the band's music and enthusiasm move me. If the band is rich, like Municipal Waste and New Found Glory are, then I get paid.

[14]The Faggot video was shot on Super 8mm, which did not cost much and looks cool!

[15]I am sure that I'll be directing music videos on some kind of digital format soon, however. I am really starting to like the new video cameras! ...and they seem to like me, too!

[16]A "grip" refers to the guy or gyno who moves things on a set like a camera, lights, cables, his bowels, etc. There were only two grips on the set of *Terror Firmer*. "Grip" is not to be confused with "gripe," of which there were many on the set of *Terror Firmer*.

film fan, he went on to direct music videos and made his directorial feature film debut with Wrong Turn 2. *Like Gabe Friedman, he now works for G4, an American cable and satellite television channel geared toward male viewers aged 12–28 and devoted to the gaming and technology world. G4 has televised many a Troma movie. He will be directing his next film in New York City and plans to give me an acting role.*

Fox saw a music video I had done that cost me literally $1K, for a band called Strapping Young Lad, where I took the band and I put them in *Evil Dead*,[17] because *Evil Dead* is one of my favorite horror movies[18] and the singer and I shared a mutual love for that film—I said to him, "What if we put you in the house from *Evil Dead*?" Long story short, they liked it, we did it and it was a big hit on *Headbanger's Ball* and the guys at Fox saw it and said, "Hmm, he must know about horror movies," and based on that, they offered me the opportunity to direct *Wrong Turn 2*.

What I did was over-prepare in my presentation pitch to the studio—and this is something I recommend to every filmmaker—you can never be too prepared for anything, I don't care if anybody says, "You don't need to bring anything except your enthusiasm." Fuck that nonsense. Go in with storyboards, a trailer, have the whole movie cut in your head. I went in there and had storyboards for the first scene of *Wrong Turn 2* and I mean literally had them all nicely boarded and everything and they were like, "Whoa, holy shit, we had no clue you were going to be this prepared for it." I was communicating just how passionate I was about making the movie. They later admitted, "Boy, we took a real risk with you." But when they saw the movie, they were really happy with it.

I've done about twelve music videos now, and believe me, I wish I could do more. I love the music video form, I love taking visuals and music and putting them together. I did my first music video through Troma with this band called Godhead. They were featured on the *Terror Firmer* soundtrack. Lloyd said to me: "These guys want Troma to produce a video, can you direct it?" I said "Of course! I have Troma's two video cameras right here, why not?" and we ended up making a really sweet video for a total budget of $40 and I'm really proud of it. That video got me a bunch more videos. That's how it works.[19] A lot of

[17] *Evil Dead* (1981), one of the all-time scariest movies, was written and directed by Sam Raimi and starred Bruce Campbell, Ellen Sandweiss and Betsy Baker. *Evil Dead* is not to be confused with *Dead Evil: The Richard Nixon Story*.

[18] *Terror Firmer* is probably Joe's favorite film of all time, but it is not a horror movie.

[19] FOOTNOTE GUY: We started reading Marianne Williamson, too, Lloyd! She says that "Just as work begets work . . . "*

*INDEX GYNO: " . . . love begets love." This is our new philosophy in the production company we're forming. We are going to go out and produce our own damn tiny music video and put it here in the margins.**

**FOOTNOTE GUY: Of course that means there will only be room for a two-second song.

times, you have to be your own producer on those projects. I had to set up my own company to produce my music videos, because I didn't have anyone else to back me. I would just have these bands that came to me saying, "We loved that metal show you did, can you do a video for us?" or "Hey, I liked that video you produced for Troma, can you produce one for us?" It was a snowball effect.

I was my own manager, I was my own producer, I was my own director, I was my own editor—I did it all. My wife was my DP. It was those projects that allowed me to really hone my craft in editing, in shooting, and *especially* producing. When you're given a budget and told "Here's when it's due," that's it. That's all you get from the studio or the label. You have to create content out of thin air. That's where being a producer is key. That's when you sit there and say to yourself, "Okay, I need to solidify my contract, deal with the insurance forms, take care of all the details." And knowing how to do all that is so essential, because then when someone tells you, "No, that's not possible," you already know the process. You can tell them, "Fuck you, yes I can!"[20] I've been doing those videos for eight or nine years now and they feel like short film productions to me. That's because I was involved in every single part of the process from writing all the way down through the moment I delivered the tape to the label. I know how to make it all work. And that is how I know how to produce.

I made a *right turn* working for Troma and ended up with Fox's *Wrong Turn 2*!

Moviemaking in the 21st century has become something that is utterly extraordinary. The availability of high quality high-def equipment at relatively inexpensive prices (compared to that of film and 35mm cameras), coupled with the immediacy of the Internet, is creating a tidal wave of new creativity. It is my hope that this tidal wave becomes a tsunami of brilliant creative producing that floods this big blue marble of ours with its diversity. Now, finally, we can all go out and produce our own damn movies, totally in control of our own content! When I started in the business 40 years ago, hardly anyone could produce his, her or its own damn movie. It was too damn expensive. Remember way back in this book how I talked about how my film *Battle of Love's Return* made in 1970 cost $8K? That was a rock-bottom budget then. But $8K in 1970 dollars

[20]It is a little known fact that while running for president, Barack Obama borrowed Joe Lynch's now-famous slogan and modified it to "Yes we can!"

would be equal to over $100K today, taking into account inflation, and *Battle of Love's Return* was technically ass. Not many people have $100K today to blow on their first movie! So, how nice that you can use a $500 HD camera from Best Buy, along with your computer to produce a movie that looks 10,000 times better than *Battle of Love's Return* for practically nothing! Also, had I had access to the Internet's Mandy.com or Craigslist.org in 1970, I could have assembled a much better cast and crew and, again, using the Internet, maybe even found some free "production stress-reducing clips" instead of having to use my very expensive (in those days) *Penthouse* magazines.

Today, there is a ready, willing and able audience available to you on the Internet—you can reach Mumbai, India; Adelaide, Australia; Okinawa, Japan; and all the little towns and villages in between. People don't need to haul their asses to a movie theatre or a video rental store—the DVDs get mailed to your house or the movie will be on the Internet or some "On Demand" cable channel pretty soon. Why shell out $12.50 (the cost of one movie ticket in most New York City movie theatres) when there's plenty of untapped entertainment just waiting for you at the tip of your fingers on any computer keyboard?

Moreover, this is a sound-byte culture. Anything Paris Hilton or the President says (usually in that order) is instantly broadcast, scrutinized and dissected around the world. Today, there is no "how to" holy grail for producing movies. We live in a world that is rapidly changing. I've been producing movies for more than 40 years and I have tried to change the way I work and adapt with the times. You, too, have to adapt and find your own way into this business, whether it's taking shitty jobs on other people's shitty movies or at other people's production companies, or skipping a liberal arts education and forking over the cash for some fancy film-school degree, or just going out with your own camera and peeps to produce a 3-minute "calling card"[21] movie. I just traveled to Bechtelsville, Pennsylvania to play a lawyer who gets disemboweled in Ted Moehring's giallo[22] feature film, *Bloodbath in the*

[21]A "calling card"* movie is usually a short one that is slick and is made to appeal to studio executives—much like the way a cheap piece of shiny metal will attract magpies.

*It is important to know that this type of calling card will not help you make a call to the studio that forgot to leave your pass at the gate and left you sweating in your bar mitzvah suit.

[22]*Giallo* means "yellow" in Italian and is a type of Italian film directed by folks like Lucio Fulci, Dario Argento and Mario Bava. *Giallo* films are based on crime detective novels printed with yellow covers. Not to be confused with Jello, a shimmering, wiggly dessert.

House of Knives. Ted has his own studio comprised of exactly three lights, a microphone, a boom pole and a Canon HD camera. The cost was under $2K for all of this, and he has been renting out the equipment to make back some of his investment. He needs nothing more. He can remain in Bechtelsville, Pennsylvania, wherever that is, and produce all his own damn movies. Also, he will use the Internet to promote his film to the many *giallo* fan sites, so he has a built-in audience. Because his entire production budget is also only $2K, Ted will distribute his own film himself over the Internet and at horror conventions and can probably make a profit.

THE DUPLASS BROTHERS SAY GO FOR THE VOLUME[23]

(And Neveldine and Taylor Interject)

DUPLASS BROTHERS: Producing movies is a complex piece of art creation that requires the synthesis of a lot of skills. We came of age as producer/filmmakers in Austin, Texas in the 1990s, a time when real indie film[24] was popular and abundant. A lot of our friends spent years and years raising money for their first feature that cost anywhere between $250K and $500K. It took five or six years to get the budget together, but in the meantime, they weren't practicing their craft. Then they'd make the movie and it wouldn't be that good. Why? Because they were practicing their fundraising, not their filmmaking. So our philosophy has always been to make cheap films and make a lot of them so that you can find your voice while you are producing them. That's what you did, Lloyd.

MARK NEVELDINE: Who cares if your fucking camera costs only $500?! Just start shooting.

BRIAN TAYLOR: What language!

MARK NEVELDINE: Young producers should get used to swearing.

DUPLASS BROTHERS: Eventually, you have to figure out what you can offer the world. While you are figuring out what your opus[25] is going to be, it's easy to make films with digital cameras and digital editing. It's easy to fail, but your mistakes are cheap and you learn from them.

---

[23]As in amount, not sound.

[24]What they mean is that the word "independent" has been hijacked and is used to describe $15 million dollar movies produced by members of Tom Hanks family or the like.

[25]An opus is usually a musical composition. In this case, it refers to your work, your movie in general. "Opus" is also occasionally effective as a noun and an insult as in, "You, opus!"

Back in the 1970s, it cost me about $500K to learn from my mistakes on *Battle of Love's Return*, *Sugar Cookies* and *Big Gus, What's the Fuss?* Today you can fuck things up like I did for less than 5 percent of that! Speaking of opii,[26] you're probably wondering what to do about getting a great music track for your own damn movie that you're producing. Because, let's face it: music for your film or viral movie or music video is crucial for the trajectory of the emotional arc you want your audience to travel. Maybe you think it's hopeless because you can't afford "great" music. Well, there are hundreds of thousands of musicians on MySpace and other sites who will let you hear their work and most likely be dying for you to give them exposure by using their songs in your movie. For free!

Also, there are the established mainstream rock bands that refuse to "sell out" or "go commercial." They like the idea of maintaining their "street cred" by allowing you to put their music in your flick. For example, Lemmy of the band Motörhead has generously donated not just his music but his amazing acting talents to more than one Troma movie because he believed in the Troma way of life (and he cracked after I called his cell phone 26 times over a three-day period).

Take *Poultrygeist* as another example. Being the musical extravaganza made for "chicken feed" that it was, Gabe Friedman and I had to write our own damn lyrics. But we needed someone to bring them to life. I put out an ad on the Internet asking for a composer seeking the acute privilege of scoring a Troma movie for no money whatsoever in exchange for a rockin' credit and incredible experience.[27] We were inundated with responses! Some were slackers, but many of the sincere responses came with great samples and compositions from talented musicians across the country and the continent. As it turned out, one of the best came from Edmonton, Canada, by way of Mr. Duggie Banas. Through the beauty of the Internet and modern technology, Duggie, Gabe Friedman and I were able to work intensively together over several months, honing and then recording the tracks until they were perfect. Duggie worked his Banas off! I didn't even meet *Poultrygeist*'s composer, film scorer

[26]Not to be confused with Opie, Ron Howard's character on the old TV show *Howdy Doody*, starring Harriet Tubman.

[27]The soundtracks to *Poultrygeist*, *Terror Firmer*, and *Citizen Toxie* are all available for purchase at Troma: http://www.troma.com: BUY TROMA!!!

and music producer in person until a *Poultrygeist* screening at a festival in Calgary, Canada, two years after Duggie and I had met on the Internet. After meeting him in person, I felt guilty that Duggie did so much hard work over so much time for free. So I sent him a big $100 dollars.

THANK YOU FOR THE MUSIC[28]

BY DENNIS DREITH

WHO IS DENNIS DREITH?

Dennis Dreith is a Los Angeles–based film composer, orchestrator, conductor and administrator of the Film Musicians Secondary Markets Fund. Dennis also wrote the score for the original Punisher *film and, more recently,* Gag, *produced by ex-Tromite Scott McKinley. He has been a loyal sponsor of the TromaDance Film Festival in Park City, Utah.*

I want to debunk some myths about music for independent films. First and foremost, it is important to state that there is no excuse for music to ever sound cheap, especially in low-budget films. Every film, no matter how modest it may be, deserves to have an original score that gives a voice to the film and defines the soul of its characters. I have heard many impressive temp scores utilizing cues edited from major motion picture scores. As remarkable as individual scenes are with these cues, taken as a whole, temp scores lack the coherence that an original score provides by connecting characters and plot elements with consistent musical themes.

Myth 1: *"I have so little money that I can't afford an original score, so I have to use library music."*

Although library music can provide what seems to be a cost-effective alternative to original scoring, if you are set on using library music, you need to resign yourself to the fact that the music you license is also available to everyone for any purpose. If you think it's OK that the music in the film you put your heart and soul into can (and will) be used in anything from a dog food commercial to a second-rate porn flick, then library music is fine for you. Don't get me wrong—there are valid uses for library music—but for the most part, it is for situations where the music is more like wallpaper, not necessarily needed to follow action or define characters.

[28]Not to be confused with the Abba song by the same name, as I'm not sure anyone can really properly *thank* Abba for their music.

Myth 2: "*An original score is too expensive.*"

Certainly, hiring an A-list composer, engaging hundreds of musicians and recording in a world-class scoring stage can all add up to a pretty high price tag. That's something that many (if not all) filmmakers aspire to. However, one has to ask first, "Is this something that is absolutely necessary for my film?" If it really is (and not just a whim), then by all means, go raise the money to do just that. I have worked on a number of big-budget films and can say that it is truly a rewarding and exhilarating experience to have your music performed by a world-class orchestra. However, I have also done a number of very small films with just a handful of wonderful musicians. Those were equally rewarding experiences. In some cases, they were even more rewarding because of the filmmakers' enthusiasm and creativity. I love the opportunity to create a memorable score with very few resources other than an active imagination and a willingness by everyone to experiment.

What makes music most important in a film is not the size of the orchestra, but how well-crafted the musical themes are and how well the music moves with action, how well it plays on/to the audience's emotions, or identifies the characters. Well-written music for a small ensemble can add to the richness of the tapestry of a film just as well as that of a large ensemble. At times, a solo instrument or intimate group, such as a string quartet, can provide even more emotional content that a full orchestra. Of course, there are times when the circumstances of a particular film require a more expansive, substantial score. When operating under budget constraints, these situations will offer greater challenges that require more than just creativity and planning. Though I don't wish to debate the pros and cons of union scoring (using members of the American Federation of Musicians under a union agreement), it is important to note that there have been many changes over the past few years within the union that allow low-budget and independent films to be scored for rates and under conditions commensurate with those budgets.

Myth 3: "*If I can't hire an orchestra, I can just simulate one with an electronic score.*"

Electronic scores can and do offer viable alternatives in the appropriate hands. What's true for an electronic score is true for any other score: a well-written score is still well-written, regardless of the performance medium or ensemble. Rather than simply replacing an orchestra, I have often found that by creatively using an arsenal of electronic equipment in combination with even just one solo instrument, or, if appropriate, a small ensemble, excellent results can be achieved.

Another tried and true technique is, if at all possible, to hire an orchestra (even a small one enhanced by electronics) for a single session to record the vital and most important cues or those cues requiring an orchestra. Then record the remainder of the cues with electronics and a soloist or, depending on the budget, a small ensemble.[29] By utilizing consistent themes, and having them played by various ensembles, you will be amazed how the score will seem larger than it really is.

Myth 4: "*It's a lot easier and cheaper to just use records instead of a score.*"

Sometimes it might be cheaper, but only if you are using obscure records, friends' records, or recordings of bands who are looking for exposure. They will allow the use of their music for little or no money. However, the first, and most important question is, "Does this recording serve the needs of the motion picture as well as an original score?" There are, of course, a number of circumstances in which records serve the needs of a film quite well. They can often define a period in time or a place in a unique manner. They can also paint an emotional picture in ways that are quite different than underscoring can.

However, the use of licensed music can be most problematic. A discussion of "master" and "synch license agreements" would be most helpful, but there isn't time. It is sufficient to say that before embarking on a course of placing records in your film, you should acquire a solid working knowledge of these costs and limitations.

Not securing the proper licensing agreements (which can cost next to nothing or much more than your entire production budget), could turn out to be a major stumbling block to securing distribution for your film. In some cases, it can result in an injunction prohibiting the exhibition of your film as long as the records in question are included in the film. There are numerous sources to assist in gaining the requisite information, including music supervisors, license experts, publishers and record companies, that can assist in securing the appropriate rights. It is important, however, not to include pre-existing material in a film without appropriate permission.

The bottom line is that a combination of songs and original scoring can tremendously enhance your film. Though I said it at the beginning, it bears repeating: there is no excuse for you to settle for anything except an excellent first-rate score.[30]

Chris Wyatt, who produced *Napoleon Dynamite,* told us at the Tromadance Film Festival a few years ago that due to his needing to save money, he licensed or acquired only "festival rights" for the music for his low-budget independent movie, *Napoleon Dynamite.*

[29]My homes Jenn Kuhn is a gorgeous, brilliant, and talented cellist who can do this . . . and act for you, too!

[30]Unless your name is Lloyd Kaufman.

So when Fox announced they were going to distribute *Napoleon Dynamite,* Chris had to go back to all the music publishers to license all of the other rights. Of course, when the music publishers discovered that a major studio was now involved, the greatest ass fucking since the classic film *Anal Lesbian Club Part XII* took place. Chris paid twice as much for music rights for his film score as the entire budget of *Napoleon Dynamite*: $800K, I believe.

And what about Nina Paley? She is a genius filmmaker who produced *Sita Sings the Blues*, the only animated movie entirely in Flash, as far as I know. She, too, has limited resources, so she decided to score her film with public domain music whose "sync" or publishing rights cost zilch. Unfortunately, Nina did not know that the "performance rights" of the folks performing the music were not public domain, and those singers, performers and musicians wanted to be paid. So far this has been a huge problem for Nina and has stood in the way of her making distribution deals.

Producing Lesson #9,572: Get *all* rights to any music that you use in your own damn production. For example, Lemmy and Motörhead gave us all rights in all media worldwide to the song *Sacrifice* used in *Tromeo & Juliet* . . . I hope.

Giuseppe Andrews composes all of his own damn music. Believe it or not, I used to do that, too. *For Battle of Love's Return* and *The Girl Who Returned,* I knew enough clarinet[31] to pick out the main melodic themes played throughout the course of the movie. As I made those movies during my time at Yale, we recorded the music in one of the piano rooms there in the Music Department using a reel-to-reel tape recorder and microphone. In *Sugar Cookies,* we worked with composer Gershon Kingsley, whose big claim to fame at that time was the Maxwell House coffee commercial jingle and a novelty song called "Popcorn." *Sugar Cookies* was one of the first movies to be scored entirely using a Moog synthesizer.[32] During an early scene within *Sugar Cookies,* Mary Woronov plunks out about five random notes on the piano. Gershon used those five notes as the theme to score the entire movie.

---

[31]Thanks, Mom.

[32]The Moog synthesizer is the first musical device to produce and mimic the sounds of various musical instruments *electronically*. It is also the reason the 1980s happened.

By the way, while you're producing your own damn movie music, you may have to write your own damn lyrics! That's what I did when I wrote the words to the top-20 hit song[33] "Big Gus, What's the Fuss?[34]" and "Have I Ever Let You Down?," both featured in *Sugar Cookies.*

EDITING AND POST-PRODUCTION: A TROMA FAN TEACHES YOU EVERYTHING YOU NEED TO KNOW ABOUT FREE SOFTWARE TO PRODUCE AND EDIT YOUR OWN DAMN MOVIE

BY DANIEL ARCHAMBEAULT-MAY

WHAT IS A TROMA FAN?

A Troma fan is brilliant, beautiful gyno or guy with a great passion for anything and everything Troma. Some fans pick Lloyd up at airports and drive him where he needs to go. Some let Lloyd sleep in their homes and eat their food. Some have tattoos of Toxie on their bodies. Some contribute money to the Tromadance Film Festival. Most important, they all spread the Troma love worldwide. A Troma fan can never get enough Troma. Aspiring filmmaker Daniel Archambeault-May is such an enlightened individual.

Software newsflash: in case it's not already clear from reading this book, nearly every aspect of film-making can now be done on computers. Writing, editing, optical effects, audio production and mastering, scoring your film and so on—it can now all be handled with the click of a mouse. Unfortunately, you need several thousand dollars to get all the software you need to do this. Well, I'm here to tell you that you can actually get all of that stuff for *free*!

For every piece of big-ticket software, there's a free or open source application that works just as well, if not better. For example, I'm writing this in OpenOffice.org (downloaded for free off the Internet!). And it's every bit as capable as the $300 name-brand application (by Microsoft). But it doesn't stop there. The entire process of making your own damn digital movie can be handled with free applications—and great ones, too. I won't mention anything here unless it's absolutely capable of professional quality work, and is 100 percent free.

[33]Top-20 list of obscure songs for movie flops.

[34]This song and its title were written and conceived a year before the vision for what became the Troma movie flop of the century (of the same name) happened.

To start your movie, you need a script. You could spend a handsome sum for a piece of software to properly format your screenplay, but you don't have to. Celtx is a full-featured preproduction suite that not only properly formats scripts for film, TV, theater, radio, and everything else, but also has built-in scheduling and storyboarding tools. This nifty piece of software will handle everything up to your first day of shooting. You haven't even started filming yet, and you've already saved a couple hundred bucks. Download it for free from *http://www.celtx.com.*

Who says mind-blowing CGI special effects are only for the big-budget studio blockbusters? Blender is a full-featured 3D modeling software that can more than hold its own. Aside from being used on *Spiderman 2*, it was also the force behind the entire CGI production of the independently made short *Elephants Dream.* Among its numerous abilities, Blender can function as a nonlinear editor. Get it without paying a dime from *http://www.blender.org.*

Now, you need to edit your feature film. That's where things get a little trickier. Quality NLEs are few and far between in the open source world, but you aren't without options. Applications like Avidemux and Kino can handle most simpler productions. So can the aforementioned Blender. If you just need to cut and paste together your talking-heads drama, these will do the job. If you need something more, with lots of effects and compositing, Cinelerra is the way to go. Its interface is horsey[35] to work with at times, but it is a very powerful piece of software, and won't leave you wanting anything but an easier interface. Visit *http://www.cinelerra.org.*

For the final touches on your film, you can use what Hollywood uses: CinePaint. CinePaint allows you to retouch your movie frame by frame without degradation of quality. It's the go-to-program for the majors as well—it was used for *Spiderman, Harry Potter and the Philosopher's Stone, The Last Samurai* and *Stuart Little*, to name only a few. CinePaint can be downloaded for free from *http://www.cinepaint.org.*

Audio will make or break your movie. Luckily, audio is where free software really shines. Ardour is the best in the business, in my humble opinion. You can record, rerecord, layer, add music, and anything else that can be considered audio production. Go to: *http://www.ardour.org.* If it's not available for your platform, Audacity will also work wonderfully. Get it from *http://audacity.sourceforge.net.*

Burn your finished flick to DVD using DeVeDe, make up some cover art and posters in GIMP or Inkscape, and call it a wrap. All can be found at *http://www.majorsilence.com/devede, http://www.gimp.org* and *http://www.inkscape.org.*

Some of these applications may not work on all platforms. I recommend using Linux (specifically, "Ubuntu Studio"), or a Mac with X11 installed. If

[35]So it seems is the smile of Julia Roberts.

you're attached to Windows, some of these will work there, too. But if not, you can always dual-boot from a Mac. There's a plethora of great software out there that I didn't even mention. All you have to do is look around for it.

If you like the big-money software, by all means, use it. It's great stuff. But don't let not having enough money for a specific application stand between you and producing your own damn movie.

FIGURE 9.3 LK is not a fan of CGI, preferring old school make-up special effects, exemplified here in a publicity still from *Tromeo & Juliet*.

Thanks, Daniel, for all those great tips, however, I am old-fashioned (or just plain old, if you will) and Troma pioneered many ingenious ways of saving money producing on celluloid. By serving as Producer, Director and Writer, we produced *The Toxic Avenger* (1982) and *Poultrygeist* (2005) for the same amount of dollars (around $500K), which meant that my fowl production, made 16 years later, taking into account inflation, actually costs only about 25 percent of what *The Toxic Avenger* cost. Mainstream budgets skyrocketed in the span of those 16 years.[36] The average mainstream movie is now $80,000,000, plus another $80,000,000 for distribution! Holy shit!

[36]INDEX GYNO: Lloyd never was very good at math. It's actually 25 years. So *Poultrygeist*, using 1982 dollars, cost about 15% of *The Toxic Avenger*.

$160 million dollars spent on one piece of celluloid fluff! Yikes! I wonder how the good folks of Darfur feel about that. Now let's get back to reality and hear from Herschell Gordon Lewis, a man who's been there and done that too—since 1960!

HERSCHELL GORDON LEWIS SAYS "DISTRIBUTION, DISTRIBUTION, DISTRIBUTION"

WHO IS HERSCHELL GORDON LEWIS?

Herschell Gordon Lewis is a producer/director who has been previously anointed the "Godfather of Gore" for being a pioneer in horror and exploitation films. Some of his most popular films include Blood Feast, *widely considered to be the first gore film,* Monster a Go-Go, *and* The Gore Gore Girls *(my personal favorite of his). Lewis has also written 31 books (mostly on the arts of advertising and marketing), some of which include* Effective E-mail Marketing: The Complete Guide to Creating Successful Campaigns *and* Open Me Now: Direct Mail Envelopes that Work . . . and Those That Don't. *Herschell was the first director to show dead people on the screen with their eyes open.*[37]

If you want to be a producer, before you begin producing, make contact with a distributor of motion pictures who distributes either to DVD outfits or movie theatres and have a solid business-like conversation—not a "Golly gee willikers!" chat, but a solid discussion of the reality, saying, "Here is my situation, Mr. Distributor. I want to make a movie, not because I am simply dazzled by the glamour of the motion picture industry, but because I think that is a profitable way to proceed. Your company has distributed movies of this type and shown that they can be profitable. Here's what I have in mind and I would like your opinion. Ultimately, I would like more then your blessing, I would like your involvement. But I would certainly cherish and benefit from anything you might tell me what will help me get this project off the ground."

When someone in our business hears sincerity, backed by some degree of talent and business acumen, that person will react to it. Lloyd and I and everyone else who do this are constantly approached by people who want to produce movies. Why do they want to do this? If you penetrate down to the nasty core of reality, they want to produce a movie because they want to produce a movie. It is just that simple.

---

[37] A concept that he originated and is still used today by most of the U.S. Congress.

[38] INDEX GYNO: You've not quite mastered that, Lloyd.

A good producer has characteristics that run parallel to those of a good executive:

1. A good producer leaves his ego at the door and is not afraid to delegate responsibility.
2. A good producer is not afraid to give compliments as well as insults.[38]
3. A good producer sets realistic goals, not pie-in-the-sky goals. That realism doesn't come from guesswork but from a knowledge of what he or she is going to do. Hence, think marketing and distribution way up front, Mr. Producer!
4. A good producer has to have a sense of humor and be reasonably unflappable in case disaster strikes. I don't care what you are shooting, how low or how high the budget is, how much help you have or don't have: something is going to happen that represents a minor catastrophe.
5. A good producer should treat himself/herself as part of a team. Problems will occur, almost always, over money—not over amount of screen time or lines of dialogue, but money. You have to understand that when you go in. A producer's function is to understand exactly how much money each person is getting paid, how much each location is going to cost, who is responsible for what and who gets what.
6. Finish strong. Pretend that you are not someone who is producing a movie, but just a person who is watching someone else's movie. Be heartless in your analysis of what you see at the tail end of the film. You've got to have a good ending. In our business there is no sin more cardinal then a half-finished picture. If you're not going to make it at all, there is no harm done. If you can't put your deal together, there is no harm done. But if you have it halfway done and you're afraid, so you stop and you think you'll never get it done, that's a big mistake. I've seen that so often: someone will start a picture, then they'll run out of money, or they'll run out of ideas, or the cast leaves, something happens, and what have you got? Nothing.

FIGURE 9.4 *Little Shop of Horrors* plant (see background) about to attack LK and legendary producer Herschell Gordon Lewis.

FIGURE 9.5 Herschell Gordon Lewis and lovely focus puller watch LK's crappy acting on set of *Grim Fairy Tale*.

I just acted in Herschell's new film, *Grim Fairy Tale*. It looks as though this may be his supreme masterpiece. Herschell stresses that all of his movies are market-driven, but I believe that he is a true artist in spite of this approach. There is no way his soul is not in his films. In spite of his intellectual devotion to his production theory that it's about marketing, I believe that Herschell is a closet "to thine own self be true" artist.[39] I'm talking about the "auteur theory" (remember the footnote in Chapter 8?), which was that the filmmaker is the author of the film and the film produced should display what is truly in his heart—like Mark Harris, who described movies in Chapter 4 such as *Million Dollar Baby* and *Crash*. Herschell produces only what he believes in. But whereas Harris uses major stars to satisfy Herschell's marketing theory, Herschell uses genre elements to guarantee a market for his productions.

Look, I give major lip service to "producing what is in my soul." But I am always also thinking about answering the question, "Will my fans be pleased with what I am producing? Will *Poultrygeist* live up to the expectations of my fans?" I also make sure that because I can't give them big stars like Mark Harris does, I use slapstick social satire, sex and violence as my stars! So I am thinking "marketing" while I am producing "personal" films that I am 100 percent behind.

[39]FOOTNOTE GUY: Are you trying to say that Herschell a closet homosexual (just like you, Lloyd) or a closet Shakespeare scholar, unlike you?

FIGURE 9.6 *Independent producers are innovators. Herschell Gordon Lewis was one of the first producers to use the Red Camera, which replaces 35mm with a comparable—if not better—look.*

And speaking about getting 100 percent behind a project (and also having a nice behind), meet my friend Mark Damon. Mark is so much further up on the Hollywood A-list ladder than I will be, ever, that he has trouble finding me, and I need a telescope to see him—he is so high up! Mark knows what it means to really get 100 percent behind a film and how a major producer has to fight major battles.

DOING THE DISTRIBUTION DANCE

BY MARK DAMON

WHO IS MARK DAMON?

Mark Damon is a producer of such Hollywood films as The Upside of Anger, Beyond the Sea *and* Monster, *which won lead actress Charlize Theron a Golden Globe and an Oscar for her performance as real-life prostitute turned serial killer, Aileen Wuornos. He started as an actor in Italian productions and then switched to producing. Mark Damon is one of the premiere American independent producers.*

Every film is a fight. I don't think I've ever had a film that has been 100 percent smooth and that I didn't have to worry about.

For example, with *Monster*, I found the script, and I was convinced that the director, a first-time director, had the chops to make a good film. Because she had never directed before, I realized that she would depend on me very much. I worked with her for about three months on the script, and we were the ones who got Charlize interested in the picture. We had been casting for a while when I saw a picture called *Trapped*, in which Charlize did an incredible job. I said, "Why don't we try for her?" Of course we didn't have the money because the picture had only a $5 million dollar budget. So, we offered her $150K and a producer credit. She warmed to that idea and then became a real producer. I was really amazed at how much she really took over as a producer of the picture.

I had to go out and pre-sell many territories. But the subject matter was so difficult that it wasn't an easy pre-sell. So we basically funded the picture out of our own pocket because we couldn't depend on a bank giving us all the money. I made it a German co-production. Germany had nothing to do with the film, but I was able to get some tax-shelter funds there as we pieced together the financing. I said to myself, "If the picture doesn't work, at least I have a picture about a serial killer and it's a real story, so there'll be interest. I have a major star, an interesting love story, and enough video value to get out of the investment."

What I didn't count on was the fact that when the picture was finished, no studio wanted to touch it. Or, if they did consider the possibility of taking it, they wouldn't do so without a minimum guarantee. They also wanted it out the following year. I sat in the cutting room for about six months with this picture because I said if the studios didn't like it, there was something problematic about it.

I realized that maybe we were making the film too sympathetic to Aileen Wuornos, our serial killer protagonist. You couldn't embrace a character committing cold-blooded murder. I turned to our editor and director Patty Jenkins and said, "Remember, we have to walk a very fine line. Empathize, but not sympathize. Try to understand what she did, but don't like her for it." Only in following that line, navigating that delicate balance, did it work. It finally made the picture acceptable. When we finished the picture, I said, "This is about as good as it can get. Let's now try to make a distribution deal." Everyone said, "Put it out next year, let it run the festival circuit. Sundance, whatever. Hope it picks up enough buzz." And I said, "No way. Right now there is a big buzz on the picture. If you wait another year, this will be old news. The picture will be stale, there'll be a backlash and we'll never get it."

So nobody would distribute the picture. We dipped into our own pockets, we independents, and put up $3 million just to launch the picture, get a Golden Globe nomination, hopefully an Oscar nomination, open in four theaters on Christmas. I went against all conventional wisdom and we took a chance. We went out in four theaters, spent $3 million dollars and if we hadn't grossed big numbers on Christmas, it would have been over. But it did. It got some of the best reviews I've ever seen. Ebert and Roper called it the best American picture in the last 10 years.

When you listen to your own gut and know that something is right, it doesn't matter how many people tell you differently. We did, and only in that

FIGURE 9.7 Producing legend Mark Damon can smile because his films make money and they win Oscars.

FIGURE 9.8 Producer LK confuses the electron microscope with a 35mm camera and discovers that he is looking at slides of his own parasite-ridden anus. It is interesting to note that the two other folks pictured here, Emma Brown and Arsenio Assin, met on the set of *Poultrygeist* and are now married.

way did we get an Oscar for Charlize. A $5 million movie made $80 million worldwide in the theatrical box office and $200 million on home video.

If not for the courage of our own conviction, the picture would have ended up making perhaps a quarter of that, because it wouldn't have received awards. It was a struggle from beginning to end. We risked so much of our own money. We were mavericks,[40] thinking outside the box. Our risk made the whole experience worthwhile. Seeing a picture open and seeing a line around the block for the first viewing—this is what makes it great to be an independent producer.

FIGURE 9.9 *LK always has his special raincoat on when he says to his attractive young fans, "Show me your T-shirt."*

A LATE-NIGHT E-MAIL FROM MY FORMER ASSISTANT AND FORMER CO-WRITER, SARA ANTILL

-----------------------Original Message-------------------------

From: santill@gmail.com

Sent: May 9, 2009 1:21AM

To: Lloyd Kaufman <lloyd@troma.com>

Subject: RE: from sHitler

---

[40] John McCain and Sarah Palin later stole this "maverick" label in McCain's 2008 presidential campaign.

Hi Lloyd,

I wanted to let you know that I got your seven texts last night asking me to help you come up with an ending for your book, and then the eighth one that I'm not even sure was in English. I know you want an ending that is "slightly touching, dark and hilarious," and I would really like to help, but as I spent my entire train ride this morning trying to come up with something, I was reminded that thinking about your life really depresses me.

You keep leaving me these voicemails saying that you don't know anything about producing, but I don't think that's true. You've been producing movies since before I was born, and you couldn't have done that unless you knew something about producing, right? Unless producing is so simple that you don't need to know anything, in which case, I guess there is no reason to write a book about it! HA! HA! Jk, Jk.

I think the best thing about you is that you inspire people. I'm not really sure how. You're kind of an asshole a lot of the time. Other filmmaking books seem to radiate with this idea that you need to have your shit together to make a film – education, equipment, money, Hollywood connections, etc. But you show people that you don't need to have your shit together. And since most people don't have their shit together most of the time, I guess that speaks to most people. It also challenges the image that big-shot Hollywood people have of themselves as some kind of master race.

Jeremy and I are leaving for Paris next week, so if you call me, I won't answer. I just wanted you to know ahead of time that I won't answer, so that when I don't answer, you won't take it personally and freak out and start calling my friends. Also, if you get desperate and end up using this email as an ending to your book, which I have a really bad feeling that you're going to do, can you at least take out the part where I called you an asshole? I don't want my Nana to read that.

XOXO,
Sara

-------------------------End Message---------------------------

---

FOOTNOTE GUY: WOW! Mark Damon was really inspiring! Look, Lloyd, we feel like Sara, too. We're done. I mean, Index Gyno and I are moving on. For real. We took your advice in Chapter 3 and networked. We net Font Gyno to pull a favor with Header Guy and move us up in this world. Taking your advice, we are going to produce our own short film, Lloyd. We're gonna shoot *How to Make Your Own Damn Footnotes*!

INDEX GYNO: We are so over being pushed to the margins of your life. We are going to be sending minutiae all over the Internet with our producing debut and then . . . who knows what's next!? *How to Make Your Own Damn Index*! Books and merchandise will follow!

Well, gee, little guys and gynos, I'm happy for you, I really am . . . in a marginal way. It's true, anything is indeed possible.[41] That is, in fact, exactly what I want you and everyone to do who's reading this book. Go out, make your dream come true and produce your own damn movie!

[41]This topic is the title of Marianne's next weekend seminar. I can't wait!

Frugal in Fargo Asks Lloyd

Dear Lloyd,

Am I legally required to feed the actors and crew on my film set? Couldn't I just give them an hour off and let them go buy their own food at the McDonald's down the street? I'm trying to put as much money as possible on the screen, and it doesn't make sense to me that I should need to feed 20 people every day. They're adults, for Pete's sake.

Cordially,
Frugal in Fargo

Dear Frugal,

In theory, you are entirely justified.

Your actors and crew members are adults, and therefore are entirely capable of feeding themselves. And if you have a small crew and are not under time constraints and you are filming in a mall parking lot, by all means, let them go to the food court and grab some authentic Mexi-Chinese pita wraps.

However, let me throw a few scenarios at you. First of all, your crew and your actors combined total 10 people or more. That means at least ten cars that have been carefully parked so as not to be on camera. Let's say you are filming in a location that is somewhat unfamiliar to the majority of your actors and crew. Let's also say that your actors and crew are being paid by the day or the length of the shoot, and not by the actual time spent filming. Or maybe they aren't being paid at all.

What all of this leads up to is a jumbled mass exodus everyday at lunch time, people getting lost, people not coming back on time, people not coming back at all, and for those who do return, all those cars that must be carefully reparked, yet again, so as not to be on camera.

Now, let's say that all of that could be avoided by putting some cheese sandwiches on a card table. That way, no one has to leave and face the temptation to take the rest of the day off, and most people will find time to eat when they have nothing else to do anyway. Time is saved and everyone is happy. And, just for the record, food on set is an expectation that most actor persons and crew members have, and if you get a reputation for stinginess, it may make it more difficult to convince people to do stuff for you for little or no money later on.

Of course I wouldn't know anything about being stingy.

xoxo,
Lloyd

Dammit! Why Are You Reading This?!

I'm feeling rather reflective today. *The Toxic Avenger Musical* opened last night to a wild crowd at New World Stages on 50th Street in New York City, followed by a standing ovation, with an appearance by New Jersey resident and rock legend Jon Bon Jovi himself. I was out until 4:00 in the morning celebrating, mistakenly interpreting my editrix's late-night e-mail asking me something about an "Afterword" as the clue for 9-down in last Sunday's *New York Times* crossword puzzle.

She was cluing me in that I had to tie everything up into a nice, neat little package.[1] Now that I think of it, in my "Course in Miracles" with Marianne Williamson she encouraged me to see everything through to the end to ensure "closure," enabling me to move on to my next project in life, be it personal or professional.

[1]Now that Footnote Guy is gone, there is no one with the balls to write a "package" pun.

FIGURE AW 1.1 *Opening night of* The Toxic Avenger Musical: *Bon Jovi's David Bryan (left) wrote the music; Joe DiPietro (right) wrote the book; and LK did nothing.*

FIGURE AW 1.2 *More opening night: New York State Film Commissioner Pat Swinney Kaufman (left) with* (Urinetown) *Tony Award–winning Director of* The Toxic Avenger Musical, *John Rando.*

But let's face it. Producing movies is no exact science and if you've learned anything in this damned book, it's that there are a million ways to go about it. I asked all of the other people in this book to give their take on producing their own damn movies so you could see that Lloyd Kaufman's Troma Way is not the ultimate zeitgeist. My movies are made for our fans above anyone else. Due to the increasing power of the devil-worshipping multi-national cartel, Troma's ability to get our movies theatrically released and distributed on video and on TV—like we used to—has grown more difficult over time. In a fair world, *Poultrygeist* would be huge!

A number of the other producers in this book are suggesting that if you, a first-time producer, actually want to get to make a movie that (a) people go to see, (or at least get a chance to see) and (b) makes its initial investment back (or better yet, actually returns a profit), you have to be able to pre-sell your movie. And holy smoke! All without having yet established a name for yourself! It's about as daunting as trying to get a 50 percent black man elected president of the United States.

The good news for producers is: YES WE CAN!

There are so many more options available to the young producer these days in terms of the path you can take. There are hundreds of film schools out there that can teach you the basics of filmmaking. Although only a precious few of them will guarantee you a leg up (though what you really need is two feet planted squarely on the ground), all of them will teach you something about the art of filmmaking. Or instead, maybe you start playing "Six Degrees of Kevin Bacon" to land you a fairly hot well-known underground movie star (who will bring a following) in fewer degrees than you may have thought possible.

And if you can't afford or don't want to go to school, you can take production jobs on other films or just start producing movies on a small scale (like a funny, disturbing or disgusting three-minute short on YouTube or a music video for your neighbor's hot daughter's band), upload it and see what happens! You never know who will see it. Then go make another and another after that, and still another one after that one. Meet people, all kinds, but most certainly talk to people in the film business; find out who'd you like to work with and see what opportunities arise. Or, write your own damn feature-length script that you and your best friend have been plotting out in your heads while wasting away your youth masturbating and watching the Wanda in the steam room scene in *The Toxic Avenger* (the scene numerous young pudgy boys have told me they first masturbated to), or while watching your home-grown pot grow. And then take that brilliant piece of writing and show it around. Talk to anyone and everyone who will listen and maybe give you a chance to make it.

You're going to make mistakes, you're going to have days you feel like you're in over your head, you're going to have days when you wish you had chosen to spend your life as lazy fuck (to which I can attest is a very undemanding job, when you work as hard at it as I do). But you'll make *your* piece of art! Put it out there and share it with the rest of the world to adore, love or shit upon. Any which way you get it done, remember this: movies live on for years and years and years. They take on an identity and life of their own, sometimes in unpredictable ways.

Who ever would have imagined that I would see *The Toxic Avenger*, which features a 12-year-old boy's cranium being crushed by the wheel of an automobile, become an environmentally correct children's cartoon show, a mass-marketed toy, and then a foot-stomping, yuppie-pleasing hit musical with music by a Bon Jovi guy? And that this musical became a reality initially by my giving away free permission for people to create and exploit a singing and dancing Toxie! Some fans in Portland wanted to make Toxie sing about his tortured existence in an environmentally polluted world and that led to other toxic musical experiments in other states and other "pirate" productions. I made no money on any of this. But because, as described earlier in this book, most of entertainment media has been a closed market to my movies, I figured that these fan musicals in a few cities might help keep Toxie and Troma on the public's radar during our time in the media desert.

And then, Jesus Christ on a pogo stick! One day, some real Broadway producers, Jean Cheever and Tom Polum, put together a package of major theatrical talent including Tony Award–winning director John Rando, hit playwright Joe DiPietro, and Bon Jovi keyboardist David Bryan. Who would have guessed? A damn hit musical happened! The point is that you need to think outside the clapstick and keep the creative juices pumping (not to mention all the others, too), stay in the game and continue producing. As Woody Allen says, "80 perecent of success is just showing up."

Troma has never been more famous. People occasionally stop me in the street to ask me for my autograph, yet business has never been worse. Pat and I paid for *Poultrygeist* out of our own pockets and Michael and I are subsidizing Troma's payroll. But things are happening and toxic green shoots are sprouting. Microsoft, Xbox, Itunes, FEARnet and other new technological distribution entities are starting to send in money as they present our films in cyber-space. Others are knocking on our Troma Building door wanting our legendary library for their "On Demand," "Pay-Per-View" and other Internet services. Lots of big money promises. My brother's movie *Mother's Day* has been signed for a big Brett Ratner-style Hollywood budget remake. Some big shots are also going to sign up *The Toxic Avenger* for a remake and give us a big check, hopefully. We are getting offers to remake *Class of Nuke 'Em High* and *Terror Firmer* and even *Poultrygeist, Night of the Chicken Dead.* Soon they'll remake our movies before we even produce them. Maybe the remakes will be brilliant—or maybe they'll suck. Our purist fans who follow me on Twitter are already expressing hostility. Some are even suggesting that we may have sold out. But if nothing else, these mainstream media remakes of our Tromasterpieces will introduce a whole new generation of young moviegoers (whose parents were not even born early enough to see them) to the original classic Troma productions.

But enough about me! Now back to myself.

I've stayed informed. I do not do this by reading *Variety* or *Hollywood Reporter*, but by watching and going to a shitload of movies. As I mentioned earlier in this book, I also act (usually for little or no pay) in movies by people like you, dear reader, just to help you! I learn a lot from these usually no-budget movies—and sometimes mega-budget movies. By being on the sets of young producers of the future, I continue my film school education! For example, I have learned a lot about lighting for nighttime and how to make darkness on high-def digital tape from what I observed while acting in Ryan Nicholson and Ted Moehring's flicks. From Glen Weiss's *Thong Girl 4,* I learned about an up-to-date no-cost Steadicam rig that you can make.[2] For example, I also learned a lot about the Red Digital Camera, a camera that may change the world of filmmaking, because I played a "genericon" robot in Neveldine and Taylor's $80 million dollar mainstream flick *Gamer* and saw the revolutionary Red Camera up front

[2]Google "make your own Steadicam." Boy, these footnotes are hard work! I wish Footnote Guy would return. I miss the little shit.

and personal. By continuing to hang out in the Troma booths at conventions and talking to the fans, I learn about what they like, what's new, and what new technologies are out there. Thanks to the fans who called it to my attention, I got on Twitter before a lot of other producers. THX, FANS! U CN B SURE OF THT. LOL. I may be 63 years old, but I am more "up to date" about state-of-the-art producing than most of the young, suited killer rabbits in the Hollywood producing world. Certainly, I am more informed than the big-budget producer for one of the megaconglomerates I spoke with recently, who thought my reference to the "revolutionary" Red Camera was referring to something Lenin[3] used during the Bolshevik Revolution. Those guys may get the power table at Mozza, but I get the power fans!

I am also starting to develop *The Toxic Avenger Part V, The Toxic Twins*! I don't know where the money to produce it will come from, but somehow we'll find it, or maybe I'll raid Pat's retirement fund again! (Please do not tell her.) I'm also thinking about putting Toxie in a Shakespeare play. *Tromeo & Juliet* worked out well, so maybe this time a Toxic Shakespeare—how about *Comedy of Twin Terror?* Perhaps I'll film digitally, with the Red Camera or maybe just my

FIGURE AW 1.3 *Lloyd plays Thomas Edison in Glen Weiss's* Thong Girl 4 *with Jim Orear (right) and Alex Baldwin in white shorts (background, left).*

[3]Lenin of course refers to John Lenin, one of the only assassinated Beatles.

Canon VIXIA HD. Some of the short films I've acted in have gotten a pantload of views on YouTube. Maybe I'll film Toxie's new movie in three-minute webisodes so they can go into cyberspace one at a time, week by week, and build a huge audience—like when 1914's *Perils of Pauline* was serialized in cinemas! Then maybe we'll edit all the three-minute webisodes together, add in some never-before-seen footage and then transfer it all to 35mm to show this "director's cut" in movie theatres. And then and THEN! Well, you can see where this is going.

You're not reading this book because you chose the easy path. You are already walking down a long and winding road, one not easily taken (as Robert Frost described in his poem "The Road Not Taken")[4], like the iconic American letter carrier – through wind, hail and blizzard conditions; a road not very welcoming to all who Tom Cruise it. But if you move forward, it *will* make all the difference Frost was right: "In three words, I can sum up everything I've learned about life—it goes on." OK, so Frost may have written it first, but I am here to tell you that it is true and I am living proof. You go on.

You, dear readers, are reading this book because … you can read … and also because you are passionate about movies. That's great. That in itself is a beautiful thing. Nothing else has more power to bring together a group of strangers and incite ecstasy or cause them to vomit. But seriously, you've read enough. Now just go out there and produce your own damn movie. Keep me posted on your progress and write me at lloyd@troma.com.

And then, when you do make it to Hollywood and win that Oscar, be sure to thank me in your televised acceptance speech. Also, write a big fat check and make it out to Lloyd Kaufman and mail it to The Troma Building, 36–40 11th Street in Long Island City, NY, 11106, so I can go produce my own (next) damn movie.

XXX,

Uncle Lloyd

P.S. For those of you wondering or hoping, I probably will not "blow my fucking brains out." Writing this book has been very therapeutic and besides, as you well know, since everything I do is fucked, I'd most likely miss my brain and accidentally kill my co-writer Ashley, who is sitting right next to me.

---

[4]EDITOR'S NOTE: Very nice touch to bring in a distinguished poet here, Lloyd! I feel you've grown from this experience.

A Trio of E-mail Exchanges Among Ashley, Elinor, and Lloyd, *and* A Final Final Ending to This Book About Producing

SOME FINAL WORDS VIA E-MAIL FROM MY CO-AUTHOR ASHLEY

----------------------Original Message------------------------

From: ashley@suckedintoworkingforlloyd.com
Sent: May 11, 2009 11:43 PM
To: Lloyd Kaufman <lloyd@troma.com>
Subject: Only a Nightmare

Lloyd:

Hey! Just a quick note to say thanks so much for working so hard to crank out the rest of the book to make our third deadline extension! I think you did a really awesome job! I will never forget these final, stellar six months that have been the highlight of my life thus far.

Also, sooooo funny, last night I had this dream I tried to kill you because you drove me nuts! Can you imagine?! Like I would ever do such a thing!

So, HA HA! I don't think you have anything to be worried about. After all, it was only a nightmare. . . HA HA HA HA HA HA HA!

In fact, I've gotten to like you soooo much MORE after doing this book together. I am going to go into total withdrawal now that it really is truly, finally over. I texted myself 47 messages about pre-selling sidebars, Index Gyno's sexaholic tendencies, Footnote Guy's throbbing member. . . exactly like you've been doing to me for the past 126 days, 13 hours, 7 minutes and 53 seconds. . . sending out your daily 47 texts and 37 excited phone messages that I loved oh so much. . . and now I can pretend we're still working together!!!!!!! You made me work so closely with you -- you made me your Siamese twin! I can't, I just can't get away from you!!!

Hold it! Hold it right there. Oh. My. God. I am not asleep and yet your face is everywhere in my room! ACKKK!!! Lloyd, get your two l's out of here. Ok, ok, ok! I'll write another stupid footnote, I'll do anything, just leave me alone!! There are six Lloyd's here. Aghhhhh!!!!!!

Hey! Wait a minute . . . Hey! Um, who are all these men in the white coats? Lloyd? Lloyd! Get away from me with that net! I'm not crazy, you know. You'll never catch me! Hey, where are they taking me?

Unhand me, men in white coats. Don't you know who I am? I am Marianne Williamson. HA HA HA HA HA HA!!!! HA HA HA HA HA HA HA HA HA HA !!!!!!!!

XOXO,
Guru Goddess

-------------------------End Message----------------------------

A NOTE FROM MY EDITRIX

-----------------------Original Message------------------------
From: elinor@repress.com
Sent: May 12, 2009 7:13 PM
To: Lloyd Kaufman <lloyd@troma.com>
Subject: Never Again

Dear Lloyd,

I am still waiting for your Afterword.

The process of this book has been torturous and my work with you has made my hair turn white. Also, I am in serious trouble with the men upstairs at Focal Press because of your tardiness and the filthy language you use and I have now been told that I may lose my job. But, may I say, Lloyd, that you are my absolute favorite author. You are so hot and I really want to sleep with —[1]

---

[1]EDITOR'S NOTE: Jesus, God, make this stop!

They've taken Ashley out of the straitjacket, but she's still in bad shape. She keeps mumbling things about footnotes and ass pirates and your pushing double l's at her and your six faces? I am taking care of her as best I can. Poor gyno. Shame on you!

Eckhart Tolle and Marianna Williamson are holding a retreat in Los Angeles the weekend of May 22nd called "Consciousness and the Higher Plane." Ashley and I are going to go! Too bad you can't join us! Too bad I won't be able to edit your next book because I'll be assigning our newest and least experienced editor to it. . . if there is a next book. Too bad I won't be seeing you ever again after this book. Too bad you were born.

Have a toxierrific summer, Lloyd.

Best,
Elinor

Sent via BlackBerry by AT&T

-------------------------End Message---------------------------

LLOYD'S E-MAIL TO THE EDITRIX

----------------------Original Message------------------------

From: lloyd@troma.com
Sent: May 12, 2009 7:39PM
To: Elinor <elinor@repress.com>
Subject: Re: Never Again

Thanks so much for the invite to Deepak and Marianne's event. Sorry to hear about Ashley's breakdown. I can't even begin to imagine how something like that could have happened. That is so nice of you to take care of her. I wish I could join you and Ashley at the retreat, but Index Gyno just informed me that she and Footnote Guy are pregnant with an asterisk, so their 1-minute movie production is now in turnaround.

The *Tromeo & Juliet* Credits Guy struck it rich and he's financing my next endeavor, so I'll be busy shooting May 22, as we are now moving ahead rather quickly.

But take some good notes and tell Marianna and Eckhart I said "Namaste[2]!"

[2]"Namaste" is a Hindu word meaning Lloyd Kaufman is the kindest film producer in the world.

XOXO,
Lloyd

-------------------------End Message----------------------------

FINAL FINAL ENDING TO THIS BOOK ABOUT PRODUCING – I SWEAR!

Over the past year, I've spent a lot of time thinking about producing—especially worrying that I don't know squat about producing, that I don't even know what I *don't* know about producing, what I *should* know about producing, or what *you* should know about producing, and how to make it seem like I know enough about producing so that you will buy this book and my editor will be happy, and you will learn something useful about producing and review this book on Amazon. I've probably spent more time worrying about my inability to write a book about producing than I actually have spent thinking about producing[3] my next movie.[4]

But I digress. The thing is, the more I think about it, the more I think that I've learned a shit ton about producing just by working on this book. I mean, some of the stuff in those interviews I conducted was really useful. If only I could go back in time to Israel circa 1972 and fix the mistakes in producing *Big Gus, What's the Fuss?*, my entire career could have been different! In fact, I have learned so much about producing that now I actually could write a book!

So, Elinor, if you're reading this, I'm feeling really confident right now! What do you say we meet at IHOP down the street and discuss? I finally feel ready to begin writing *Produce Your Own Damn Movie!* And then, after I finish that, *Market Your Own Damn Movie!* and then *Edit Your Own Damn Movie!* The creative juices are flowing!

XOXO,
Lloyd

---

[3]In an effort to keep me on track with this book, my editrix instituted a rule that the word "producing" or "producer" or some variation of such had to be mentioned at least twice on each page, for a total of 400 times. Because I have obviously not done that, I am hoping that by using the word "producing" as much as possible in this last section, Elinor will consider my obligation met. My fingers are crossed!

[4]For which I am still looking for a script. If you have an extreme character-driven ensemble piece with a small cast, please send it to me at The Troma Building, 36–40 11th Street, Long Island City, New York 11106!

THE EDITRIX STRIKES BACK

-----------------------Original Message------------------------

From: elinor@repress.com

Sent: May 12, 2009 7:47PM

To: Lloyd Kaufman <lloyd@troma.com>

Subject: Re: Re: Never Again

Dear Lloyd,

Fuckity Bye!

XO,
Elinor

Sent via BlackBerry by AT&T

-------------------------End Message---------------------------

Index Gyno's Bitchin' Index

16 Blocks, 218

A

Abatement, 173
Accidental business plan, 117–120
Accidents, on movie sets, 186–187
Ace Ventura, 227
Ackerman, Stanley, 87
AFI. *See* American Film Institute (AFI)
AFM. *See* American Film Market (AFM)
Alexander, 20
Allen, India, 182
Allen, Woody, 68, 157
All-rights deal, 154
American Film Institute (AFI), 22, 151
American Film Market (AFM), 136, 159–160
American Idol, 18
A Midsummer Night's Dream, 178
Anal Lesbian Club Part XII, 255
Andrews, Giuseppe, 255
Any Given Sunday, 21
Apocalypse Soon, 54
Archambeault, Daniel, 256
Ardour, 257
Ashley, conversation with, 98–101
Ashley's e-mail, 97–101, 279–280
Associate producer, defined, 133–134
Austin Powers, 226

B

"Bad of taste", 119
BAFTA. *See* British American Film and Television Alliance (BAFTA)
Baron, Caroline, 215
Bay, Michael, 214
Begelman, David
  history of, 68–69
Behind the Green Door, 40
Benson, Robby, 230
Beyond a Reasonable Doubt, 18
Beyond the Sea, 262
Big Gus, What's the Fuss?, 20, 27, 251
  release of, 28–30
Big Hollywood Movie Model, 10–12
Bloodbath, 249
Blood Feast, 259
Bloodsucking Freaks, 84, 119
Body Double, 36
Bone Eater, 85
Brando, Marlon, 47
Brian Taylor, 250
British American Film and Television Alliance (BAFTA), 88
Brokeback Mountain, 181
Brooklyn's Finest, 11
Burton, Richard, 68
Bush, George W., 69
Buyer, defined, 158–159
Byrne, Rhonda, 50

C

CAA. *See* Creative Artists Agency (CAA)
Cage, Nicholas, 23
Cahiers du Cinéma, 229
Calling card movie, 249
Cannes Film Festival, 78, 147, 148, 219, 241
Cannibal the Musical, 118, 146
Carolco, 217
Carpenter, John
  interview with, 65–66
Carrey, Jim, 224, 226, 227
Carroll, Alan, 210
Celtx, 257
CGI. *See* Computer-generated images (CGI)
Cheyenne Autumn, 229
Chien, David
  conversation with, 41–47
Chinese Cultural Revolution, 38
Cinelerra, 257
CinePaint, 257
CineTel Films, 85
Citizen Kane, 183
Citizen Toxie, 54, 55, 182
Class of Nuke' Em High, 118, 124
Close Encounters of the Third Kind, 68
Co-executive producer, 15
Cohen, Larry, 231, 232
Combat Shock, 88, 99, 220
Comedy Central, 146
Computer-generated images (CGI), 150

Contract
for location, 168
Co-producer, defined, 63–64
Corey, Irwin, 88
Corman, Roger, 37, 49, 119–120
Crank, 221
Crank 2: High Voltage, 221, 232
Crash, 21, 72–73
Creative Artists Agency (CAA), 68, 224
Credit Card Model, 8, 10
Crocodile Dundee in L.A., 153, 154
Crypts, 80
Cry Uncle, 84
Cuatro, 149

D

Damon, Mark, 18
Dance of the Sun, 134
Dante, Joe, 27
Deadgirl, 52
Deemer, Andy, production diaries, 125–130
Deep Throat, 39
Def by Temptation, 118
Defective Man!, 52
Delivery, defined, 159
DeNiro, Robert, 218
De Palma, Brian, 36
DGA. *See* Director's Guild of America (DGA)
Dialing for Dingbats, 99
Dickerson, Ernest, 47
Die Hard, 84
"Director's cut", 119
Director's Guild of America (DGA), 86–87
Direct Your Own Damn Movie!, 8, 16
Discounting agreements, defined, 154
Disney, 6
Divine Obsession, 40
Doggie Tails, 84
Douglas, Michael, 18
Draven, Danny, 80–81
Dreith, Dennis, 252
Dumb and Dumber, 223–224, 228
Duplass, Jay, 216, 222–223, 250
Duplass, Mark, 216, 222–223, 250

E

Easter Bunny, Kill! Kill! 52, 53, 55
Eisner, Michael, 224
Elephants Dream, 257
Erik the Viking, 77
Evil Dead, 247
Executive producer, 5
defined, 11

F

Farrelly, Bobby, 224
Farrelly, Peter, 224
FCC. *See* Federal Communications Commission (FCC)
Federal Communications Commission (FCC), 140
Field of Dreams, 140
FilmAid, 215
Film Musicians Secondary Markets Fund, 252
Film producing models, 5
Big Hollywood Movie Model, 10–12
Credit Card Model, 8
No-Budget Model, 7–8
Presale/Cross-National Model, 10
Troma Model, 8–9
Financial Interest and Syndication Rules (Fin-Syn), 140
Fin-Syn. *See* Financial Interest and Syndication Rules (Fin-Syn)
First Turn-On, 20
Focal Press, 146
Fonda, Jane, 191
Ford, Henry, 8
Ford, John, 229
Fortress of Amerikkka, 100
Friedman, Gabe, 183
Frozen River, 43

G

Gargoyle, 85
Garland, Judy, 68
Garris, Mick, 31–32
General Electric, 185
Gerbus, Jack, 181
Gershuny, Theodore, 19
Ghost in the Shell, 23
Ghostmonth, 80
Ghost Rider, 23
Giallo, 249
Gigli, 188
Giovinazzo, Buddy, 88, 99, 220
Lerner, Avi, conversation with, 89
Girls School Screamers, 99
Gladden Entertainment, 69
Glenn, Garrard L., 16, 20
Godfather of Gore, 259
Godhead, 247

Gods and Monsters, 21
Golan, Menahem, 25–26
Goldstone, John, 78
Gooding, Cuba, Jr., 192
Good Night and Good Cluck. *See Poultrygeist, Night of the Chicken Dead*
Gottschalk, Thomas, 224
Green room, 169
Gremlins and Gremlins 2: The New Batch, 27
Grim Fairy Tale, 261
Guitar Hero, 134
Gunn, James, 210, 213

H

Haaga, Trent, 52, 88
  conversation with, 52–56
Ha Balash Ha'Amitz Shvartz. *See* Big Gus, What's the Fuss ?
Hackmen, Gene, 231
Haggis, Paul, 21, 72–73
Hanger, case study, 169–172
Happy Birthday, 23
Hard Wire, 192
Harris, Mark, 21, 74, 261
  conversation with, 72–73
Harry Potter, 257
Headbanger's Ball, 247
Heffner, Hugh, 183
Hemdale Film Corporation, 219
Hertzberg, Paul, 85–86
  conversation with, 148–152, 180–181
Herz, Michael, 25, 28, 84, 98, 182
  conversation with, 215–216
Hessel, Lee, 84
Hill, Jonah, 222
Hitchcock, Alfred, 18
Hoffs, Tamar Simon, 81–82
Hollywood producing model, 6
Holy Grail, 77
House of Knives, 250
House of the Rising, 100
Hughes, John, 225
Hutchinson, Tessie, 67

I

Icarus, 85
Ice Tornadoes, 150
IFTA. *See* Independent Film & Television Alliance (IFTA)
Igor and the Lunatics, 99
IHOP. *See* International House of Pancakes (IHOP)
IMDB. *See* Internet Movie DataBase (IMDB)
"Independent Film," defined, 136–137
Independent Film & Television Alliance (IFTA), 135–137
  as chairperson of, role, 137–141
  Prewitt, Jean, CEO of, 158–161
Indie film producer
  qualities for, 188–189
Inducement, 173
Insurance
  film making and, 190–191
International House of Pancakes (IHOP), 75–77
Internet, role of, 245
Internet Movie DataBase (IMDB), 99
  website, Lloyd's credits on, 108–116
In the Land of Women, 156, 157
Invasion of the Space Preachers, 68
I Spit on Your Grave, 85

J

Jackson, Shirley, 67, 69
Jakarta
  language in, 198
  reality about, 199
  religion in, 198–199
  weather in, 198
Jakarta, 197
Jenkins, Patty, 263
JFK, 22
Joe Lynch, 246
Jones, Terry, 77–79

K

Kappelman, Jeffrey, 20
Kaufman, Charles, 197, 200, 201
Keener, Catherine, 222
Killer Bike Chicks, 52
Kingpin, 223, 224, 228
Kingsley, Gershon, 255
Krevoy, Brad, 223

L

Lack, Andy, 28, 30
Lang, Herr Fritz, 18
Lawrence, Matt, 70–72
Lee, Stan, 75
Lemmon, Jack, 231

Lerner, Avi, 11, 121–122, 185, 216
  conversation with, 217–220
  Giovinazzo, Buddy, conversation with, 89
Letter
  from Barack H. Obama, 243–244
  to president Obama, 142–145
Lewis, Herschell Gordon, 259–261
Life Is Hot in Cracktown, 88, 89, 220
Life of Brian, 77
Limited Liability Company (LLC)
  setting up, 184–186
Line producer, 96–97
Line Watch, 192
Lion's Gate, 218
LLC. *See* Limited Liability Company (LLC)
Location
  choosing a, 167–169
  contract for, 168
Lord of the Rings, 10
Louis Su, 38
  dinner with, 35–59
Lovett, Richard, 224
Lowry, Lynn, 20
Lucky Lady, 231
Luna Chicks, 245
Lust for Freedom, 98

M

MAD Magazine, 211
Mad Money, 219
Major Movie Star, 11
Make Your Own Damn Movie!, 16
Maloney, Jim, 206
Mark Neveldine, 250
Martian Child, 12
Masters of Horror, 31, 32
McDowell, Malcolm, 81–82
Metiva, Jake, 178
Metropolis, 18
Meyer, Russ, 212
Michigan
  tax incentives in, 173
Midnight Express, 229
Million Dollar Baby, 21, 72
Minnelli, Liza, 231
Model Sales Agency agreement, 160
Moehring, Ted, 249
Moishe, hot Israeli actor, 26
Monroe, Marilyn, 68
Monster, 263
Monster a Go-Go, 259
Monster in the Closet, 118
Monty Python, 77
Moog synthesizer, 255
Morano, Reed, 43–47, 69
Morgan, Kathy, 152
  conversation with, 153–157
Morgan Creek Productions, 227
Mother's Day, 235
Motion Picture Association of America (MPAA), 17, 82
MPAA. *See* Motion Picture Association of America (MPAA)
MPAA lottery, 82–88
Mudhoney, 212
1969 Mustang deal, 4
Myers, Mike, 226

N

Napoleon Dynamite, 254–255
Natural-born Killers, 21
Negative insurance, 186
Neveldine, Mark, 220, 231
  conversation with, 221
News Corporation, 6
New York Daily News, 86, 87
New York Post, 183
New York State
  tax incentives in, 172, 176
New York State Film Commission, 174
New York Times, 99
New York University (NYU), 230
Nicholson, Ryan, 169–170
Night Flight Comics, 246
Nixon, 22
No-Budget Model, 7–8
No Country for Old Men, 181
NYU. *See* New York University (NYU)

O

Obama, Barack, 243–244
  letter to, 142–145
One on One, 230
On the Waterfront, 47
Orman, Suze, 118
Oscar-winning producers
  Haggis, Paul, 21
  Harris, Mark, 21, 74
Overture Films, 218

P

Paar, Jack, 68
Pacino, Al, 218
Paley, Nina, 255
Parker, Sarah Jessica, 172

Parker, Trey, 90–91, 245
Paul, Steven, 23–24
Payout, 21
Penthouse magazine, 249
Personal Services, 77
Philadelphia Art Museum, 36
Philosopher's Stone, 257
Pilot, 176
Plan B, 56
Playboy Mansion, 182
Popcorn song, 255
Poultrygeist, 8, 131, 140, 179, 251–252, 258
  Night of the Chicken Dead, 6–7, 71
Pound of Flesh, 81
Presale/Cross-National Model, 10
Pre-selling, 148–152, 155
Prewitt, Jean, 158–161
Producer, 35
  characteristics of, 259–260
  defined, 5
Puffy Chair, 222

R

Rambo IV, 11, 217, 220
Rappacini, 16
Ratner, Brett, 214
Reagan, Nancy, 137
Reagan, Ronald, 140
Re-Animator, 194
Red Camera, 221
Red Roses and Petrol, 81
Reilly, John C., 222
Reynolds, Burt, 231
Righteous Kill, 218, 219
R.I.P.. *See* Rest in peace (R.I.P.)
Roberts, Julia, 10, 257
Robertson, Cliff, 68–69
Robson, Mark, 23
Rochon, Debbie, 171, 177, 186–192
Rocky, 36, 86
The Rowdy Girls, 182
Rysher Entertainment, 219

S

SAG. *See* Screen Actors Guild (SAG)
Sandler, Adam, 226
Sara Antill
  e-mail from, 265–267
Saturday Night Fever, 36
Saving Private Ryan, 99
SciFi Channel, 151
Screen Actors Guild (SAG), 55, 88
Seizure, 20
Sellers, Peter, 68
Selznick, David O., 79, 87
Shanley, John Patrick, 70
Sita Sings the Blues, 255
Slither, 212
Sly, 217
Snake Eyes, 36
Sony, 6
Sony Classics, 42
South Park, 146, 245
Spiderman, 257
Spiderman, 2, 257
Spielberg, Steven, 23
Spirit of Christmas, 245
Squeeze Play, 59, 139, 140, 212
Stallone, Sylvester, 217
Step Up Part II: The Streets, 192
Stillness Speaks, 48
Stone, Matt, 90–91, 245
Stone, Oliver, 16, 20, 21, 22, 30, 46
Stonehenge Apocalypse, 150
Strain, Julie, 182
Strapping Young Lad, 247
Stuart Little, 257
Sturges, Tom, 20
Sugar Cookies, 16, 18, 19–20, 21, 251, 255
Sweet Smell of Success, 19
Swinney Kaufman, pat, 173–178

T

Tax incentives
  defined, 173
  in Michigan, 173
  in New York State, 172
Taylor, Brian, 220, 231
  conversation with, 221
Team America, 91
Terror Firmer, 18, 55, 245, 247
Thalberg, Irving, 79
The Alchemist, 155
The Battle of Love's Return, 18, 36, 248–249, 251, 255
The Big Heat, 18
The Blair Witch Project, 74–75
The Dark Side of Midnight, 98
The Danish Girl, 155
The Devil in Miss Jones, 40
The Doors, 21
The Final Countdown, 208
The Five People You Meet in Heaven, 88
The Girl Who Returned, 16, 255

The Gore Gore Girls, 259
The Haircut, 81
The Hole, 27
The Hollywood Reporter, 84
The Howling, 27
The Incredible Torture Show, 118
The In-Laws, 139
The Killer Bra, 70
The Last Samurai, 257
The Lottery, 67
The Mask, 227, 228
The Meaning of Life, 77
The Newcomers, 48–49
The Puffy Chair, 222
The Rowdy Girls, 182
The Searchers, 229
The Secret, 50
The Sopranos, 176
The Sorcerer's Apprentice, 71
The Toxic Avenger, 13, 43, 98, 100, 118, 124, 210, 215, 235
The Toxic Avenger II, 27, 148
The Toxic Avenger Musical, 241, 242, 258
The Untitled Duplass Brothers Project, 222
The Upside of Anger, 262
The Wedding Party, 36
The Wind in the Willows, 77
The Yale Murders, 25
Theron, Charlize, 262
Thick as Thieves, 11
Time Warner, 6
Titanic, 22
Tomei, Marisa, 222
Touch Me in the Morning, 51, 100–101
Tovah, hot israeli actress, 26
Toxie II, 182
Trailer Town, 51
Tribune Broadcasting group, 224
Troma Building in North Carolina, 123
TromaDance Film Festival, 134, 254
Troma Entertainment, 43, 71
Troma Entertainment, Inc., 173
Troma fan, 256
Troma Model, 8–9
Troma movies, 6, 55, 118
Tromapalooza event, 202
Troma's Edge TV, 52
Troma's War, 84, 87
Tromeo & Juliet, 210, 211, 258
Tweed, Shannon, 182
Twilight, 155

U

United States v. Paramount Pictures, Inc., 138–139, 161
Unit Production Manager, 97

V

Vampire in Vegas, 11
Vertigo, 18
Viacom, 6
Video boom to modern age, evolution from, 147
Voight, Jon, 88

W

Wall Street, 21
Wanda June, 23
Waters, John, 212
Watson, Diane, Congresswoman, 181
Website
  acting list on, 105–107
  producing list on, 102–104
Weinstein, Harvey, 85, 155
Williams, Robin, 227
Williamson, Marianne, 21, 209
Willis, Bruce, 218
Woronov, Mary, 19–20, 255
Wrong Turn, 2, 247
Wuornos, Aileen, 262
Wyatt, Chris, 254

X

X-Ray Eyes, 37

Y

Yuzna, Brian, 123, 124
  conversation with, 192–193, 194–196
  video boom to modern age, evolution from, 147

For Product Safety Concerns and Information please contact our EU representative GPSR@taylorandfrancis.com Taylor & Francis Verlag GmbH, Kaufingerstraße 24, 80331 München, Germany

Printed and bound by CPI Group (UK) Ltd, Croydon, CR0 4YY

11/04/2025

01844014-0001